PENGUIN BOOKS

THE PENGUIN DICTIONARY FOR WRITERS AND EDITORS

Bill Bryson was born in 1951 in Des Moines, Iowa, and grew up there, but has spent most of his adult life in Britain. He has worked for the *Bournemouth Evening Echo*, *Financial Weekly* and *The Times*, and was one of the founding journalists on the *Independent*. His other books include *The Penguin Dictionary of Troublesome Words*, *Mother Tongue: The English Language*, also published by Penguin, and the travel books *The Lost Continent* and *Neither Here Nor There*. He is married, with four children, and lives in North Yorkshire.

Bill Bryson

THE PENGUIN DICTIONARY FOR WRITERS AND EDITORS

PENGUIN BOOKS

PENGUIN BOOKS

Published by the Penguin Group
Penguin Books Ltd, 27 Wrights Lane, London W8 5TZ, England
Penguin Books USA Inc., 375 Hudson Street, New York, New York 10014, USA
Penguin Books Australia Ltd, Ringwood, Victoria, Australia
Penguin Books Canada Ltd, 10 Alcorn Avenue, Toronto, Ontario, Canada M4V 3B2
Penguin Books (NZ) Ltd, 182–190 Wairau Road, Auckland 10, New Zealand

Penguin Books Ltd, Registered Offices: Harmondsworth, Middlesex, England

First published by Viking 1991
Published with revisions in Penguin Books 1994
10 9 8 7 6 5 4 3 2

Set in 10/12 pt Monotype Bembo
Typeset by Datix International Limited, Bungay, Suffolk
Printed in England by Clays Ltd, St Ives plc

CONTENTS

PREFACE

This book is intended as a quick, concise guide to the problems of English spelling and usage most commonly encountered by writers and editors. To keep it simple, I have freely resorted to certain short cuts. Pronunciations have been simplified. I have scorned the International Phonetic Alphabet, with its dogged reliance on symbols such as *θ*, i:, *δ* and u: on the grounds that hardly anyone understands them and instead have attempted to convert tricky pronunciations into straightforward phonetic equivalents. Often these are intended as no more than rough guides – anyone who has ever heard a Dutchman growl 's-Gravenhage' will instantly realize what a pitiable thing my suggested pronunciation is – and I unhesitatingly apologize for any shortcomings in this respect.

I have also been forced on occasion to be arbitrary over spelling. Dictionaries are sometimes remarkably out of step with the rest of the world on certain matters of usage and orthography, but there is usually a rough consensus, which I have sought to follow. Sometimes, however, there is no consensus, particularly with the spellings of foreign names. Where this has happened I have tried to indicate at least some of the alternative spellings.

I have tried also to keep cross-references to a minimum. In my view one of the great irritants of research is to pore through several pages looking for Khayyám, Omar, only to be told: 'See Omar Khayyám'. So I have tried, where possible, to put such information not only where it should be but also where a hurried reader might mistakenly look for it. The consequence of this is occasional repetition.

Some issues of style – such as whether you should write shopkeeper, shop-keeper or shop keeper – have been deliberately ignored. Such matters are so overwhelmingly a question of preference, house style and fashion that my choices would be simply that: my choices. I would suggest that in such instances you should choose what you wish. You will not be any more inconsistent than most of the authorities.

DICTIONARY

A

a, an A is used before words beginning with consonants other than silent *h* and with vowels pronounced as *w* or *y*. An is unarguably correct before just four words beginning with *h*, in which that letter is never aspirated: hour, honest, honour/honor and heir. In Britain an is also often used before hotel and historian (then pronounced with a silent *h*), but many authorities prefer a hotel and a historian

Aachen (Ger.) /**Aix-la-Chapelle** (Fr.) city in Germany

Aalto, (Hugh) Alvar (Henrik) (1898–1976) Finnish architect and designer

Aarhus/Århus (Dan.) city in Denmark

abacus, *pl.* **abacuses**

Abadan, Iran

abaft towards the stern, or rear, of a boat

abattoir

Abbado, Claudio (1933–) Italian conductor

Abbotsinch Airport, Glasgow

Abbot's Salford, Warwickshire

ABC American Broadcasting Companies (note plural); the television network (*not* station) is ABC-TV (hyphen). Australian Broadcasting Commission

abdomen, abdominal

Abdulaziz International Airport, King Jeddah, Saudi Arabia

Abdul-Jabbar, Kareem (1947–) born Lew Alcindor; American basketball player

Abélard/Abailard, **Pierre/Peter** (1079–1142) French theologian, known for his affair with his pupil Héloïse. The poem by Alexander Pope is 'Eloisa to Abelard' (1717)

Aberdonian of or from Aberdeen

Aberfan coal-mining village in Mid Glamorgan, Wales, scene of 1966 landslide in which 144 people died

Abergavenny, Gwent, Wales. Pronounced ab-er-guh-ven'-nee for the town, but ab-er-ghen'-nee for the Marquess of Abergavenny

aberrant, **aberration**

Aberystwyth, Dyfed, Wales

abhorrent

Abidjan capital of Ivory Coast

ab incunabulis (Lat.) from the cradle

abiogenesis the concept that living matter can arise from non-living matter; spontaneous generation

-able In adding this suffix to a verb, the general rule is to drop a silent *e* (livable, losable) except after a soft *g* (manageable) or sibilant *c* (peaceable). When a verb ends with a consonant and a *y* (justify or indemnify) change the *y* to *i* before adding -able (justifiable, indemnifiable). Verbs ending in -ate drop that syllable before adding -able (appreciable, demonstrable)

-able/-ible There are no reliable rules for knowing when a word ends in -able and when in -ible; *see* Appendix for a list of some of the more frequently confused spellings

ABM anti-ballistic missile

Åbo (Swed.)/**Turku** (Fin.) Finnish seaport

ab origine (Lat.) from the beginning

abracadabra

abridgement (UK, alt. US)/**abridgment** (US, alt. UK)

abrogate to abolish

Absalom in the Old Testament, third son of David

Absalom, Absalom! novel by William Faulkner (1936)

Absaroka Range range of Rocky Mountains in Montana and Wyoming

abscess

abseil (UK), **rappel** (US) to descend a rockface by means of a rope

absinth a plant native to the Mediterranean region and (US) a liquorice-flavoured liqueur

absinthe (UK) a liquorice-flavoured liqueur

absquatulate (mock Lat.) to depart in haste

abstemious

Abu Dhabi largest member state of United Arab Emirates, and capital city of that state

Abu Simbel, Egypt. Site of temples built by Rameses II

abyss, abyssal, but **abysmal**

Abyssinia former name of Ethiopia

acacia

Académie française French literary society whose 40 members act as custodians of the French language; in English contexts, Française is usually capitalized

a cappella singing without instrumental accompaniment

Acapulco, Mexico. Officially, Acapulco de Juárez

ACAS (UK) Advisory, Conciliation, and Arbitration Service

Accademia della Crusca Italian literary academy

accelerator

accessible

accessory

acciaccatura grace note in music

accidentally *not* -tly

accolade

accommodate note -cc-, -mm-

accompanist *not* -iest

accouterment (US)/**accoutrement** (UK)

Accra capital of Ghana

Accrington, Lancashire

Achebe, Chinua (1930–) Nigerian novelist

Acheson, Dean (Gooderham) (1893–1971) American diplomat and politician, Secretary of State 1949–53

Achilles King of the Myrmidons, most famous of the Greek heroes of the Trojan War

Achilles' heel (apos.)

Achilles' tendon (US)/**Achilles tendon** (UK)

Achillini, Alessandro (1463–1512) Italian philosopher and physician

acidulous, assiduous Acidulous means tart or acid; assiduous means diligent

acknowledgement (UK)/**acknowledgment** (US)

Acland, Sir Antony (Arthur) (1930-) British diplomat; note unusual spellings of both first name and surname

acolyte *not* -ite; a follower

Aconcagua, Cerro mountain in the Andes in Argentina, highest peak (22,835 ft/6,960 m) in the Western Hemisphere

Açores Portuguese spelling of Azores

acoustics As a science it is singular ('Acoustics was his line of work'), but as a collection of properties it is plural ('The acoustics in the auditorium were not good')

acquiesce, acquiescence

acquit, acquittal, acquitted

Acre/Akko (Heb.), Israel

acre a unit of land measuring 43,560 sq ft, 4,840 sq yd; equivalent to 4,047 sq m, 0.405 hectare

acronym a word formed from the initial letter or letters of a group of words, as in NATO (North Atlantic Treaty Organization) and laser (light amplification by stimulated emission of radiation). Abbreviations that are not pronounced as words (IBM, CBS, TUC) are not acronyms

acrostic writing in which the first, and sometimes the last, letter of each line spells a word when read vertically

Actaeon in Greek mythology, a hunter who is turned into a stag by Artemis after he watches her bathing, and subsequently is killed by his own dogs

Action française, L' right-wing French political group and newspaper

ACTT (UK) Association of Cinematograph, Television and Allied Technicians

acute, chronic Acute, applied to an illness or situation, means approaching a crisis or at a critical stage, and is the opposite of chronic, which means lasting, of long standing or constant

AD *anno Domini* (Lat.) in the year of the Lord. AD should be written before the year (AD 25), but after the century (fourth century AD), and is usually set in small caps, as here; *see also* BC

adagio slowly; slow movement; *pl.* **adagios**

Adams, John (1735–1826) US President 1797–1801; father of **John Quincy Adams** (1767–1848), US President 1825–9

Addams, Charles (Samuel) (1912–88) American cartoonist, long associated with the *New Yorker*

Addams, Jane (1860–1935) American social activist and reformer; Nobel Peace Prize 1931

Addenbrooke's Hospital, Cambridge

addendum, *pl.* **addenda**

Addis Ababa capital of Ethiopia

adducible/adduceable (alt. US) capable of being proved

Ade, George (1866–1944) American playwright

Adenauer, Konrad (1876–1967) West German Chancellor 1949–63 and Foreign Minister 1951–5

adenoid, **adenoidal**

ad hoc (Lat.) towards this, for a particular purpose

Adirondack Mountains mountain range in New York State, part of the Appalachians

adjudicator

administer *not* administrate

Admiral's Cup series of yachting races held every two years

admissible, but **admittable**

ad nauseam (Lat.) *not* -um; to the point of nausea

adolescence, **adolescent**

Adoula, Cyrille (1921–) Prime Minister of Zaïre 1962–4

ADR American depository (*not* -ary) receipt; a financial instrument that enables the shares of non-American companies to be traded on Wall Street

à droite (Fr.) to the right

advance planning is a tautology; all planning must be done in advance.

adverse, **averse** Adverse means contrary or opposed; averse means disinclined

advisable

adviser. Advisor is an acceptable alternative, but most authorities prefer adviser

advisory

advocaat a liqueur
Aeaea in Greek mythology, the island inhabited by Circe
Aegean Sea area of the Mediterranean between Greece, Turkey and Crete
Aegina town and island off the south-eastern coast of Greece
Aeneid epic poem by Virgil
Aeolian Islands group of islands off north-eastern Sicily; also called Lipari Islands
Aeolus Greek god of winds
aeon (UK)/**eon** (US)
aerate pronounced air-ate, *not* air-e-ate
Aer Lingus Irish national airline
Aeroparque Jorge Newbery Buenos Aires airport
aeroplane (UK)/**airplane** (US)
aerosol
Aérospatiale French aviation company
Aerovias de Mexico Mexican airline, formerly called Aeromexico
Aeschylus (*c*. 525–*c*. 456 BC) Greek playwright
Aesculapius (Lat.)/**Asclepius** (Grk) Roman and Greek god of medicine
Afars and Issas, French Territory of former name of Djibouti
AFBD (UK) Association of Futures Brokers and Dealers
affaire de coeur (Fr.) love affair
affaire d'honneur (Fr.) duel
affect, effect As a verb, affect means to influence ('Smoking may affect your health') or to adopt a pose or manner ('He affected ignorance'), and effect means to accomplish ('The prisoners effected an escape'). As a noun, effect is almost always the desired word (as in 'personal effects' and 'the damaging effects of war'); affect as a noun has a narrow psychological meaning.
affettuoso in music, to play with feeling
affidavit
affrettando in music, speeding up
affright
aficionado, *pl.* ***aficionados*** not -ff-

AFL-CIO American Federation of Labor and Congress of Industrial Organizations

à fond (Fr.) thoroughly

a fortiori (Lat.) with even stronger reason

Afrikaans, **Afrikaners** The first is a language; the second, a people

Ag chemical symbol for silver

AG *Aktiengesellschaft* (Ger.), roughly equivalent to Inc. or PLC

Agamemnon in Greek mythology, King of Argos and commander of Greek army in the Trojan War; title of play by Aeschylus, the first part of the Oresteian trilogy

Agassiz, (Jean) Louis (Rodolphe) (1807–73) Swiss-born American naturalist

agenda, *pl.* **agendas**

ageing (UK)/**aging** (US)

agent provocateur, *pl.* ***agents provocateurs***

à gauche (Fr.) to the left

aggrieve

Agincourt, Battle of (1415)

Agnelli, **Giovanni** (1921–) pronounced an-yell'-ee; Italian businessman

AGR advanced gas-cooled reactor, a type of nuclear power station

agreeable

Aguascalientes city and state in central Mexico

Agusta *not* Aug-; formally, Gruppo Agusta; Italian helicopter company

à huis clos (Fr.) behind closed doors

Ah, Wilderness! comedy by Eugene O'Neill (1933)

aide-de-camp abbr. ADC; *pl.* **aides-de-camp**

aide-mémoire, *pl.* ***aides-mémoire***

AIDS Acquired Immune Deficiency Syndrome

aiguillette ornamental braid worn on the shoulder of a uniform

Ailesbury, Marquess of but the town in Buckinghamshire is Aylesbury

Aintree, Merseyside, site of Grand National race course

Airbus Industrie European aircraft manufacturer

Airedale (cap.) a breed of terrier, named after valley in Yorkshire

Air-India (hyphen) airline

Air Line Pilots Association (US) *not* Airline; trade union

airplane (US)/**aeroplane** (UK)

airports *See* Appendix for a table of some of the world's main airports and their international baggage and ticket codes.

Airy, George Biddell (1801–92) English astronomer

aitch the eighth letter of the alphabet

Aix-en-Provence (hyphens)

Aix-la-Chapelle (hyphens) French name for Aachen

Aix-les-Bains (hyphens)

Ajaccio capital of Corsica and birthplace of Napoleon

AK postal abbr. of Alaska

Akihito (1933–) Emperor of Japan 1989–

AL postal abbr. of Alabama

Ala. Alabama

à la The adjectival forms of proper nouns in French do not take capital letters after *à la*: *à la française, à la russe, à la lyonnaise*

alabaster

Aladdin

Alamein, El/Al Egyptian village that gave its name to two battles of World War II

Alamogordo, New Mexico; site of first atomic bomb explosion

Alanbrooke, Alan Francis Brooke, Viscount (1883–1963) British field marshal

A la recherche du temps perdu novel by Marcel Proust, published in English as *Remembrance of Things Past*

Albigenses, **Albigensians** religious sect during 11th to 13th centuries, also known as Cathars, exterminated at the behest of the Inquisition

albumen, albumin Albumen is the white of an egg; albumin is a protein within the albumen.

Albuquerque New Mexico; pronounced al-buh-ker-kee

Alcaeus (*c.* 600 BC) Greek poet

Alcatraz, San Francisco Bay, California

Alcibiades (*c*. 450–404 BC) Athenian statesman and general

Alcock, Sir John William (1892–1919) British aviator who with Sir Arthur Whitten Brown was the first to fly nonstop across the Atlantic (1919)

Alcott, Louisa May (1833–88) American writer, daughter of **Amos Bronson Alcott** (1799–1888), author and philosopher

Aleixandre, Vicente (1898–1984) pronounced ah-lay-hahn'-dray; Spanish poet, Nobel Prize for Literature 1977

Alembert, Jean le Rond d' (1717–83) French mathematician and philosopher

Aleutian Islands long range of islands in northern Pacific, part of Alaska

Alexanders Laing & Cruickshank (no punc.) UK stockbroking firm

alfalfa

Alfa-Romeo Italian car company, a subsidiary of Fiat

Alfieri, Vittorio (1749–1803) Italian poet and dramatist

Alfonsín (Foulkes), Dr Raúl (1923–) President of Argentina 1983–9

Algeciras, Spain

Algonquin Hotel, New York; **Algonquin** Indians

algorithm

Ali, Muhammad (1942–) born Cassius Marcellus Clay; American heavyweight boxer, three times world champion

Alitalia Italian national airline

à l'italienne (Fr., no caps.) in the Italian style

alkali, *pl.* **alkalis/alkalies**

al-Khwarizmi, Muhammad ibn-Musa (*c*. 780–850) Arab mathematician, often called the father of algebra

Allahabad city in Uttar Pradesh, India

allege, **allegedly**, **allegation**

Allegheny Mountains, *pl.* **Alleghenies**

Allegheny River, **Allegheny Airlines**, *but* **Alleghany Corporation** and **Allegany State Park**, New York

Allen, (William) Hervey (1889–1949) *not* Harvey; American novelist

Allenby, Edmund Henry Hynman, Viscount (1861–1936) British general

Allende (Gossens), Salvador (1908–73) pronounced a-yen'-day; President of Chile 1970–73

All Fools' Day, April Fools' Day (US), but **April Fool's Day** (UK) 1 April

All God's Chillun Got Wings play by Eugene O'Neill (1924)

Allhallows, Kent

all intents and purposes is a tautology; use just 'to all intents'

allophone one of the variant sounds of a phoneme; in Canadian usage, someone who does not speak French

allot, allotted, allotting, allottable

all right Alright is never all right

All Saints' Day 1 November

All Souls College, Oxford

All Souls' Day 2 November

Allyson, June (1917–) American film actress

Alma-Ata capital of Kazakhstan

Al Manama/Al Manamah capital of Bahrain

Alnwick, Northumberland, pronounced ann'-ick

Alpes-de-Haute-Provence *département* of France

Al Qahirah/El Qahira Arabic name for Cairo

Alsatian (cap.) common UK name for breed of dog officially called German Shepherd

Althing parliament of Iceland

although, though The two are interchangeable except as an adverb placed after the verb, where only though is correct, and with the expressions 'as though' and 'even though', where idiom precludes although.

aluminium (UK)/**aluminum** (US)

alyssum border plant

Alzheimer's disease type of dementia associated with old age; named after Alois Alzheimer, the German physician who first described it

a.m./AM *ante meridiem* (Lat.) before midday

Amalienborg Palace, Copenhagen, residence of Danish royal family

amanuensis one who takes dictation; *pl.* **amanuenses**
Amarillo, Texas
amaryllis
Ambassadors Theatre, London (no apos.)
ambergris substance used in the manufacture of perfumes
ambidextrous *not* -erous
ambience (UK, US)/**ambiance** (Fr., alt. US)
ameba (alt. US)/**amoeba** (UK, US)
Amenhotep name of four kings in 18th dynasty of ancient Egypt
America's Cup race held every three to four years (since 1851) between an American yacht and one from another country
Amharic the official language of Ethiopia
amicus curiae (Lat.) friend of the court; *pl.* ***amici curiae***
amid, among Among applies to things that can be separated and counted; amid to things that cannot. Rescuers might search among survivors, but amid wreckage
Amman capital of Jordan
amniocentesis the withdrawing of amniotic fluid from a pregnant woman's uterus to check for the presence of disease or genetic defects in, or to determine the sex of, the foetus
amoeba, *pl.* **amoebas/amoebae**; *see also* **ameba**
a moitié (Fr.) in part, halfway
amok (pref.)/**amuck** (alt.)
among, between A few authorities insist that among applies to more than two things and between to only two. But by this logic you would have to say that St Louis is among California, New York and Michigan, not between them. In so far as the two words can be distinguished, among should be applied to collective arrangements (trade talks among the members of the European Community) and between to reciprocal arrangements (a treaty between the UK, the US and Canada).
amoral, immoral Amoral applies to matters in which questions of morality do not arise or are disregarded; immoral applies to things that are evil
amour propre (Fr.) self-respect
Ampère, André Marie (1775–1836) French physicist; the unit of electricity named after him is **ampere** (no cap., no accent)

amphetamine
amphibian, **amphibious**
Amphitryon in Greek mythology, a Mycenaean king whose wife, Alcmene, gave birth to Hercules after Zeus tricked her into sleeping with him
amphora, *pl.* **amphorae/amphoras**
ampoule (UK, alt. US)/**ampul**, **ampule** (US)
Amtrak US railway company; official name: National Railroad Passenger Corporation
amuck (alt.)/**amok** (pref.)
Amundsen, Roald (1872–1928) Norwegian explorer, first person to reach the South Pole (1911)
Anacreon (*c.* 563–*c.* 478 BC) Greek poet
anaesthesia, **anaesthetic** (UK)/**anesthesia**, **anesthetic** (US)
anaesthetist (UK), **anesthesiologist** (US) doctor who administers anaesthetics and/or specializes in anaesthesia; in the US an **anesthetist** may be a nurse or a doctor
analyse (UK)/**analyze** (US)
anathema, *pl.* **anathemas**
Anaxagoras (*c.* 500–428 BC) Greek philosopher
Anaximander (*c.* 611–*c.* 547 BC) Greek philosopher
anchovy, *pl.* **anchovies**
ancien régime (Fr.) the old order
ancillary
Andalusia/Andalucía (Sp.) region of Spain
Andersen, Arthur *not* -son; accountancy firm
Andersen, Hans Christian (1805–75) Danish author of fairy-tales
Andhra Pradesh Indian state
Andorra a principality; capital, Andorra la Vella
Andretti, Mario (Gabriele) (1940–) American racing driver
Andrewes, Lancelot (1555–1626) English scholar and prelate, one of the principal translators of the King James Bible
androgenous producing male offspring
androgynous having male and female characteristics
Andromache in Greek mythology, the wife of Hector
Andropov, Yuri (1914–84) General Secretary of the Communist Party of the USSR 1982–4; President of the USSR 1983–4

Andrzejewski, Jerzy (1909–83) Polish novelist

anesthesia, anesthetic (US)/**anaesthesia, anaesthetic** (UK); *see also* anaesthetist/anesthesiologist

aneurysm (pref.)/**aneurism** (alt.)

Angelico, Fra (1387–1455) Florentine painter, also known as Fra Giovanni da Fiesole

Angleterre (Fr.) England

Anglo American Corporation (no hyphen) South African mining conglomerate

Angkor complex of ruins in Cambodia. **Angkor Wat/Vat** is a single temple within the compound.

angora hair of the angora goat or rabbit, and fabric made from it

Angostura Bitters

Ångström, Anders Jonas Jöns (1814–74) Swedish physicist

ångström/angstrom unit abbr. Å; used to measure wavelengths of light, and equal to one ten-billionth of a metre, or one hundred-millionth of a centimetre

Anheuser-Busch pronounced an'-hie-zer bush; US brewer

Anhui (Pinyin)/**Anhwei** Chinese province

animus, but **animosity**

aniseed a flavourful seed

anisette a drink flavoured with aniseed

Ankara capital of Turkey

Annapolis capital of Maryland and home of the US Naval Academy

Annapurna a cluster of mountains in the Himalayas, of which the highest peak is Annapurna I (26,545 ft/8,091 m)

Ann Arbor, Michigan, home of the University of Michigan

Anne of Cleves (1515–57) fourth wife of Henry VIII

annex (US noun, vb; UK vb)/**annexe** (UK noun)

annihilate

Ann-Margret (1941–) born Ann-Margret Olsson; note hyphen and irregular spelling of Margret; American actress

anno Domini (Lat., cap. D only) the year of the Lord; *see also* AD

annus mirabilis (Lat.) remarkable year; also title of a poem by Dryden (1667)

anomaly, **anomalous**
anonymous, **anonymity**
anorak
anorexia nervosa
anorexic
Anouilh, Jean (1910–87) pronounced an-wee'; French playwright
Anschluss (Ger.) a union; particularly applied to that of Germany and Austria in 1938
Antananarivo capital of Madagascar
Antarctic, **Antarctica**
ante bellum (Lat.) before the war; especially applied to the period before the American Civil War
antecedence, **antecedents** Antecedence means precedence; antecedents are ancestors or other things that have gone before.
antediluvian antiquated, primitive
ante meridiem (Lat.) before midday; abbr. a.m./AM
antenna, *pl.* **antennas** (radio, etc.) **antennae** (zoology)
Antigone in Greek mythology, the daughter of Oedipus; also the title of a play by Sophocles
Antigua and Barbuda Caribbean state; capital, St John's
antipasto (It.) appetizer, hors-d'oeuvre; *pl.* antipasti/antipastos
Antipodean (cap.) of Australia or New Zealand
antirrhinum note -rr-; a flower, sometimes called snapdragon
antitrust (one word)
Antofagasta, Chile
Antonioni, Michelangelo (1912–) Italian film director
Antony and Cleopatra *not* Anth-; play by Shakespeare (*c.* 1606)
Antwerp/Anvers (Fr.)/**Antwerpen** (Flem.) Belgian city and province
ANZAC Australian and New Zealand Army Corps, a combined unit that fought in World War I
ANZUS Pact (1951) security treaty between Australia, New Zealand and the US
août (Fr.) August
à outrance (Fr.) *not* à l'outrance; to the very last, to the death
apartheid pronounced apart-(h)ite/apart-(h)ate; South African system of racial segregation

Apeldoorn, The Netherlands

Apennines mountain range running the length of Italy; in Italian, Appennini

aperitif, *pl.* **aperitifs**

APEX advance payment excursion fare; Association of Professional, Executive, Clerical and Computer Staff (UK)

apfelstrudel (Ger.) apple strudel

Aphrodite Greek goddess of love, identified with the Roman goddess Venus

aplomb

apocalypse, **apocalyptic**

Apollinaire, Guillaume (1880–1918) born Wilhelm Apollinaris de Kostrowitzky; French writer and critic

Apollo Greek god of light, son of Zeus

Apologie for Poetrie, An title of the essay by Sir Philip Sidney, also published as *The Defence of Poesie* (1595)

apophthegm (UK)/**apothegm** (US) a witty or pithy maxim

aposiopesis sudden breaking off of a thought or statement; *pl.* **aposiopeses**

apostasy, *pl.* **apostasies** the abandoning of one's faith

apostatize

a posteriori (Lat.) from what is after; in logic, moving from effect to cause, reasoning from experience

apotheosis, *pl.* **apotheoses** deification (generally used figuratively)

Appalachian Mountains system of mountains extending 1,600 miles/2,570 km up the eastern seaboard of North America, from Alabama to Quebec; includes the Great Smoky Mountains, Catskills, Adirondacks and Alleghenies

appaloosa North American horse with black and white markings, particularly on the rump

apparatchik party functionary, especially the Communist Party; *pl.* **apparatchiks**/**apparatchiki**

apparel

apparition

appellant, **appellate**

appellation

appendices/appendixes

applicator

appoggiatura in music, an accented non-harmonized note that precedes a harmonized note

Appomattox town in Virginia where the Confederacy surrendered to the Union to end the American Civil War (9 April 1865)

appraise, **apprise**, **apprize** Appraise means to evaluate; apprise means to inform; apprize is a synonym for appraise and US alt. spelling of apprise.

apprehensible

après-midi (Fr.) afternoon

après-ski (Fr., hyphen) the period after a day's skiing

April Fool's Day (UK)/**April Fools' Day** (US)

a principio (Lat.) from the beginning

a priori (Lat.) from what is before; in logic, an argument proceeding from cause to effect

apropos/*à propos* (Fr.)

Apuleius, Lucius (*fl.* second century AD) Roman satirist

Apulia/Puglia (It.) region of Italy

Aqaba, Gulf of an arm of the Red Sea between the Sinai Peninsula and Saudi Arabia

aqua vitae (Lat.) water of life; used to describe whiskies and other alcoholic spirits

aqueduct

aquiline like an eagle

Aquinas, St Thomas (1225–74) Italian theologian, canonized 1323

à quoi bon? (Fr.) what for?, what's the point?

AR postal abbr. of Arkansas

Arafat, Yasir (1929–) born Mohammed Abed Ar'ouf Arafat; leader, Palestine Liberation Organization 1969–

Aramaic Semitic language widely spoken for centuries throughout the Middle East

Aran Islands, off Galway, Ireland; **Aran Island**, off Donegal, Ireland; **Isle of Arran**, Scotland

arbitrageur/arbitrager one who tries to make a quick killing in the trading of shares

Arc de Triomphe, Paris. Officially, Arc de Triomphe de l'Etoile
arc-en-ciel (Fr.) rainbow; *pl.* ***arcs-en-ciel***
archaeology (UK, US)/**archeology** (alt. US)
archaic, **archaism**
archetype
Archilochus of Paros (*c.* 714–*c.* 676 BC) Greek poet
archipelago, *pl.* **archipelagos**
Archimedes' principle a body displaces its own weight in water; named after the Greek mathematician and engineer Archimedes (*c.* 287–212 BC)
Arctic Circle, **Arctic Ocean** (caps.), but **arctic fox** (no caps.)
Ardennes wooded plateau region in southern Belgium, north-eastern France and Luxembourg
Ardizzone, Edward Jeffrey Irving (1900–79) British illustrator
Arezzo, Italy
arguable
Argyll Group UK supermarkets company
Århus (Dan.)/**Aarhus** city in Denmark
Arianism an early Christian heresy
Aristides (*c.* 530–*c.* 468 BC) Athenian statesman
Aristophanes (*c.* 448–*c.*380 BC) Greek dramatist
Aristotle (384–322 BC) Greek philosopher
Ariz. Arizona
Ark. Arkansas, pronounced Arkansaw
Arliss, George (1868–1946) English actor
armadillo, *pl.* **armadillos**
Armageddon
armature
armament
Armenia formerly part of Soviet Union, capital Erevan
armour (UK)/**armor** (US)
aroma applies only to agreeable smells; there is no such thing as a bad aroma
Aroostook River centre of border dispute between Maine and New Brunswick (Canada), focus of Aroostook War

Arran, Isle of, Scotland. *See also* Aran Islands
arrière-pensée (Fr.) ulterior motive, mental reservation
arrivederci (It.) goodbye
arriviste disagreeably ambitious person
Arrol-Johnston British motor car of early 1900s
arrondissement principal division of French *départements* and some larger cities
Arrows of the Chace *not* Chase; by John Ruskin
artefact (UK)/**artifact** (US) The word should be applied only to things fashioned by humans, not to animal bones or fossils
Artemis Greek goddess of the moon, associated with hunting; Roman equivalent is Diana
arteriosclerosis
Arthur Andersen *not* -son; accountancy firm
Arthur, Chester Alan (1830–86) US President 1881–5
artichoke *not* arte-
Article Six article of the USSR constitution amended in 1990 to remove Communist Party's guarantee of total authority
Aruba Caribbean island, a self-governing territory of The Netherlands; capital, Oranjestad
Asahi Shimbun Japanese newspaper
ascendancy, **ascendant**
Ascension remote island in south Atlantic, administered as a dependency of St Helena, itself a colony of Britain
Asch, Sholem (1880–1957) Polish-born American novelist
Asclepius use Aesculapius
Asea Brown Boveri Swedish-Swiss electrical equipment company
ASEAN Association of South East Asian Nations, formed 1967; members are Brunei, Indonesia, Malaysia, the Philippines, Singapore and Thailand
aseptic
Ashby de la Zouch, Leicestershire (no hyphens)
Asheville, North Carolina
Ashihara, Yoshinobu (1918–) Japanese architect
Ashkenazi an East or Central European Jew; *pl.* **Ashkenazim**
Ashkenazy, Vladimir (1937–) Russian pianist and conductor

Ashkhabad capital of Turkmenistan
Ashmolean Museum, Oxford
Asimov, Isaac (1920–92) American biochemist and prolific science-fiction writer
asinine
ASLEF (UK) Associated Society of Locomotive Engineers and Firemen
asparagus
Asquith, Herbert Henry (1852–1928) British Liberal statesman
assailant
assassinate
assegai/assagai African spear
assessor
asseverate to declare
assiduous, **acidulous** Assiduous means diligent; acidulous means tart or acid
Assisi town in Umbria, Italy, birthplace of St Francis
assonance words that rhyme in consonants but not vowels (e.g., cat and kit) or in vowels but not consonants (e.g., bun and sponge)
assuage, **assuaging**
ASTMS (UK) Association of Scientific, Technical, and Managerial Staffs
Asunción capital of Paraguay
asymmetry, **asymmetric**, **asymmetrical**
Atarot Airport, Jerusalem
Atatürk, Mustapha Kemal (1881–1938) Turkish leader and President 1923–38
Athenaeum a London club and a leading British literary review 1828–1921
Athene Greek goddess of wisdom
Atheneum US book publisher
Athinai Greek spelling of Athens
à tout prix (Fr.) at any price
attaché
Attawapiskat Canadian river
Attenborough, Richard, Lord (1923–   ) British film actor and

director; brother of **Sir David Attenborough** (1926–), zoologist and TV presenter

Attila (*c.* 405–53) king of the Huns

Attlee, Clement (Richard), Earl (1883–1967) British Prime Minister 1945–51

attorney-general, *pl.* **attorneys-general**

attributable

Attucks, Crispus (*c.* 1723–1770) black American martyr, killed in the Boston Massacre

Atwater, (Harvey) Lee (1951–91) American political figure

Atwood, Margaret (1939–) Canadian author and critic

Atwood's machine *not* Att-

AU ångstrom unit; astronomical unit

Au *aurum* (Lat.) gold

aubergine (UK, Fr.), **eggplant** (US)

au besoin (Fr.) if need be

aubrietia flowering plant named after Claude Aubriet (1655–1742), French painter

Auchinleck, Sir Claude John Eyre (1884–1981) British field marshal; also family title of James Boswell, whose contemporaries pronounced it aff'-leck

Auchinloss, Louis (Stanton) (1917–) American novelist

Auden, W(ystan) H(ugh) (1907–73) English-born American poet

audible

Audubon, John James (1785–1851) American artist and naturalist

Auerbach, Berthold (1812–82) German writer

Auerbach, Frank (1931–) German-born English artist

au fait (Fr.) to be in the know

au fond (Fr.) basically, at the bottom

auf Wiedersehen (Ger.) goodbye, until we meet again

auger, **augur** An auger is a tool for boring holes in wood or soil; an augur is a prophet or soothsayer.

auld lang syne (Scot.) literally, 'old long since', the good old days; also the title (caps.) of the traditional end-of-year song with words by Robert Burns

Auld Reekie (Scot.) Old Smoky, nickname for Edinburgh
au mieux (Fr.) for the best; at best
au naturel (Fr.) in the natural state
Ausable River, **Ausable Chasm**, New York State
Au Sable River, **Au Sable Point**, Michigan
Auschwitz/Oświęcim (Pol.) German concentration camp in Poland during World War II
au secours (Fr.) a cry for help
Ausländer (Ger.) foreigner
auspicious means propitious, of good omen, *not* memorable or important
Austen, Jane (1775–1817) English novelist
Austral (adj.) of or relating to Australia or Australasia
austral (noun) former currency of Argentina; reverted to pesos in 1992; *pl.* **australes**
austral (adj.) southern
Australia, Commonwealth of is divided into six states (New South Wales, Queensland, South Australia, Tasmania, Victoria, Western Australia) and two territories (Australian Capital Territory, Northern Territory); capital, Canberra
autobahn (Ger.) express motorway; *pl.* **autobahns/*Autobahnen***
auto-da-fé execution of heretics during the Inquisition; *pl.* **autos-da-fé**
autostrada (It.) express motorway; *pl.* **autostrade**
Auvergne region of France
auxiliary *not* -ll-
avant-garde
Avenue of the Americas, New York City. Often still referred to as Sixth Avenue, its former name
averse, **adverse** averse means disinclined; adverse means hostile
avocado, *pl.* **avocados**
avoirdupois weights the system of weights used throughout the English-speaking world, based on 1 pound equalling 16 ounces. Originally there were two other common systems of measurement: the troy system, which is still used by jewellers, and the apothecaries' system, which is no longer generally used

Avon county of England formed in 1974; also the name of several rivers in England, and the title of the former Prime Minister Anthony Eden (Earl of Avon)

à votre santé (Fr.) to your health

a while, **awhile** To write 'for awhile' is wrong because the idea of 'for' is implicit in 'awhile'. Write either 'I will stay here for a while' (two words) or 'I will stay here awhile' (one word)

axel, **axle** An axel is an ice-skating jump; an axle is a rod connecting two wheels

Axelrod, George (1922–   ) American screenwriter

axis, *pl.* **axes**

ayatollah Shiite Muslim religious leader, particularly associated with Iran

Ayckbourn, Alan (1939–   ) British playwright

Ayer, Sir Alfred Jules (1910–89) English philosopher

Aykroyd, Dan (1952–   ) Canadian-born actor and screenwriter

Aylesbury, Buckinghamshire, but Marquess of Ailesbury

Ayres, Gillian (1930–   ) British artist

AZ postal abbr. of Arizona

Azerbaijan a former republic of the Soviet Union; capital Baku

Azikiwe, Nnamdi (1904–   ) Nigerian nationalist leader; President 1963–6

Azores/Açores (Port.)

B

BA British Airways

Baader-Meinhof Group West German underground group named after Andreas Baader (1943–77) and Ulrike Meinhof (1934–76)

Ba'ath Socialist Party Middle Eastern political group

Babangida, Major-General Ibrahim (1941–) President of Nigeria 1985–

Babbitt a novel by Sinclair Lewis (1922)

Babington, Antony (1561–86) Roman Catholic who led a plot, called Babington's Conspiracy, to assassinate Queen Elizabeth I

Babi Yar site near Kiev where Nazis massacred Russian Jews in 1941; also title of a poem by Yevgeny Yevtushenko and a novel by Anatoly Kuznetsov

babushka (Russ.) grandmother; also a kind of head scarf often worn by Eastern European peasant women

Bacardi brand of rum

baccalaureate

baccarat/*baccara* (Fr.)

Bacchae, The a play by Euripides

Bacchus Roman god of wine; Greek equivalent is Dionysus; note -cc- in all spellings arising from Bacchus; Bacchanal, Bacchanalian, Bacchic, Bacchantic, etc.; in the US these words usually do not have caps.

Bach, Johann Sebastian (1685–1750) German composer and father of four others: **Wilhelm Friedemann Bach** (1710–84), **Carl Philipp** (note -pp) **Emanuel Bach** (1714–88), **Johann**

Christoph Friedrich Bach (1732–95) and **Johann Christian Bach** (1735–82)
bachelor *not* batchelor
bacillus, *pl.* **bacilli**
back benches, **backbencher** (UK) Backbenchers are Members of Parliament not holding a senior office; they sit behind the Members of Parliament on the front benches, who are leading members of the Government or Opposition
Bacon, Francis, Baron Verulam of Verulam, Viscount St Albans (1561–1626) English philosopher and essayist
Bacon, Francis (1909–92) Irish artist
bacterium, *pl.* **bacteria**
Baden-Powell, Robert Stephenson Smyth, Baron (1857–1941) founder of Boy Scouts (1908) and, with his sister **Agnes Baden-Powell** (1858–1945), Girl Guides (1910)
Baden-Württemberg German state; capital, Stuttgart
Badlands National Park, South Dakota
BAe British Aerospace; not be be confused with BA, which is British Airways
Baedeker famous series of guidebooks first published in Germany by Karl Baedeker (1801–59)
Baekeland, Leo Hendrik (1863–1944) Belgian-born American chemist, invented Bakelite
Baeyer, Johann Friedrich Wilhelm Adolf von (1835–1917) German chemist; Nobel Prize for Chemistry 1905
bagatelle a trifle; also the name of a board game
Bagehot, Walter (1826-77) pronounced badge'–ut; English economist, journalist and authority on the English Constitution
Baghdad capital of Iraq
Bahadur title of respect in India
Baha'i a religion
Bahamian of or from the Bahamas
Bahnhof (Ger.) railway station
Bahrain island state in the Persian Gulf; capital, Al Manama
bail, **bale** Bail is a prisoner's bond, the pieces that rest atop the stumps in cricket and the act of scooping water. Bale is a

bundle of cotton or hay. You bail out a boat, but bale out of an aircraft. A malicious person wears a baleful expression

Baile Atha Cliath Gaelic for Dublin

bailiff

Baird, John Logie (1888–1946) Scottish pioneer of television

baited breath is wrong; breath is bated.

Bakelite (cap.) type of plastic

baksheesh

Bakst, Léon (Nikolayevich) (1866–1924) born Lev Samoilovich Rosenberg; Russian designer

Baku capital of Azerbaijan

Bakunin, Mikhail (Aleksandrovich) (1814–76) Russian revolutionary

balaclava knitted hats named after Ukrainian town where battle was fought (1854) during the Crimean War

balalaika stringed instrument

Balanchine, George (1904–83) pronounced bal'-len-sheen; born Georgi Melitonovich Balanchivadze; Russian-born American choreographer

Balboa, Vasco Núñez de (1475–1517) Spanish explorer, discovered the Pacific Ocean

baldachin/baldaquin pronounced baldakin; a canopy over a throne or altar; in Italian, *baldacchino*

Baldrige, Malcolm (1922–87) *not* -ridge; American statesman

Baldwin, Stanley (1867–1947) British Conservative statesman

Balearic Islands/Islas Baleares (Sp.) cluster of Spanish islands in the Mediterranean, comprising Majorca (in Spanish, Mallorca), Ibiza, Minorca (in Spanish, Menorca), Formentera, Cabrera, and eleven smaller islands

bale, bail Bale is a bundle of cotton or hay. Bail is a prisoner's bond, the pieces that rest atop the stumps in cricket and the act of scooping water. You bail out a boat, but bale out of an aircraft. A malicious person wears a baleful expression.

Balfour, Arthur (James), Earl (1848–1930) British Prime Minister 1902–06; issued Balfour Declaration (1917) calling for creation of a Jewish state in Palestine. It should be noted that there are now three Lord Balfours – the Earl of Balfour, Lord

Balfour of Inchrye and Lord Balfour of Burleigh – and care must be taken in distinguishing between them.

balk (UK vb; US vb, noun)/**baulk** (UK noun)

Balladur, Édouard Prime Minister of France 1993-

Ballesteros, Severiano (1957–) nickname 'Sevvy'; Spanish golfer

Balliol College, Oxford

balloted, balloting

Balmoral Castle royal residence near Braemar, Grampian, Scotland

Baluchistan region in Pakistan bordered by Iran and Afghanistan

Balzac, Honoré de (1799–1850) French writer

bandanna *not* -dana; coloured handkerchief

Banda Oriental former name of Uruguay

Bandaranaike, Sirimavo (1916–) Prime Minister of Sri Lanka 1960–65, 1970–77; the widow of **Solomon Bandaranaike**, who was Prime Minister 1956–9

bandicoot ratlike marsupial

banister handrail on a staircase

banjo, *pl.* **banjos**

BankAmerica Corporation (one word), but **Bank of America** for individual branches

BankAmericard

Bankers Trust (no apos.) US bank

Bank for International Settlements *not* of

Bankhead, Tallulah (1903–68) American actress

bank holiday (no caps.)

Bannister, Sir Roger (Gilbert) (1929–) first person to run a mile in less than four minutes (3 minutes, 59.4 seconds; 1954)

banns notice in church of intended marriage

banshee/bean sídhe (Gaelic) evil spirit

Bantustan a South African black homeland; *see also* Bophuthatswana

banzai, **bonsai** *Banzai* is a Japanese salute, literally, 'May you live 10,000 years'; bonsai is the Japanese art of growing dwarf trees and shrubs

baptistery

Barabbas in the New Testament, condemned thief released instead of Jesus by Pilate

Barbarossa *not* -rosa; nickname of Frederick I (*c.* 1123–90), Holy Roman Emperor; German code-name for invasion of USSR in 1941

barbecue *not* -que

Barbirolli, Sir John (1899–1970) British conductor

Barbizon School group of French landscape painters, among them Daubigny, Millet and Rousseau

Barclays Bank (no apos.)

Barclays de Zoete Wedd abbr. BZW; UK financial services company

Barco Vargas, Virgilio (1921–) President of Colombia 1986–90;

Barents Sea

bar mitzvah religious coming-of-age ceremony for Jewish boys; the ceremony for girls is a bat mitzvah

Barnard, Christiaan (Neethling) (1922–) note -aa- in first name; South African heart surgeon

Barnstable (town and county), Cape Cod, Massachusetts

Barnstaple, Devon

Barnum, Phineas T(aylor) (1810–91) American circus showman

baron, baroness, baronet A baron is the lowest rank in the British nobility. A baronage can be either hereditary or non-hereditary. Holders of the latter are called life peers. A baroness is a woman who is the wife or widow of a baron, or a peer in her own right. In British contexts, Lord or Lady can be substituted for Baron or Baroness, e.g., Baron Baden-Powell is called Lord Baden-Powell. A baronet is not a peer; it is a hereditary title ranking below a peer but above a knight. *See also* peerage.

Barons Court, London (no apos.)

barracuda

Barratt Homes (UK)

Barratt, Michael (1928–) British broadcaster

Barrault, Jean-Louis (1910–) French actor, mime, director and producer

Barre, Raymond (1924–) French Prime Minister 1976–81

Barrie, Sir J(ames) M(atthew) (1860–1937) Scottish writer

Barrow-in-Furness, Cumbria (hyphens)

Bartholdi, Frédéric Auguste (1834–1904) French sculptor, designed Statue of Liberty

Bartholomew Day 24 August; but the **St Bartholomew's Day Massacre** (1572)

Bartók, Béla (1881–1945) Hungarian pianist and composer

Bartolommeo, Fra (1475–1517) Florentine painter

Bart's nickname for St Bartholomew's Hospital, London

Baruch, Bernard (Mannes) (1870–1965) American financier

Baryshnikov, Mikhail Nikolayevich (1948–) Russian-born ballet dancer and actor

BASIC Beginner's All-purpose Symbolic Instruction Code, a computer language

Basle (UK, Switz.)/**Basel** (US, Ger.)/**Bâle** (Fr.) pronounced bazz'-ul/bahl; third largest city in Switzerland

Basotho the people of Lesotho

Bastille Day 14 July (1789)

Bataan peninsula of the Philippines, famous for long forced march of defeated Allied soldiers by Japanese in which many thousands died in World War II

bated breath, *not* baited

Bathsheba in Old Testament, wife of Uriah and then David, mother of Solomon

Batista (y Zaldívar), Fulgencio (1901–73) Cuban President 1940–44 and dictator 1952–9

Baton Rouge pronounced batt'-un roojzhe; capital of Louisiana

battalion

Battelle Memorial Institute, Columbus, Ohio

Battenberg cake (cap. B)

Baudelaire, Charles (Pierre) (1821–67) French poet

Baudouin (Albert Charles Léopold Axel Marie Gustave) (1930–93) King of the Belgians 1951–93

Bauhaus German school of arts and architecture founded by Walter Gropius (1883–1969)

baulk (UK noun)/**balk** (UK vb; US vb, noun)

Baum, L(yman) Frank (1856–1919) American writer of children's stories

Bayern German for Bavaria

Bayonne name of cities in France and New Jersey

Bayreuth, Bavaria

BC always goes after the year (e.g., 42 BC); usually set in small caps.; *see also* AD

Beachy Head, East Sussex

Beaconsfield, Buckinghamshire, pronounced bek'-uns-field; the model village at Beaconsfield is Bekonscot

Beardsley, Aubrey (Vincent) (1872–98) British artist

béarnaise sauce

Bearwardcote, Derbyshire, pronounced bear'-a-kot

Beatrix (Wilhelmina Armgard) (1938–) Queen of The Netherlands, 1980–

Beatty, Warren (1937–) born Warren Beaty; pronounced bate'-ee, *not* beet'-ee; American film actor and director

Beaufort scale measures wind velocity on a scale of 0 to 12, with 0 representing dead calm and 12 representing a hurricane

Beaufort, South Carolina, pronounced bew'-furt

Beaujolais

Beaulieu, Hampshire, pronounced bew'-lee

Beaumarchais, Pierre Augustin Caron de (1732–99) French playwright whose works inspired the operas *The Barber of Seville* and *The Marriage of Figaro*

beau monde the fashionable world; *pl.* **beaux mondes**

Beauregard, Pierre (Gustave Toutant de) (1818–1893) American Confederate general

Beauvoir, Simone (Lucie Ernestine Maria Bertrand) de (1908–86) French author

beaux arts pronounced bo-zar'; the fine arts

Beaverbrook, Max (William Maxwell Aitken), Baron (1879–1964) Canadian-born British press baron

béchamel sauce

Becher's Brook formidable jump on Grand National course
Bechuanaland former name of Botswana
Becket, St Thomas (à) (1118–70) Archbishop of Canterbury, murdered by followers of Henry II
Beckett, Samuel (1906–89) Irish poet, novelist and playwright
becquerel a unit of radioactivity, named after Antoine Henri Becquerel (1852–1908), French physicist
Bede (*c.* 673–735) British clerical scholar, known as the Venerable Bede
Bedloe's Island former name of Liberty Island, New York, site of Statue of Liberty
bedouin this is actually a double plural; *sing.* **bedi** *pl.* **bedu**
Beecher, Henry Ward (1813–87) American preacher
Beelzebub Satan; 'prince of demons' in New Testament; Satan's chief lieutenant in John Milton's *Paradise Lost*
Beene, Geoffrey (1927–) American fashion designer
Beerbohm, Sir (Henry) Max(imilian) (1872–1956) British writer and critic
Beethoven, Ludwig van (1770–1827) German composer
Beggar's Opera, The *not* Beggars'; by John Gay (1728)
Begin, Menachem (1913–) Polish-born Israeli Prime Minister 1977–83; Nobel Peace Prize 1978
Behn, Aphra (1640–89) English playwright, poet and novelist
behoove (US)/**behove** (UK)
Beiderbecke, Bix (1903–31) born Leon Bismarck Beiderbecke; American jazz musician
Beijing (Pinyin)/**Peking**
Bekonscot model village in Buckinghamshire
Belarus (pref.)/**Bielarus/Byelorussia/Belorussia** former republic of Soviet Union, now independent state, capital Minsk
beleaguered *not* -ured
Belém Brazilian city, formerly Pará
Belgrade/Beograd (Serbo-Croat) capital of Yugoslavia
Belisha beacon (UK) a flashing amber light at pedestrian crossings
Belize Central American republic, formerly British Honduras, pronounced beleez'

belladonna deadly nightshade

Bellany, John (1942–) British artist

belle époque (no caps.) the period just before World War I

Belleisle, County Fermanagh, Northern Ireland; but **Belle-Isle**, Brittany; **Belle Isle Straits**, Canada

Bellerophon in Greek mythology, warrior who killed the Chimera and was crippled trying to fly the winged horse Pegasus over Mount Olympus

belles-lettres writing having literary or aesthetic, as opposed to purely informational, value. A writer of belles-lettres is a **belletrist**. The art is called **belletrism** and the adjectival form is **belletristic**. Belles-lettres is usually treated as a plural, but may be used as a singular.

bellicose warlike

belligerence, belligerency

Bellini, Jacopo (*c.* 1400–65) Venetian painter and father of two others: **Gentile Bellini** (*c.* 1428–*c.* 1508) and **Giovanni Bellini** (*c.* 1430–1516)

Bellini, Vincenzo (1801–35) Italian composer

Bellona Roman goddess of war

bellwether *not* -weather

Belorussia /Byelorussia *see* Belarus

Belsen full name, Bergen-Belsen; concentration camp in Lower Saxony, Germany, during World War II

beluga caviare (no caps.) beluga is a type of sturgeon from which the caviare comes, not a manufacturer

Belvoir Castle, **Vale of Belvoir**, Leicestershire, both pronounced beaver

Bendl, Karel (1838–97) Czech composer

Benedick character in Shakespeare's *Much Ado about Nothing*

beneficence

benefit, benefited, benefiting

Benelux Belgium, The Netherlands and Luxembourg

Beneš Eduard (1884–1948) Czechoslovakian Prime Minister 1921–2 and President 1935–8, 1939–45 in exile, 1945–8

Benét, Stephen Vincent (1898–1943) American writer, brother of writer **William Rose Benét** (1886–1950)

Bene't Street, Cambridge
Benetton Italian clothing company
Benghazi Libyan city
Ben-Gurion, David (1886–1973) born David Grün; Polish-born Israeli Prime Minister 1948–53, 1955–63
benignancy/benignity
benison a blessing
Bennet family in Jane Austen's *Pride and Prejudice*
Bentsen, Lloyd (Millard Jr) (1921–) American politician
ben venuto (It.) welcome
Benzedrine (cap.)
benzene, **benzine** Both are liquid hydrocarbons and both are used as solvents, but they are different chemically; benzene is used largely in the production of plastics, benzine as a solvent in dry-cleaning establishments
Beowulf Anglo-Saxon epic written sometime between 650 and 750
Berchtesgaden, Bavarian walking and tourist centre where Hitler had a country retreat
bereft means to be dispossessed of something, not simply to lack it. A widow is bereft of her husband, but a poor person is not bereft of money unless he once had it
Bérégovoy, Pierre (1925-93) French politician, Prime Minister 1992-3
Berenson, Bernard/Bernhard (1865–1959) Lithuanian-born American art critic
Beretta Italian manufacturer of handguns
Berg, Alban (1885–1935) Austrian composer
Bergdorf Goodman New York department store
Bergesen Norwegian shipping company
Bergman, Ingmar (1918–) Swedish film director and writer
Bergman, Ingrid (1915–82) Swedish actress
Bergson, Henri (1859–1941) French philosopher
Bering Sea
berk a boorish or foolish person; rhyming slang derived from Berkshire or Berkeley Hunt
Berkeleian a follower of the philosopher George Berkeley (1685–1753)

Berkeley, Sir Lennox (Randal Francis) (1903–89) British composer

Berkeley Square, London, pronounced bark'-lee; **Berkeley,** California, pronounced birk'-lee;

Berklee Performance Center, Boston, Massachusetts

Berlin, Irving (1888–1989) born Israel Baline; Russian-born American composer

Berlin, Sir Isaiah (1909–) Latvian-born British philosopher

Berlioz, (Louis) Hector (1803–69) French composer

Bermudian

Bern/Berne capital of Switzerland

Bern Convention (1886) an international agreement on copyright

Bernhardt, Sarah (1844–1923) born Henriette Rosine Bernard; French actress, called 'the Divine Sarah'

Bernini, (Giovanni) Lorenzo (1598–1680) Italian sculptor and architect

Bertelsmann German communications group

Berthelot, Pierre-Eugène Marcelin (1827–1907) French chemist and politician; not to be confused with the next entry

Berthollet, Claude-Louis, Comte (1748–1822) French chemist

Bertolucci, Bernardo (1940–) Italian film director

Besant, Annie (1847–1933) British Theosophist and advocate of birth control

Besant, Sir Walter (1836–1901) British novelist and critic, brother-in-law of Annie Besant

beseech

besiege

Bessarabia former name of Moldova

Bessemer process, **Bessemer converter** (cap. B) named after Sir Henry Bessemer (1813–98), English metallurgist

bête noire (Fr.) something much disliked; *pl.* ***bêtes noires***

Betjeman, Sir John (1906–84) British poet; Poet Laureate 1972–84

Bettelheim, Bruno (1903–90) Austrian-born American child-psychologist

between, **among** A few authorities insist that between applies only to two things and among to more than two. But by this logic you would have to say that St Louis is among California, New York and Michigan, not between them. In so far as the two words can be distinguished, between should be applied to reciprocal arrangements (a treaty between the UK, the US and Canada) and among to collective arrangements (trade talks among the members of the European Community)

between you and I is always wrong; use 'between you and me'

Betws-y-coed, Gwynedd, Wales, pronounced bettoos-a-koyd

Bevan, Aneurin (1897–1960) British Labour politician; as Minister of Health, introduced the National Health Service (1948)

Beveridge, William Henry, Baron (1879–1963) British economist, best known as the author of the *Beveridge Report* (1942) (formally *A Report on Social Insurance and Allied Services*) which led to the setting-up of a comprehensive social security system in Britain

Beverley, Humberside

Beverly Hills, California

Bevin, Ernest (1881–1951) British politician and trade union leader; founder of National Transport and General Workers' Union; Foreign Secretary 1945–51

Bexleyheath, Kent

Bhagavadgita sacred Hindu text, part of the Sanskrit epic *Mahabharata*

Bhumibol (Adulyadej) (1927–) King of Thailand 1946–

Bhutto, Benazir (1953–) Prime Minister of Pakistan 1988–90; daughter of **Zulfiqar Ali Bhutto** (1928–79), founder of the Pakistan People's Party, President of Pakistan 1971–3, Prime Minister 1973–7

biannual, biennial Biannual means twice a year; biennial means every two years; see also bimonthly/biweekly

Biarritz French resort on Atlantic coast

biased

biathlon sport in which competitors must ski across country and shoot set targets

Bible (cap.), but **biblical** (no cap.)

Bicester, Oxfordshire, pronounced biss'-ter

Bierce, Ambrose (Gwinett) (1842–1914) American journalist and writer

Big Ben, strictly speaking, is not the famous clock on the Houses of Parliament, but just the great hour bell. The formal name for the clock is the clock on St Stephen's Tower on the Palace of Westminster

Bildungsroman (Ger.) novel dealing with character's early life and psychological development

billabong, Australian backwater; literally, 'dead stream'

Billericay, Essex, pronounced bill-a-rik'-ee

billet-doux (Fr.) love letter; *pl.* **billets-doux**

billion, **trillion** In the US and now almost always in the UK billion signifies one thousand million (1,000,000,000), but in France and Germany (and formerly in the UK) it signifies one million million (1,000,000,000,000). In the US and generally but not invariably in Britain trillion signifies one million million, but in France and Germany it is one million million million (1,000,000,000,000,000,000)

Biloxi, Mississippi, pronounced buh-luk'-see

bimonthly, **biweekly** and similar designations are almost always ambiguous. It is far better to say 'every two months', 'twice a month', etc., as appropriate

Birds Eye (US)/**Birds Eye Walls** (UK) frozen food companies named after Clarence Birdseye (1886–1956), the American who invented methods of quick-freezing food

biretta hat worn by Catholic priests

Bishkek capital of Kyrgyzstan

Bishops Cannings, Wiltshire; **Bishops Sutton**, Hampshire **Bishop's Castle**, Shropshire; **Bishop's Caundle**, Dorset; **Bishop's Cleeve**, Gloucestershire; **Bishop's Clyst**, Devon; **Bishop's Frome**, Hereford & Worcester; **Bishop's Hull**, Somerset; **Bishop's Itchington**, Leicestershire; **Bishop's Lydeard**, Somerset; **Bishop's Nympton**, Devon; **Bishop's Offley**, Avon; **Bishop's Stortford**, Hertfordshire; **Bishop's Tawton**, Devon; **Bishop's Tachbrook**, Warwickshire

Bishopstone, Buckinghamshire, Hereford & Worcester, Kent, East Sussex, Wiltshire

Bishop Sutton, Avon

Bishopton, Avon, County Durham, North Yorkshire, Strathclyde, West Glamorgan

Bismarck, (Otto Eduard Leopold), Prince von (1815–98) German Chancellor 1871–90

Bizet, (Alexandre César Léopold) Georges (1838–75) French composer

Black Friars Dominicans

Blackfriars, London

Blackley, Greater Manchester, pronounced blake'-lee

Blackmoor, Hampshire, but **Blackmore**, Essex

Blackmore, R(ichard) D(oddridge) (1825–1900) English novelist

Black Rod formally Gentleman Usher of the Black Rod; the officer of the House of Lords who summons Members of the Commons to hear the Queen's speech at the opening of Parliament and to hear her assent to bills, etc.

Black Watch nickname of the Scottish Royal Highland Regiment

blamable (US)/**blameable** (UK)

Blavatsky, Helena Petrovna (1831–91) Russian spiritualist, founded Theosophical Society in New York

blaze, **blazon** Blaze means make a trail; blazon means display ostentatiously. You do not blazon a trail

Bleecker Street, New York

Blenheim, Battle of (1704)

Blériot, Louis (1872–1936) French aviator, first person to cross English Channel in aeroplane (1909)

blitzkrieg (Ger.) 'lightning war'; overwhelming, violent attack

Blixen, Karen, Baroness (1885–1962) Danish writer, who used pseudonym Isak Dinesen

Bloemfontein, South Africa, capital of Orange Free State

Blumberg, Baruch S(amuel) (1926–) Master of Balliol College, Oxford 1988– , the first American to hold that position; joint winner of Nobel Prize for Physiology or Medicine 1976

Blu-Tack

BMW Bayerische Motoren Werke

B'nai B'rith Jewish organization

Boadicea/Boudicca (d. AD 62) queen of Iceni, a British tribe;

led unsuccessful revolt against the Romans

Boboli Gardens, Florence

Boccaccio, Giovanni (1313–75) Italian writer

Boccherini, Luigi (1743–1805) Italian composer and cellist

Böcklin, Arnold (1827–1901) Swiss painter

Bodhisattva in Buddhism, an enlightened one

Bodleian Library, Oxford

Boehme, Jakob (1575–1624) German philosopher

Boeotia region of ancient Greece, centred on Thebes

Boethius, Anicius Manlius Severinus (*c.* 480–*c.* 524) Roman statesman and philosopher

Boettcher Concert Hall, Denver, Colorado

Bogarde, Sir Dirk (1921–) born Derek Niven van den Bogaerde; English actor and writer

Bogdanovich, Peter (1939–) American film director and writer

bogey, **bogie**, **bogy** A bogey is one stroke over par in golf; a bogie is a wheeled undercarriage; and a bogy is an evil spirit

Bogotá capital of Colombia

Bohème, La opera by Puccini

Bohr, Niels (Henrik David) (1885–1962) Danish scientist; Nobel Prize for Physics 1922

Boiardo, Matteo Maria, Conte di Scandiano (1434–94) Italian poet

Bois de Boulogne Paris park

Boise pronounced boyce'-ee by locals, but boyz'-ee by almost all other Americans; capital of Idaho

Bokassa, Jean Bédel (1921–) self-proclaimed emperor of Central African Republic (called Central African Empire during his reign) 1966–79

Bokhara a river in Australia; but **Bukhara**, a town in Uzbekistan

Boldiszár, Ivan (1912–) Hungarian writer

Boleyn, Anne (*c.* 1507–36) second wife of Henry VIII

Bolingbroke, Henry St John, Viscount (1678–1751) English statesman

bolívar monetary unit of Venezuela, after Simón Bolívar (1783–1830), Venezuelan-born revolutionary

Bolivia The seat of government is La Paz, but the official capital is Sucre

Böll, Heinrich (1917–85) German author

bon appétit (Fr.) eat well, enjoy your food

Bonhams (no apos.) London auction house

bonhomie (Fr.) good nature

Bonington, Chris(tian John Storey) (1934–) *not* Bonn-; English mountaineer

Bonington, Richard Parkes (1802-28) English painter

Bonnard, Pierre (1867–1947) French painter

bonne nuit (Fr.) good night

bonsai, *banzai* Bonsai is the Japanese art of growing dwarf trees and shrubs; *banzai* is a Japanese salute, literally, 'May you live 10,000 years'

bonsoir (Fr.) good evening

bon vivant, **bon viveur** A bon vivant is a person who enjoys luxurious food; a bon viveur is one who lives well (this term is not in current French usage)

Booker Prize British literary award

Book-of-the-Month Club (US)

Boorstin, Daniel (1914–) American historian, author and former Librarian of Congress

Booth, Edwin (1833–93) the greatest American actor of his day and brother of **John Wilkes Booth** (1831–65), the assassin of Abraham Lincoln

Bophuthatswana South African black homeland; capital Mmabatho

Borges, Jorge Luis (1899–1986) Argentinian writer

Borgia, Rodrigo (1431–1503) Pope Alexander VI, father of **Cesare Borgia** (1476–1507) and **Lucrezia Borgia** (1480–1519)

Borghese noble Italian family of Siena and, later, Rome; the Villa Borghese in Rome contains a fine collection of art

Borglum, (John) Gutzon (de la Mothe) (1871–1941) American sculptor, the guiding force behind Mount Rushmore

Boris Godunov play by Pushkin and opera by Mussorgsky; *see also* Godunov, Boris

Borlaug, Norman Ernest (1914–) American agricultural scientist; Nobel Peace Prize 1970

Bormann, Martin (1900-?45) German Nazi politician

born, borne Born is limited to the idea of birth ('He was born in December'). Borne should be used for the sense of supporting or tolerating ('He has borne the burden with dignity'), but is also used to refer to giving birth in active constructions ('She has borne three children') and in passive constructions followed by 'by' ('The three children borne by her')

Borodin, Alexander (Porfiryevich) (1833–87) Russian composer

Bosch, Hieronymus (*c.* 1450–1516) born Hieronymus van Aken; Dutch painter

Bosnia-Hercegovina (Serbo-Croat)/**Bosnia and Herzegovina** a former Yugoslavian republic; capital Sarajevo

Bosporus *not* Bosph-; strait separating Europe and Asia

BOSS Bureau for (*not* of) State Security; former South African intelligence department, replaced by the National Intelligence Service

Bossuet, Jacques Bénigne (1627–1704) French theologian and orator

Bosworth Field, Leicestershire, scene of decisive battle in War of the Roses, in which Henry Tudor defeated Richard III (22 August 1485)

Botswana southern African republic, formerly Bechuanaland; capital Gaborone; the people are Batswana (*sing.* and *pl.*)

Botticelli, Sandro (*c.* 1445–1510) born Alessandro di Mariano di Vanni Filipepi; Italian painter

Boucher, François (1703–70) French painter

Boucicault, Dion (1822–90) pronounced boo'-see-ko; Irish playwright and actor

Boudicca/Boadicea (d. AD 62) queen of the Iceni, a British tribe; led unsuccessful revolt against the Romans

bougainvillaea (UK)/**bougainvillea** (US)

bouillabaisse pronounced boo-yah-base'; fish stew

bouillon *not* -ion; broth

Boulez, Pierre (1925–) French conductor and composer

Boumédienne, Houari (1925–78) President and Prime Minister of Algeria 1965–78

bourgeois, **bourgeoisie**

Bourgogne (Fr.)/**Burgundy**

Bourguiba, Habib ibn Ali (1903–) Tunisian President 1957–87

Bourn, Cambridgeshire, but **Bourne**, Lincolnshire

Bournville, greater Birmingham; **Bournville** chocolate

boustrophedon writing in which alternate lines go from right to left and left to right

boutonnière flower for buttonhole

Boutros-Ghali, Boutros (1922–) Egyptian politician and civil servant; Secretary-General of United Nations 1992–

Bouygues Group French construction company

bouzouki Greek stringed musical instrument

Bow Bells (caps.) were located in the Church of St Mary-le-Bow, Cheapside, London. Those born within their sound are said to be Cockneys

Bowes Lyon (no hyphen) family name of British Queen Mother and the Earl of Strathmore

Boyd Orr, John, Baron (1880–1971) British nutritionist; Nobel Peace Prize 1949

'Brabançonne (La)' Belgian national anthem

braggadocio hollow boasting, after the character Braggadochio in Spenser's *Faerie Queene*

Brahe, Tycho (1546–1601) Danish astronomer

Brahmaputra river that flows through Tibet, India and Bangladesh

brahmin (UK)/**Brahman** (US) member of Hindu caste (after the Hindu god Brahma). In the US Brahmin is used to describe long-established socially exclusive people ('Boston Brahmins').

Brahms, Johannes (1833–97) German composer

Braille, Louis (1809–52) French inventor of embossed reading system for the blind

Bramante, Donato di Pascuccio d'Antonio (1444–1514) Italian architect and artist

Brancusi, Constantin (1876–1957) Romanian sculptor

Brandeis, Louis D(embitz) (1856–1941) Associate Justice of the US Supreme Court; Brandeis University in Massachusetts is named after him

Brandywine creek in Pennsylvania and Delaware, site of a battle in the American War of Independence

Braque, Georges (1882–1963) French Cubist painter

Brasenose College, Oxford

Brasília capital of Brazil

Braun, Wernher von (1912–77) German-born American space scientist

Brazil formally, República Federativa do Brasil; capital Brasília. The language is Portuguese; for forms of address, *see* señor/senhor

Brazzaville Declaration (1914) guaranteed people of French colonies full rights as French citizens

BRD Bundesrepublik Deutschland: West Germany 1949–90, now formal name of united Germany; *see* Germany

breach, breech A breach is an infraction, while breech means the rear or lower portion. The main expressions are breach of promise, breech birth, breeches buoy, breechcloth, breech-loading gun

Breakspear, Nicolas (*c.* 1100–59) Pope Adrian IV, the only English Pope

Brearley, Mike (John Michael) (1942–) English cricketer

Breathalyser (UK)/**Breathalyzer** (US) a trade-marked device that analyses exhaled breath to determine the amount of alcohol in the body

Brecht, Bertolt (Eugen Friedrich) (1898–1956) German dramatist

Brenninkmeyer, C&A German retail group

Brescia, Italy

Brest-Litovsk, Treaty of (1918) ended Russian involvement in World War I

Bretagne (Fr.)/**Brittany** a region of France; a native is a Breton

Bretton Woods mountain resort in New Hampshire, site of the conference in 1944 that led to the establishment of the International Monetary Fund and World Bank

Breuer, Marcel (Lajos) (1902–81) Hungarian-born American architect and designer

Breugel/Breughel use Brueghel

Brezhnev, Leonid (Ilyich) (1906–82) General Secretary of the USSR Communist Party 1964–82, President of the Supreme Soviet 1977–82

Briand, Aristide (1862–1932) French statesman; joint winner of the Nobel Peace Prize 1926

bric-à-brac (UK)/**bric-a-brac** (US)

Bridge of San Luis Rey, The a novel by Thornton Wilder (1927)

Bridgwater, Somerset, but **Bridgewater**, Nova Scotia, the **Earl of Bridgewater** and the **Bridgewater Treatises**

Brillat-Savarin, Anthelme (1755–1826) French gastronome

briquette piece of compressed coal dust

Bristol-Myers Squibb US pharmaceuticals company

Britannia, **Britannic** *not* -tt-. The song is 'Rule, Britannia' (note comma); *see also* Brittany

British Guiana former name of Guyana

British Honduras former name of Belize

British Indian Ocean Territory group of 2,300 islands in the Indian Ocean run as a British colony; principal island, Diego Garcia

British Midland Airways

British monarchs *see* Appendix

British Printing & Communication Corporation former name of Maxwell Communication (*not* -tions) Corporation

British Thermal Unit abbr. BTU; the amount of heat required to raise the temperature of 1 lb of water by 1 °F

Brittain, Vera (Mary) (1893–1970) British feminist and writer, mother of British politician Shirley Williams (1930–)

Brittan, Sir Leon (1939–) British politician

Brittany/Bretagne (Fr.) region of France; *see also* Britannia, Britannic

Britten, (Edward) Benjamin, Baron Britten of Aldeburgh (1913–76) English composer

Broackes, Sir Nigel (1934–) British businessman

Brobdingnag *not* -dig-; place inhabited by giants in *Gulliver's Travels*

broccoli

Bronfman, Edgar M(iles) (1929–) Canadian businessman

Brontë, Anne (1820–49); **(Patrick) Branwell** (1817–48), **Charlotte** (1816–55) and **Emily (Jane)** (1818–48) English literary family. Among their best-known works are Emily's *Wuthering Heights*, Charlotte's *Jane Eyre*, and Anne's *The Tenant of Wildfell Hall*

brontosaurus *not* bronta-; type of dinosaur

Brooke, Rupert (Chawner) (1887–1915) English poet

Brookings Institution (*not* Institute), Washington, DC, named after **Robert Somers Brookings** (1850–1932), American philanthropist

Brooks, Van Wyck (1886–1963) American critic, writer and historian

brouhaha uproar

Brown, Sir Arthur Whitten (1886–1948) British aviator who with Sir John William Alcock was the first to fly nonstop across the Atlantic (1919)

Brown* v *Board of Education (1954) landmark civil rights case in which US Supreme Court ruled that segregated schools were illegal

Brown, Ford Madox (1821–93) English painter

Browne, Sir Thomas (1605–82) English physician and writer

Browne-Wilkinson, Sir Nicolas (Christopher Henry) (1930–) note unusual spelling of first name; British judge, Vice-Chancellor of the Supreme Court 1985–

Bruckner, Anton (1824–96) Austrian composer

brucellosis disease of cattle

Brueghel, Pieter, the Elder (*c.* 1520–69) *not* Breu-; Flemish painter and father of two others: **Pieter Brueghel the Younger** (1564–1638) and **Jan Brueghel** (1568–1625)

Bruges (Fr.)/**Brugge** (Fl.) city in Flanders, Belgium

Brummell, (George Bryan) Beau (1778–1840) English dandy

Brundtland, Gro Harlem (1939–) Norwegian Prime Minister 1986–9, 1990–

Brunei independent oil-rich state on Borneo; capital Bandar Seri Begawan

Brunei, Sultan of (1946–) working title: HM Sultan Sir Muda Hassanal Bolkiah Mu'izaddin Waddaulah; full title: Duli Yang Maha Mulia Paduka Seri Baginda Sultan and Yang di-Pertuan Negeri Brunei Sir Muda Hassanal Bolkiah Mu'izaddin Waddaulah ibni Duli Yang Teramat Mulia Paduka Seri Begawan Sultan Soir Muda Omar Ali Saifuddin Sa'adul Khairi Waddin, DK, PGGUB, DPKG, DPKT, PSPNB, PSNB, PSLJ, SPMB, PANB, GCMG, DMN, DK (Kelantan), DK (Johore), DK (Negeri Sembilan)

Brunel, Isambard Kingdom (1806–59) British engineer; son of **Sir Marc Isambard Brunel** (1769–1849), also an engineer

Brunelleschi, Filippo (*c.* 1377–1446) Renaissance architect and sculptor

Brunhild In Scandinavian sagas she is a Valkyrie, or priestess, in a deep sleep. In Wagner's *Ring* cycle, the name is spelled Brünnhilde

Brussels/Bruxelles (Fr.)/**Brussel** (Fl.) capital of Belgium

Brussels sprouts (cap. B, no apos.)

Bryan, William Jennings (1860–1925) American lawyer, orator and politician

Bryant, William Cullen (1794–1878) American journalist, critic and poet

Brymon Airways (UK)

Brzezinski, Zbigniew K. (1928–) Polish-born American academic, statesman and writer

BSC British Steel Corporation

BSE bovine spongiform encephalopathy, commonly called mad cow disease

BST bovine somatotropin, controversial genetically engineered hormone used to increase milk production in cows

BTA British Tourist Authority

BTU British Thermal Unit, the amount of heat required to raise the temperature of 1 lb of water by 1 °F

Buccleuch, Duke of pronounced buck-loo'

Buchan, John, Baron Tweedsmuir (1875–1940) Scottish writer and government administrator

Bucharest/Bucureşti (Rom.) capital of Romania

Büchner, Georg (1813–37) German poet and playwright

Buddenbrooks novel by Thomas Mann (1901)

Buddha, **Buddhist**, **Buddhism**

buddleia genus of shrub

budgerigar parakeet

Buenos Aires capital of Argentina

buenos días (Sp.) good-day, hello; but ***buenas*** (*not* -os) ***noches*** (good-night) and ***buenas tardes*** (good-afternoon)

buffalo, *pl.* **buffalo/buffaloes**

Bugatti sports car named after Ettore Bugatti (1881–1947) and his son, Gianoberto (or Jean) Bugatti (1909–39)

Bujumbura capital of Burundi

Bukhara town in Uzbekistan, not to be confused with **Bokhara**, a river in Australia

Bulfinch, Charles (1763–1844) American architect

Bulfinch's Mythology *not* Bull-; subtitle of *The Age of Fable* by **Thomas Bulfinch** (1796–1867)

Bulgakov, Mikhail (Afanasievich) (1891–1940) Soviet writer

Bull Run stream in Virginia, near city of Manassas; site of two battles (1861, 1862), called the Battles of Bull Run or the Battles of Manassas, in American Civil War in which the Confederate Army forces defeated Union forces

Bülow, Claus von (1927–) born Claus Borberg; international socialite, acquitted of the attempted murder of his wealthy American wife, Sunny

Bulwer-Lytton, Edward George Earle, Baron Lytton (1803–73) British politician, poet and playwright

bumf assorted papers

Bumppo, Natty *not* Bumpo; hero of James Fenimore Cooper stories

Bunche, Ralph Johnson (1904–71) American statesman; one of the founders of the United Nations; Nobel Peace Prize 1950

Bundesbank central bank of Germany

Bundesrat/Bundestag The Bundesrat (Federal Council) is the upper house of the German parliament, the Bundestag (Federal Assembly) is the lower house

Bundesrepublik Deutschland (BRD) Federal Republic of Germany; *see* Germany

Bundeswehr German armed forces

Bunsen burner (one cap.)

Buñuel, Luis (1900–83) *not* Louis; Spanish film director

buon giorno (It.) good-morning; but ***buona*** (*not* -o) ***sera*** (good-afternoon, good-evening) and ***buona notte*** (good night)

buoy, **buoyant**, **buoyancy** *not* bouy

BUPA (UK) British United Provident Association; private medical insurance company

Burckhardt, Jacob Christoph (1818–97) Swiss historian

Burdett-Coutts, Angela Georgina, Baroness (1814–1906) British philanthropist

burgemeester (Dut.) pronounced bur-guh-may-ster; mayor

bürgermeister (Ger.) pronounced bur-ger-my-ster; mayor

Burges, William (1827–81) English architect and designer

Burgess, (Frank) Gelett (1866–1951) American humorist

Burghley/Burleigh, William Cecil, Lord (1520–98) English statesman, confidant of Elizabeth I

Burgundy/Bourgogne (Fr.) a region of eastern France

burgundy wine from the Burgundy region

Burke and Hare body snatchers and murderers in Edinburgh in the early 19th century; they were both named William

Burke, Edmund (1729–97) Irish-born British politician and political theorist

Burke's Peerage formally *A Genealogical and Heraldic History of the Peerage, Baronetage and Knightage of the United Kingdom*

Burkina Faso land-locked west African state, formerly Upper Volta; capital Ouagadougou

Burma Asian state, now called Myanmar

Burne-Jones, Sir Edward Coley (1833–98) British painter and designer

Burnet, Sir Alastair (1929–) British journalist and broadcaster

burnous (UK)/**burnoose** (US) a hooded Arab cloak

Burns Night 25 January; annual celebration in Scotland commemorating the birth of the poet Robert Burns (1759–96)

Burnt-Out Case, A a novel by Graham Greene (1960)

burnt sienna *not* siena

Burrell Collection, Glasgow

Burton, Richard, originally **Jenkins** (1925–84) Welsh stage and film actor

Burton, Sir Richard Francis (1821–90) English orientalist and explorer

Burton, Robert (1577–1640) English writer and clergyman

Burton upon Trent, Staffordshire (no hyphens)

Burundi African republic; capital Bujumbura

Bury St Edmunds, Suffolk, pronounced berry

bus, **buses**, **bused**, **busing** are words relating to a form of transport and should not be confused with **buss**, **busses**, etc., meaning kiss(es)

Bushey, Hertfordshire, but **Bushy Park**, London

Bustamante, Sir (William) Alexander (1884–1977) Jamaican politician; Prime Minister 1962–7

Buthelezi, Mangosuthu (1929-), President of Inkatha Freedom Party, South Africa

Butte pronounced bewt; a small city in Montana; a steep-sided hill with a flat top (no cap.)

BWIA British West India Airways; *not* Indies

by-election *not* bye-

by-law *not* bye-

Byrd, William (1543–1623) English composer

byte in computing, a set of eight bits

BZW Barclays de Zoete Wedd, British financial services company

C

CA postal abbr. of California
cacao the tree from whose seed cocoa and chocolate are made
Cadbury Schweppes (no hyphen) British foods group
CAD computer-aided design
caddie, caddy A caddie is a golfer's assistant; a caddy is a container for storing tea
Cadmean victory one that leaves the victor ruined
Caedmon (*fl.* seventh c.) the first English poet known by name
Caernarfon/Caernarvon, Gwynedd, Wales. *See also* Carnarvon
Caerphilly/Caerffili (Wel.) town in Mid Glamorgan, Wales, and the cheese named after it
Caesar, (Gaius) Julius (*c.* 102–44 BC) Roman leader
Caesarean section (cap. C) *not* -ian
Caetano, Marcelo (José das Neves Alves) (1906–80) Prime Minister of Portugal 1968–74
Cain, James M(allahan) (1892–1977) American novelist
caisson
Caius College, Cambridge, pronounced keys; formally, Gonville and Caius College
Cajun native of French-speaking region of Louisiana; derived from Acadian
calamine lotion
Calaveras County, California, scene of the Mark Twain story *The Celebrated Jumping Frog of Calaveras County*
Calderón de la Barca (y Henao), Pedro (1600–1681) Spanish playwright
calendar record of a year

calender type of press

Caliban character in Shakespeare's *The Tempest*

calico a kind of plain (UK) or patterned (US) cloth; *pl.* **calicoes**

Calif. California

caliper (US)/**calliper** (UK) instrument for measuring thickness or diameter of objects

Callaghan, (Leonard) James, Baron (1912–) British Prime Minister 1976–9

Callicrates (*fl.* fifth c. BC) Greek architect, co-designer (with Ictinus) of the Parthenon

calligraphy

Callimachus (*fl.* third c. BC) Greek scholar

calliope fairground steam-organ, named after Calliope, the Greek muse of epic poetry

calliper (UK)/**caliper** (US) instrument for measuring thickness or diameter of objects

Calmann-Lévy French publisher

Calypso nymph who delayed Odysseus for seven years on his way home from Troy

CAM computer-aided manufacturing

camaraderie

Cambodia has been variously known over the past twenty years as the Khmer Republic, Democratic Kampuchea and the People's Republic of Kampuchea. However, since April 1989 it has resumed its historic name of Cambodia. The capital is Phnom Penh.

Cambridge University colleges: Christ's, Churchill, Clare, Clare Hall, Corpus Christi, Darwin, Downing, Emmanuel, Fitzwilliam, Girton, Gonville and Caius, Jesus, King's, Magdalene, New Hall, Newnham, Pembroke, Peterhouse, Queens', Robinson, St Catharine's, St Edmund's House, St John's, Selwyn, Sidney Sussex, Trinity, Trinity Hall, Wolfson

Cambs. Cambridgeshire

camellia

Camembert village in Normandy, and the cheese named after it

Cameroon, United Republic of/Cameroun, République du

(Fr.) West African state formed from the union of British and French protectorates, formerly called the Cameroons; capital Yaoundé

Camisards French Calvinists disaffected by the revocation of the Edict of Nantes (1703)

camisole

camomile (UK)/**chamomile** (US)

Camorra Mafia-type secret society of Naples

Campagna di Roma countryside around Rome

campanile bell tower

Campbell-Bannerman, Sir Henry (1836–1908) British Prime Minister 1905–08

Canada a dominion, comprising 10 provinces (Alberta, British Columbia, Manitoba, New Brunswick, Newfoundland and Labrador, Nova Scotia, Ontario, Prince Edward Island, Quebec, and Saskatchewan) and 2 territories (Northwest Territories and Yukon Territory); capital Ottawa

Canaletto, Giovanni Antonio Canal (1697–1768), Venetian painter

canard a ridiculous story or rumour. 'Gross canard' is a cliché. The French satirical magazine is *Le Canard Enchaîné*

Candlemas the Feast of the Purification of the Virgin Mary; 2 February

Canetti, Elias (1905–) Bulgarian-born British writer; Nobel Prize for Literature 1981

canister

cannabis

Cannae site of battle in southern Italy where Hannibal routed the Romans

cannon, **canon** A cannon is a gun; canon is an ecclesiastical title, a body of religious writings or the works of a particular author

cannelloni

cannibal

Cannizzaro, Stanisloa (1826–1910) Italian chemist

canoodle

canopy

Canova, Antonio (1757–1822) Italian sculptor

cant, jargon Both apply to words or expressions used by particular groups. Cant has derogatory overtones and applies to the private vocabulary and colloquialisms of professions, social groups and sects. Jargon is a slightly more impartial word and usually suggests terms used in a particular profession

Cantab. *Cantabrigiensis* (Lat.), of Cambridge University

cantaloup (UK)/**cantaloupe** (US)

Canton/Guangzhou (Pinyin)/**Kuang-chou** (Wade-Giles, now seldom used) capital of Guangdong Province, China

Canute/Cnut (*c.* 995–1035) King of England, Norway and Denmark

canvas, canvass Canvas is a fabric; to canvass is to solicit, especially for votes

CAP Common Agricultural Policy, the farm policy of the European Community

Cape Canaveral, Florida, called Cape Kennedy 1963–73

Čapek, Karel (1890–1938) Czech author

Cape Town, South Africa

capital, Capitol A capital is the city that is the seat of government of a state or nation; Capitol refers to a building in which a legislature meets in the US, or to the temple of Jupiter on Capitoline Hill in ancient Rome

Capitol Hill, Washington, DC, the site of the building in which the US Congress meets

Capitol Reef National Park, Utah *not* -al

cappuccino (It.)

carabiniere (It.) *not* carib-; Italian soldier-policeman; *pl.* ***carabinieri***

Caracalla, Marcus Aurelius Antoninus (186–217) Roman emperor

Caracas capital of Venezuela

carafe

carat unit of weight for precious stones, equal to 200 mg; *see also* caret

carat (UK)/**karat** (US) one twenty-fourth part of pure gold; *see also* caret

Caravaggio, Michelangelo Merisi/Amerighi da (*c.* 1569–1609) Italian painter

caraway seeds

carbon monoxide, carbon dioxide Carbon dioxide is the gas people exhale; carbon monoxide is the highly poisonous gas associated with car exhausts

carburetor (US)/**carburettor** (UK)

carcass

Carcassonne walled city in Southern France

cardamom

cardinal numbers one, two, three, etc.; *see also* ordinal numbers

Carducci, Giosuè (1835–1907) Italian poet and critic; Nobel Prize for Literature 1906

CARE Cooperative for American Relief Everywhere; originally the R stood for Remittances and the E for Europe

careen, career Careen means to tilt dangerously, while career means to move forward at speed. A runaway car would be more likely to career than to careen

caret an insertion mark (ʌ); *see also* carat

Carey, George Archbishop of Canterbury 1991-

Carey Street To 'go to Carey Street' is to become bankrupt, as the entrance to the London bankruptcy courts was on Carey Street

cargoes

Caribbean

Cariboo Mountains, Canada, part of the Rockies

caribou North American reindeer; *pl.* **caribou/caribous**

caricature

carillon

Carisbrooke castle and village on the Isle of Wight

Carl XVI Gustaf (1946–) King of Sweden 1973–

Carlisle, Cumbria, and Earl of; *see also* Carlyle

Carlsbad (Ger.)/**Karlovy Vary** (Czech) Czechoslovakian resort

Carlsberg Danish brewer

Carlsson, Ingvar (1934–) Swedish Prime Minister 1986–

Carlyle Hotel, New York City

Carlyle, Thomas (1795–1881) Scottish historian; the word for his style, if it must be used, is **Carlylean.**

Carmichael, Hoagy (Hoagland Howard) (1899–1981) American songwriter

Carnap, Rudolf (1891–1970) German-born American philosopher and logician

Carnarvon, George Edward Stanhope Molyneux Herbert, Earl of (1866–1923) English archaeologist, co-discoverer (with Howard Carter) of the tomb of Tutankhamun in Egypt; *see also* Caernarfon.

Carnegie Institute, Pittsburgh

Carnegie Institution, Washington, DC

Carnoustie, Tayside, Scotland

Carolina, North and **South** They are separate states. There is no state of Carolina in the US

carom

Carothers, Wallace (Hume) (1896–1937) American scientist

carotid arteries

Carpaccio, Vittore (*c.* 1460–*c.* 1526) Italian painter

carpe diem (Lat.) seize the day, make the most of the present

Carracci, Lodovico (1555–1619), **Agostino** (1557–1602) and **Annibale** (1560–1609) family of Italian painters

Carrantuohill highest mountain in Ireland (3,414 ft/1,041 m), in Macgillicuddy's Reeks, County Kerry

Carrara town in Tuscany, Italy, and the fine white marble quarried near by

Carrefour French supermarkets group

Carrington, Peter Alexander Rupert Carington, Baron (1919–) note -r- in the family name and -rr- in title; British Conservative politician; Secretary-General of Nato 1984–8

Carroll, Lewis pen name of Charles Lutwidge Dodgson (1832–98)

Carter Barron Amphitheatre, Washington, DC; note that Amphitheatre is spelled -re

Carthusian member of order of monks or a past or present student of Charterhouse School; the name is derived from Chartreuse

Cartier-Bresson, Henri (1908–) French photographer

cartilage

Carton, Sydney principal character in Dickens's *A Tale of Two Cities*

Caruso, Enrico (1874–1921) Italian tenor

Cary (Arthur) Joyce (Lunel) (1888–1957) British author

caryatid in architecture, a female form used as a supporting pillar

Casablanca, Morocco

Casals, Pablo/Pau (1876–1973) Spanish cellist

Casamassima*, *The Princess novel by Henry James (1886)

Casanova (de Seingalt), Giovanni Jacopo/Giacomo (1725–98) Italian adventurer remembered for his *Mémoires* and sexual exploits

cashmere

Cassandra In Greek mythology, she was given the power of prophecy by Apollo but doomed never to be believed. The name is now used as a synonym for any prophet of doom

Cassatt, Mary (1845–1926) American Impressionist painter

cassava

Cassavetes, John (1930–89) American film actor and writer-director

cassette

Cassiopeia, a constellation in the northern hemisphere named for the mother of Andromeda in Greek mythology

cassowary flightless bird

castanets Spanish rhythm instruments

Castile/Castilla (Sp.) area of northern Spain. The name appears in two Spanish regions: Castilla-La Mancha and Castilla-León. A native is a **Castilian.** The soap is **castile soap** (no caps.)

Castlereagh, Robert Stewart, Viscount (1769–1822) British statesman

castrato castrated soprano; *pl.* **castrati**

casus belli (Lat.) act that gives rise to war

CAT scan short for computerized axial tomography; process for viewing a cross-section of a brain or other organ

catamaran

catarrh

Catharine's College, St, Cambridge

Catharism a heresy

Cathays Park, Cardiff, (no apos.)

Catherine's College, St, Oxford

Catullus, Gaius Valerius (*c.* 84–*c.* 55 BC) Roman poet

Caudillo (Sp.) leader, title assumed by General Francisco Franco of Spain

cauliflower

cause célèbre

Cavaço Silva, Anibal (1939–) Prime Minister of Portugal 1985–

caveat emptor (Lat.) let the buyer beware

caviar (US)/**caviare** (UK)

Cavour, Conte Camillo Benso di (1810–61) Italian statesman

Cayenne capital of French Guiana

CBC Canadian Broadcasting Corporation

CBI Confederation of British Industry

CBS (US) Columbia Broadcasting System, which is a network, not a station

CCCP Soyuz Sovyetskikh Sotsialistcheskikh Respublik (Union of Soviet Socialist Republics); in the Cyrillic alphabet *S*s are rendered as *C*s, and *R*s as *P*s

Ceauşescu, Nicolae (1918–89) pronounced chow'-shess-coo; President of Romania 1967–89

Cecil, William *see* Burghley

cedilla mark [,] placed under a *c* to indicate that it is pronounced in French as an *s*, in Turkish as *ch* and in Portuguese as *sh*

Ceefax (UK) teletext system used by the BBC

ceilidh (Gaelic) pronounced kay-lee; gathering for music, singing and dancing

Cela, Camilo José (1916–) Spanish novelist; Nobel Prize for Literature 1989

celebrant, celebrator A celebrant is a participant in a religious ceremony; a celebrator is someone engaged in revelry

celibacy means only to be unmarried; it does not necessarily indicate abstinence from sex, which is chastity

Cellini, Benvenuto (1500–71) Italian sculptor, goldsmith and author

Celsius, centigrade abbr. C ; interchangeable terms referring to the scale of temperature invented by Anders Celsius (1701–44), a Swedish astronomer. To convert Celsius to Fahrenheit, multiply the Celsius temperature by 1.8 and add 32, or use the table in the Appendix

cement, concrete not interchangeable; the first is merely a constituent of the second

cemetery *not* -ary

centavo a monetary unit in many countries of South and Central America equivalent to one one-hundredth of the country's main unit of currency; *pl.* **centavos**

Centers for Disease Control *not* Center; US national medical research facility, Atlanta, Georgia

centi- prefix meaning one-hundredth

centigrade *see* Celsius

centimeter (US)/**centimetre** (UK) abbr. cm

Central Criminal Court formal title of the Old Bailey, London

centre round (or around) is incorrect; use 'centre on' or 'revolve around'

centrifugal force pulling away from

centripetal force drawing towards

Cephalonia/Kephallinia (Grk) Greek island in the Ionian chain

Cerberus in Greek mythology, three-headed dog that stood guard over the gates to the underworld

Ceres Roman goddess of grain, identified with the Greek goddess Demeter

cerise purplish red colour

CERN originally Conseil Européen de Recherches Nucléaires, now Organisation Européenne de Recherches Nucléaires, the European Organization for Nuclear Research, based in Geneva

Cervantes (Saavedra), Miguel de (1547–1616) Spanish author

c'est la guerre (Fr.) that is the way of war

Cévennes mountains in southern France

Ceylon former name of Sri Lanka

Cézanne, Paul (1839–1906) French Impressionist painter

cf. *confer* (Lat.), compare; used in cross-references

CFTC (US) Commodities Futures Trading Commission
Chablais region of Haute-Savoie, France, pronounced 'shablay'
Chablis white burgundy wine, pronounced 'shably'
chacun à son goût (Fr.) everyone to his own taste
chacun pour soi (Fr.) everyone for himself
chador a large piece of cloth worn by Muslim women in some countries, which is wrapped around the body to leave only the face exposed
chafe, **chaff** Chafe means to rub until sore; chaff means to tease
Chagall, Marc (1889–1985) Russian-born French artist
chagrined
chaise-longue *pl.* ***chaises-longues*** *not* -lounge
Chaliapin, Feodor (Ivanovich) (1873-1938) Russian operatic singer
Chamberlain, Sir (Joseph) Austen (1863–1937) British politician; Nobel Peace Prize 1925; son of **Joseph Chamberlain** (1836–1914), also a politician; half-brother of **(Arthur) Neville Chamberlain** (1869–1940), British Prime Minister 1937–40
Chambers's Encyclopaedia
chameleon
chamois pronounced sham'-wa; antelope whose hide makes the soft leather (pronounced sham'-ee) commonly used to polish cars; *pl.* **chamois**
Champagne region of France; formally Champagne-Ardenne; the wine is champagne (no cap.)
champaign an open plain
Champaign/Champaign-Urbana, Illinois
Champaigne, Philippe de (1602–74) French painter
Champigny-sur-Marne suburb of Paris
Champlain, Samuel de (1567–1635) founder of Quebec
Champollion, Jean François (1790–1832) French Egyptologist who helped decipher the Egyptian hieroglyphics on the Rosetta Stone
Champs-Élysées, Paris (hyphen)
Chancellor of the Duchy of Lancaster post in the British Cabinet that has no formal duties, enabling the holder to take up special assignments for the Prime Minister

Chancellorsville, Battle of, *not* -orville; battle in the American Civil War

Chandigarh Indian city laid out by Le Corbusier; joint state capital of Haryana and the Punjab

Changi Prison, Singapore

Chang Jiang (Pinyin)/**Yangtze River** If you use the Pinyin spelling, you should make at least a passing reference to the Yangtze, as that name is much more widely known in the English-speaking world

Channel Islands They are not part of the UK, but are Crown dependencies. The principal islands are Jersey, Guernsey, Alderney, Brechou, Sark, Herm and Jethou.

Chanukah use Hanuka (US)/Hanukkah (UK)

chaparral scrubby thicket of the American West

chapati/chapatti type of unleavened bread from India

chaperon

Chappaquiddick island off the coast of Massachusetts

chargé d'affaires, *pl.* **chargés d'affaires**

Charlemagne Charles I (742–814), first Holy Roman Emperor (800–814)

Charleston, South Carolina, not to be confused with Charleston, West Virginia, or Charlotte, North Carolina. The Charleston (cap.) is a dance named after the city in South Carolina.

Charlestown, Massachusetts, and Nevis Island, St Kitts-Nevis

Charlottenburg suburb of Berlin

Charollais cattle

chary cautious, doubtful; but **chariness**

Charybdis pronounced kuh-rib'-dis; in Greek mythology a whirlpool off the coast of Sicily. It is often paired metaphorically with Scylla (pronounced sill'-a), a six-headed monster who lived near by. In this sense Charybdis and Scylla signify a highly unattractive and unavoidable dilemma

Chase, Chevy (1949–) American comedy actor; *see also* Chevy Chase

chastise *not* -ize

Chateaubriand, François-René, Vicomte de (1768–1848) French statesman and writer

châteaubriand (no cap.; circumflex) grilled fillet of beef

Châteaubriant, France

Château-Lafite, **Château-Margaux** French red wines

Chattahoochee River, Georgia and Alabama

Chattanooga, Tennessee

Chatterton, Thomas (1752–70) English poet

Chatto & Windus Ltd British publisher

Chaucer, Geoffrey (?1345–1400) English poet

chauffeur

Chayefsky, Paddy (1923–) American playwright and screenwriter

cheap, **cheep** The first means inexpensive; the second refers to the sound birds make

Cheeryble brothers characters in Dickens's *Nicholas Nickleby*

Chekhov, Anton (Pavlovich) (1860–1904) Russian playwright and short-story writer

Chelyabinsk, Siberia, USSR

Chemnitz, Germany called Karl-Marx-Stadt during the period of East German sovereignty

Chennault, Claire (Lee) (1890–1958) American general, organized Flying Tigers air corps in World War II

Chequers official country house of British Prime Minister, near Princes Risborough, Buckinghamshire

Chernenko, Konstantin (Ustinovich) (1911–85) General Secretary of the USSR Communist Party, and President of the USSR 1984–5

Chernobyl Ukrainian site of world's worst known nuclear accident, 1986

Cherokee North American Indian people

Chesapeake Bay between Maryland and Virginia

Chesebrough-Pond's US cosmetics and household products company

Chesil Beach, Dorset

Chester-le-Street, Co. Durham

Chevalier, Maurice (1888–1972) French entertainer

Cheviot Hills range of hills on the English-Scottish border; the highest is The Cheviot (2,676 ft/816 m)

Chevy Chase, Maryland

Cheyenne North American Indian people; capital city of, and river running through, Wyoming

Cheyne Walk, Chelsea, London, pronounced chay'-nee

Chiang Ching-kuo, General (1910–88) son of Chiang Kai-shek and President of Taiwan 1978–87

Chiang Kai-shek (1887–1975) leader of Nationalist Republic of China 1928–49 and first President of Taiwan 1950–75

chiaroscuro interplay of light and shade

Chicago, Illinois, the first two letters are pronounced sh as in sheet, *not* ch as in chicken

Chicano (cap.) American citizen or resident of Mexican descent; *pl.* **Chicanos**

Chickamauga, Georgia, *not* -magua; site of American Civil War battle (1863)

chicory

Chihuahua city and state in Mexico and breed of dog

chilblain *not* chill-

Childe Harold's Pilgrimage *not Child;* poem by Lord Byron

Childermas former name for Holy Innocents' Day, 28 December

Childers, (Robert) Erskine (1870–1922) Irish nationalist and writer, and father of **Erskine Childers** (1905–74), President of Ireland 1973–4

children's is the only possible spelling of the possessive form of children

Chile South American country

chili, *pl.* **chilies** (US)/**chilli**, *pl.* **chillies** (UK) hot peppers

Chiltern Hundreds Because British MPs are not permitted to resign, they must apply to become stewards of the Chiltern Hundreds – effectively a nonexistent position – which disqualifies them from Parliament

chimera pronounced kī-mir'-a; a wild or fanciful creation, taken from Chimera (sometimes Chimaera), a mythological beast with the head of a lion, the body of a goat and the tail of a serpent

chimpanzee

China, Republic of official name of Taiwan, used almost nowhere except in Taiwan itself. The mainland country is the People's Republic of China

chinchilla

Chinese names The two main international systems for romanizing Chinese names are Wade-Giles and Pinyin. Wade-Giles, dating from 1859, is the traditional system; Pinyin was devised in 1953 but has been in widespread international use only since about 1977. The result is that many names are now commonly spelled two or more ways; e.g., Peking (the traditional English name), Pei-ching (Wade-Giles) and Beijing (Pinyin), or Canton (traditional English name), Guangzhou (Pinyin) and Kuang-chou (Wade-Giles). The same difficulty arises with the names of many people; e.g., Chou En-lai (Wade-Giles), Zhou Enlai (Pinyin). Common practice is to use traditional spellings for long-established names (Canton, Peking, Shanghai, Mao Tse-tung) and Pinyin for all others. Taiwan and Hong Kong do not use Pinyin spellings.

chinook warm dry wind that blows off the Rocky Mountains

chipmunk *not* -monk; North American ground squirrel

chipolata small sausage

Chippendale, Thomas (*c.* 1718–79) English furniture designer and maker

Chipping Campden, Gloucestershire, *not* Camden

Chirac, Jacques (René) (1932–) French politician and Mayor of Paris 1977–

chivvy to hurry or harass

chlorophyll

chocolate

Choctaw North American Indian people

cholesterol

Chomsky, (Avram) Noam (1928–) American linguist and political writer

Chongqing (Pinyin)/**Chungking**, Sichuan province, China

Chopin, Frédéric François (1810–49) Polish composer and pianist

chord, cord A chord is a group of musical notes, while a cord is a length of rope or similar material of twisted strands. You speak with your vocal cords

Chou En-lai/Zhou Enlai (Pinyin) (1898–1976) pronounced jo'-enn-lie; Prime Minister of China 1949–76

Chrétien de Troyes (*fl.* 1170–90) French poet

Christ Church the Oxford college; *not* called Christ Church College and not to be confused with Christ's College, Cambridge

Christchurch, New Zealand; **Christchurch**, Dorset; **Christchurch**, Gloucestershire

Christiania original name of Oslo

Christie, Dame Agatha (Mary Clarissa) (1891–1976) prolific English mystery writer

Christie's London auction house; formally, Christie, Manson, & Woods, but the parent company styles itself Christies International (no apos.)

Christ's College, Cambridge not to be confused with Christ Church, Oxford

Christy Minstrels

chromosome

chronic, **acute** Chronic means lasting, of long standing or constant, and is the opposite of acute, which, applied to an illness or situation, means approaching a crisis or at a critical stage.

chrysalis, *pl.* **chrysalides/chrysalises**

chrysanthemum

Chrysostom, St John (*c.* 345–407) Greek orator and religious figure

chukka (UK)/**chukker** (US) period of play in polo

Chun Doo-hwan (1931–) President of South Korea 1980–88. After the first reference he is Mr Chun

Chur/Coire (Fr.)/**Coira** (It.)/**Cuoira** (Romansh), Switzerland

Churchill, Sir Winston Leonard Spencer (1874–1965) British statesman

Church of Jesus Christ of Latter-Day Saints formal title of the Mormon Church

chutzpah (Yidd.) pronounced hootz'-pah; shameless impudence, brashness, forwardness

ciao (It.) salutation meaning either hello or goodbye

Ciba-Geigy Swiss pharmaceuticals company

Cicero, Marcus Tullius (106–43 BC) Roman orator and statesman

Cincinnati, Ohio

Cincinnatus, Lucius Quinctius (*c.* 519–*c.* 439 BC) Roman general

Cinderella

CinemaScope

cineraria, *pl.* **cinerarias**

cinnamon

cinquecento (It.) literally, 'the five hundreds'; Italian name for the 16th century and Renaissance art

Cinque Ports pronounced sink; originally Dover, Hastings, Hythe, Romney and Sandwich, and later Rye and Winchelsea

CIPFA (UK) Chartered Institute for Public Finance and Accountancy

cipher *not* cypher

circadian taking place in 24-hour cycles

Circe in Greek mythology, an enchantress on the island of Aeaea who detained Odysseus and his men, turning the latter into swine and bearing a son by the former

cirrhosis the expression 'cirrhosis of the liver' is almost always tautological

Citicorp US bank group; its branches use the name Citibank

Citlaltépetl dormant volcano in Mexico

C. Itoh Japanese trading company

Citroën French car

Ciudad Trujillo former name of Santo Domingo, capital of the Dominican Republic

civet cat-like mammal and fluid taken from it used in the manufacture of perfume

Civil List annual payment for expenses made to Queen and other members of the British royal family

civil servant, but **Civil Service**

Civitavecchia Italian coastal city, north of Rome in Latium

clamour, clamorous (UK)/**clamor** (US)
Clare, **County**, Ireland
Claridge's Hotel, London, but the **Hôtel Claridge,** Paris
clarinetist (US)/**clarinettist** (UK)
Clark, Sir Kenneth (Mackenzie), Baron (1903–83) English art historian
Clarke, Arthur C(harles) (1917–) English science-fiction writer
Clarke, Kenneth (Harry) (1940–) British politician
Clemenceau, Georges (Eugène Benjamin) (1841–1929) Prime Minister of France 1906–09, 1917–20
Clemens, Samuel Langhorne (1835–1910) American author, used pen name Mark Twain
clerestory
clerihew four-line nonsense poem devised by Edmund Clerihew Bentley (1875–1956)
Cleveland, (Stephen) Grover (1837–1908) US President 1885–89, 1893–97
Cley, Norfolk, pronounced 'klye'
cloisonné a type of enamel work
Clouseau, Inspector fictional character portrayed by Peter Sellers in *Pink Panther* films
Clwyd pronounced kloo'-wid; county of northern Wales, comprising the former county of Flintshire and most of the former county of Denbighshire
Clytemnestra in Greek mythology, the wife of Agamemnon
cm centimeter (US)/centimetre (UK)
Cnossus (US)/**Knossos** (UK) ancient capital of Crete
Cnut/Canute (*c*. 995–1035) King of England, Norway and Denmark
CO postal abbr. of Colorado
Coahuila state in north-eastern Mexico
Coats Viyella British textiles company
Cobb, Irvin S(hrewsbury) (1876–1944) American journalist and humorist
Cobbett, William (1762–1835) British writer
Cobh Co. Cork, Ireland, pronounced 'Cove'

COBOL Common Business Oriented Language, a computer language
Coca-Cola (hyphen) The diminutive term Coke should always be capitalized
coccyx tailbone; *pl.* **coccyxes/coccyges** (rare)
cock-a-leekie soup
Cockburn's Port, Lord Cockburn pronounced ko'-burn
cockney (no cap.) native of London's East End; traditionally, one born within the sound of Bow Bells; *pl.* **cockneys**
cocky
cocoa
COCOM Coordinating Committee on Multilateral Export Controls, Paris-based organization that decides which Western goods should or should not be exported to Communist countries. Its members are Australia, Belgium, Canada, Denmark, West Germany, Greece, Italy, Japan, Luxembourg, The Netherlands, Norway, Portugal, Spain, Turkey, the UK and the US
coconut
cocoon
Cody, William Frederick (1846–1917) nickname 'Buffalo Bill', Wild West showman
coequal is a pointless word, as co- adds nothing to the meaning of equal
Coetzee, J. M. (1940–) South African author
Coeur de Lion, Richard (1157–99) Richard the Lionheart, Richard I of England
cogito, ergo sum (Lat.) I think, therefore I am. Descartes's aphorism
cognoscente, *pl.* ***cognoscenti***
Cohan, George M(ichael) (1878–1942) American songwriter and performer, playwright and producer
COHSE (UK) Confederation of Health Service Employees
Cointreau orange-flavoured liqueur
colander *not* -dar; a perforated bowl
Coleg Prifysgol Cymru (Wel.) University College of Wales
coleus plant with brightly coloured leaves

Colgate-Palmolive (hyphen) US personal products company
colic, but **colicky**
Coliseum, the London theatre, but the **Colosseum,** Rome
collapsible
collectable (UK, alt. US)/**collectible** (US, alt. UK)
collide, collision A collision can occur only between two or more moving objects. If a car runs into a wall it is not a collision
Collor de Mello, Fernando (1949–) President of Brazil 1990–1993
Colman, Ronald (1891–1958) English actor
Colo. Colorado
Colombey-les-Deux-Églises town east of Paris where Charles de Gaulle is buried
Colombia, South American country; *not* -um-
Colombo capital of Sri Lanka
colonnade *not* -ll-
coloration, **colorific** *not* -our-
colossal
Colosseum, Rome
Colossus of Rhodes
colostomy
Colquhoun pronounced ko-hoon', Scottish name
Columba, St (521–97) Irish saint associated with Scottish island of Iona
Columbus, Christopher/Colombo, Cristoforo (It.)/**Colon, Cristóbal** (Sp.) (*c.* 1451–1506) Italian explorer
Columbus Day US holiday, formerly observed on 12 October (the date of Christopher Columbus's first landfall in the New World in 1492), now observed on the Monday nearest that date
combatant, **combated, combating**
combustible capable of being burned
COMECON Council for Mutual Economic Assistance; Eastern European common market, formed 1949 by Albania (expelled 1961), Bulgaria, Cuba, Czechoslovakia, East Germany, Hungary, Mongolia, Poland, Romania, the USSR and Vietnam; disbanded 1991

Comédie-Française national theatre of France; formally, the Théâtre Français
comestible foodstuff
Comiskey Park Chicago baseball stadium, home of the White Sox
commedia dell'arte type of farcical Italian comedy
commingle *not* comingle; to mix together
commiserate
commitment, but **committal**, **committed**, **committing**
committee
Commodus, Lucius Aelius Aurelius (AD 161–92) Roman emperor (AD 180–92)
Commonwealth, The *not* the British Commonwealth; members: Antigua and Barbuda, Australia, Bahamas, Bangladesh, Barbados, Belize, Botswana, Brunei, Canada, Cyprus, Dominica, Gambia, Ghana, Grenada, Guyana, India, Jamaica, Kenya, Kiribati, Lesotho, Malawi, Malaysia, Maldives, Malta, Mauritius, Nauru, New Zealand, Nigeria, Papua New Guinea, St Kitts-Nevis, St Lucia, St Vincent and the Grenadines, Seychelles, Sierra Leone, Singapore, Solomon Islands, Sri Lanka, Swaziland, Tanzania, Tonga, Trinidad and Tobago, Tuvalu, Uganda, United Kingdom, Vanuatu, Western Samoa, Zambia, Zimbabwe
Common Market *see* European Economic Community
Comoros island state off Madagascar; capital Moroni
comparability, **comparable**, **comparative**
compatible
compatriot, but **expatriate**
compendium does not mean vast and all-embracing but a succinct summary or abridgement. A compendium provides a complete summary in a brief way
complacent, **complaisant** Complacent means content; complaisant means obliging
Compleat Angler*, *The book by Izaak Walton (1653)
complement, **compliment** Both are nouns and verbs; the first refers to making complete, the second to praise
complexion
compos mentis (Lat.) of sound mind

comprehensible
compressor
Concertgebouw Orchestra, Amsterdam
concur, concurred, concurring
condescension
Coney Island, New York
confectionery *not* -ary; the products of a confectioner
confer (Lat.) compare; abbr. cf., used for cross-references
confidant (masc.)/**confidante** (fem.) a person entrusted with private information
conga a rhythmic dance
conger species of eel
Congo formally the People's Republic of the Congo. The native dialect is Kongo. The country formerly known as the Democratic Republic of Congo is now Zaïre
Congressional Medal of Honor, for the highest US military award, is wrong. It is awarded by Congress, but its correct title is simply the Medal of Honor
Congreve, William (1670–1729) English playwright
Connacht province of Ireland comprising five counties: Galway, Leitrim, Mayo, Roscommon and Sligo
Connecticut pronounced ko-net'-i-kut, *not* ko-nekt'-i-cut; postal abbr. CT; traditional abbr. Conn.
Connelly, Marc(us) (Cook) (1890–1980) American writer and playwright
Connemara, Galway, Ireland
connoisseur
Connolly, Billy (1942–) Scottish comic
Connolly, Cyril (Vernon) (1903–74) British journalist, critic and writer
Conrad, Joseph (1857–1924) born Teodor Jósef Konrad Nałecz Korzeniowski; Polish-born English novelist
consensus *not* -census; 'consensus of opinion' is redundant
consols consolidated annuities, a stock-market term
Constance/Bodensee (Ger.) lake bounded by Switzerland, Germany and Austria; the city of the lake is Constance/Konstanz (Ger.)

Constantinople former name of Istanbul

Consumers' Association (UK) consumer interest group, publisher of *Which?* and other consumer-interest magazines and books

contagious, **infectious** Contagious describes diseases spread by contact; infectious describes those spread by air or water

contemptible deserving contempt

contemptuous showing contempt

conterminous/coterminous Both words mean to share a common boundary

continual, **continuous** Continual refers to events that happen repeatedly but not constantly; continous indicates an unbroken sequence

convener *not* -or; one who convenes

convertibility

Cooke, Alistair (Alfred) (1908–) British-born American journalist, broadcaster and television presenter

Coolidge, (John) Calvin (1872–1933) US President 1923–8

cooperate, **coordinate** In the US these words appear without a hyphen, but in the UK many dictionaries are curiously inconsistent, calling for a hyphen when the word is unencumbered (co-operate, co-ordinate), but dropping it when a prefix is added (uncooperative, noncooperation, uncoordinated, etc.). It is hard to see how anyone could defend the first while allowing the second. However, there is a move towards dropping the hyphen, with a few dictionaries including this as the preferred form and most others showing it as an acceptable alternative – an option I would suggest you exercise

Cooper, James Fenimore (1789–1851) American writer

Coopers & Lybrand Deloitte (no apos.) UK accountancy firm

Coordinating Committee on Multilateral Export Controls abbr. COCOM; body that decides which Western goods should or should not be exported to Communist countries

Copenhagen/København (Dan.) pronounced (roughly) koop'-en-how-en. The preferred English pronunciation among Danes is co'-pen-hay-gen, rather than co'-pen-hah-gen

Copernicus, Nicolas (or **Nicolaus)/Kopernik**, **Mikołaj** (Pol.)

(1473–1543) Polish astronomer

Copland, Aaron (1900–90) American composer

Copley, John Singleton (1737–1815) American portrait and historical painter

Coppola, Francis Ford (1939–) American screenwriter and film director

Corbière, (Édouard Joachim) Tristan (1845–75) French poet

Corbusier, Le pseudonym of Charles Édouard Jeanneret (1887–1965) Swiss architect and city planner

Corcoran Gallery of Art, Washington DC

cord, **chord** A cord is a length of rope or similar material of twisted strands, while a chord is a group of musical notes. You speak with your vocal cords

corduroy

CORE (US) Congress of (*not* for) Racial Equality, civil rights organization

Corfu/Kerkyra (Grk)

Corneille, Pierre (1606–84) French playwright

corona, *pl.* **coronae/coronas**

Coronada, Francisco Vásquez de (*c.* 1500–54) Spanish explorer of the New World

Corot, (Jean Baptiste) Camille (1796–1875) French painter

Correggio, Antonio Allegri da (1494–1534) Italian painter

corrigible capable of being corrected or improved

corruptible

Cortes legislative assembly of Spain

Cortés/Cortéz, Hernando/Hernán (1485–1547) Spanish conqueror of Aztecs

coruscate *not -rr-*; glittering, dazzling, as in 'coruscating wit'

Così fan tutte opera by Mozart (1790)

cosset, cosseted, cosseting

Cossiga, Francesco (1928–) Italian politician, President of Italy 1985–7

Costa-Gavras, (Henri) Constantin (1933–) born Kostantin Gavras; Greek-born French film director

cosy (UK)/**cozy** (US)

Côte d'Azur

coterminous/conterminous having a common boundary
cotoneaster
Cotten, Joseph (1905–) *not* -on; American film actor
Council of Europe an association of European states separate from the European Community, or Common Market. It has a Consultative Assembly, based in Strasbourg, but is best known for its European Court of Human Rights
Countess Cathleen, The *not* Kath-; a play by William Butler Yeats (1899)
County NatWest (one word) UK merchant bank
coup d'état
courgette (UK, Fr.), **zucchini** (US, It.)
Courtneidge, Dame (Esmerelda) Cicely (1893–1980) British actress, often paired theatrically with her husband, Jack Hulbert
Court of St James's note -s's; the place to which ambassadors are posted in the UK
Court of Session the supreme court of Scotland
Cousy, (Robert Joseph) Bob (1928–) American basketball player
Coutts & Co, UK bank
Covarrubias, Miguel (1902–57) Mexican artist
Cowper, William (1731–1800) pronounced cooper; English poet
cozy (US)/**cosy** (UK)
Cozzens, James Gould (1903–78) American author
Cranach, Lucas (1472–1553) German artist
Crane, Stephen (1871–1900) American writer
Cratchit, Bob character in Dickens's *A Christmas Carol*
crèche, *pl.* **crèches**
Crécy, Battle of (1346)
crevasse, **crevice** A crevasse is a deep fissure, particularly in ice; a crevice is a narrow and generally shallow fissure
Crèvecoeur, J. Hector St John (1735–1813) born Michel Guillaume Jean de Crèvecoeur; French-born American essayist
Criccieth, Gwynedd, pronounced crick'-ee-eth; small Welsh resort
cri de cœur (Fr.) an impassioned plea

Crimean War (1854–6) England, France, Sardinia and Turkey versus Russia

crime passionnel (Fr.) a crime motivated by sexual jealousy

crisis, *pl.* **crises**

criterion, *pl.* **criteria**

Croce, Benedetto (1866–1952) Italian writer, philosopher and politician

crocheted, **crocheting**

Crockett, (David) Davy (1786–1836) American frontiersman and politician

Croesus (reigned 560–546 BC) last king of Lydia, byword for wealth, pronounced 'Creesus'

Cro-Magnon early form of *Homo sapiens*, named after a hill in France and therefore the correct pronunciation is cro-man-yon, not cro-mag-non

Crome Yellow *not* Chrome; a novel by Aldous Huxley (1921)

Cromwell, Oliver (1599–1658) English soldier and statesman

Cromwell, Richard (1626–1712) English statesman and third son of **Oliver Cromwell**

Cromwell, Thomas, Earl of Essex (*c.* 1485–1540) English statesman

Cronos (US)/**Kronos** (UK) in Greek mythology, a Titan dethroned by his son Zeus; equivalent to the Roman god Saturn

crony

Crosland, (Charles) Anthony (Raven) (1918–77) British politician and writer

cross-Channel ferry is a tautology; delete cross-

Crossman, Richard Howard Stafford (1907–74) Labour politician

crotch (US)/**crutch** (UK) the area between the legs

Crowley, Aleister (1875–1947) born Edward Alexander Crowley; English writer and diabolist

Crown Estate Commissioners *not* Estates

Cruft's Dog Show (UK)

Cruikshank, George (1792–1878) English cartoonist and illustrator

crummy

crutch (UK)/**crotch** (US) the area between the legs
cruzado main Brazilian unit of currency 1986–90, reverted to its former name of cruzeiro
Cry, the Beloved Country note comma; a novel by Alan Paton (1948)
csar use **czar** (US)/**tsar** (UK)
CSCE Council for Security and Cooperation in Europe
CT postal abbr. for Connecticut
Cucamonga, Los Angeles, California, pronounced kook'-a-mon'-ga
Cuchulain pronounced koo-hoo'-lin; warrior hero of Irish mythology
cuckoo
cueing
Culloden, Battle of (1746) battle near Inverness, in the Highland Region of Scotland, in which Scottish clans were routed by the English army under the command of the Duke of Cumberland
Culpeper, Virginia
Culzean Castle, Strathclyde, pronounced kuh-lane'
cumbrous *not* -erous
cuneiform, wedge-shaped writing
cupful, *pl.* **cupfuls**
cupola
curaçao a liqueur, named after the island of Curaçao in the Netherlands Antilles in the Caribbean
curb (US)/**kerb** (UK) raised edging along street
curette a surgical instrument
curettage a surgical scraping procedure using a curette
Curie, Marie (1867–1934) born Marie Skłodowska; Polish-born French physicist; joint winner, with her husband, Pierre Curie, and Henri Becquerel, Nobel Prize for Physics 1903 for the discovery of radioactivity; Nobel Prize for Chemistry 1911 for the isolation of radium
curlicue
Curragh Incident a near-mutiny in 1914 by British officers stationed at The Curragh, near Dublin, who refused to fire on civilians in Ulster

currencies for a list of some of the main world currencies, *see* Appendix

curriculum vitae abbr. c.v.

Curtiss aircraft named after Glenn Curtiss (1878–1930), American inventor and aviator

Curtiz, Michael (1888–1962) born Mihály Kertész; prolific Hungarian-born Hollywood film director

curvaceous *not* -ious

Cuthbertson, Iain (1930–) British actor

c.v. curriculum vitae

Cwmbran, Gwent, Wales, pronounced koom'-brahn

Cwmtwrch, West Glamorgan, Wales, pronounced koom'-too-erch

cyanosis turning blue from lack of oxygen

cyclamen

cymbal percussion instrument

Cynewulf (*fl.* eighth c.) Anglo-Saxon poet

cynosure focal point, guiding star

Cyrillic alphabet Alphabet widely used for Slavonic languages and non-Slavonic languages in the USSR and other countries. It is named after St Cyril, who is popularly credited with its invention. Some of the characters vary slightly between Russian, Belorussian, Bulgarian and other languages

Cyrus the Great (*d.* 529 BC) founder of the Persian empire

cystic fibrosis

cystitis

czar (US)/**tsar** (UK)

Czechoslovakia federal state created in 1919 (as Czecho-Slovakia), dissolved 1993; now Czech Republic (capital Prague) and Slovakia (capital Bratislava), two sovereign states

Czechoslovak Air Lines *not* Airlines

D

Dachau town near Munich, site of infamous concentration camp in World War II

Daedalus in Greek mythology, father of Icarus and builder of the Labyrinth; *see also* Dedalus

Dafydd (Wel.) *not* Daffyd; David

daguerreotype early photographic process, named after Louis Daguerre (1789–1851), French painter and photographer

Dahl, Roald (1916–90) British author

Dahomey former name of Benin

Dai-Ichi Kangyo Bank Japanese bank

Dáil Éireann pronounced doyle air-ann; lower house of Irish Parliament

daiquiri

Dalai Lama the high priest of Tibet

d'Alembert, Jean le Rond (1717–83) French mathematician

Dali, Salvador (1904–89) Spanish surrealist artist

Dallapiccola, Luigi (1904–75) Italian composer

Daly City suburb of San Francisco, California

Damocles a courtier in ancient Syracuse who was forced by his king, Dionysius the Elder, to sit at a banquet with a sword suspended by a hair above his head

Danaë in Greek mythology, mother of Perseus

Danegeld tax levied in England in the 10th–12th centuries initially to pay for defending against Viking incursions

Danelaw section of England occupied by Danes in the 9th–11th centuries and the laws that prevailed there

danke schön (Ger.) thank you very much

d'Annunzio, Gabriele (1863–1938) Italian writer and adventurer

danse macabre *not* dance

Dante Alighieri (1265–1321) Italian poet; the adjective is Dantesque

Danzig former name of Gdańsk

Darby and Joan *not* Derby; after a couple in an 18th-century English song

D'Arcy Masins Benton & Bowles, advertising agency

Dardanelles the narrow channel linking the Aegean Sea and the Sea of Marmara, known in antiquity as the Hellespont

Dar es Salaam former capital of Tanzania; *see also* Dodoma

data is a plural. Although this fact is widely disregarded, by some good writers as well as poor ones, you should at least be aware that 'The data is incomplete' is incorrect

Datta, Michael Madhusudan (1824–73) Bengali poet and dramatist

Datta, Sudhindranath (1901–60) Indian poet

Daubeny, Sir Peter Lauderdale (1921–75) German-born English impresario

d'Aubuisson (Arrieta), Roberto (1943–) Salvadoran politician

Daumier, Honoré (1808–79) French painter

Davenant/D'Avenant, Sir William (1606–68) English poet and dramatist

Davies, (William) Robertson (1913–) Canadian novelist and playwright

Davies, Sharron (1962–) British swimmer; note -rr-in first name

da Vinci, Leonardo (1452–1519) the Italian artist and genius. A work by him is a Leonardo, not a da Vinci.

Davy, Sir Humphry (1778–1829) *not* Humphrey; English chemist

Dawes Plan abortive plan to extract reparations from Germany after World War I; named after Charles G. Dawes, later US Vice-President

Dayan, Moshe (1915–81) Israeli general and politician

Day-Lewis, Cecil (1904–72) Irish-born British poet

dB decibel

DC District of Columbia, coextensive with US capital, Washington

D-Day 6 June 1944

DDR Deutsche Demokratische Republik; East Germany; *see* Germany

DDT dichlorodiphenyltrichloroethane, an insecticide

DE postal abbr. of Delaware

Deakin, Alfred (1856–1919) Australian statesman

Dearborn, Michigan, suburb of Detroit, home of Ford Motor Company

Debach, Suffolk, pronounced debb-itch

débâcle

DeBakey, Michael (Ellis) (1908–) American heart surgeon

debatable

de Beauvoir, Simone (Lucie Ernestine Marie Bertrand) (1908–86) French author

debonair/débonnaire (Fr.)

Debrett's The full title is *Debrett's Peerage and Baronetage*

Debs, Eugene V(ictor) (1855–1926) American socialist and labour leader

Debusschere, Dave (1940–) American baseball and basketball player and basketball executive

Debussy, (Achille-) Claude (1862–1918) French composer

débutante

decathlon athletic event comprising ten events: long jump, high jump, pole vault, discus, shot put, javelin, 110 metre hurdles, and 100, 400 and 1,500 metre races

deceit

deceive

deci- prefix meaning one-tenth

decibel abbr. dB

decimate originally meant to reduce by a tenth. It is now used to describe any heavy loss, but should never be used to mean annihilate

De Clercq, Willy (1927–) Belgian politician

décolletage plunging neckline on clothing

Dedalus, Stephen character in James Joyce works; *see also* Daedalus

de facto (Lat.) existing in fact but not in law; *see also de jure*

defective not working properly; not to be confused with deficient

defence (UK)/**defense** (US), but **defensive**, **defensible** (UK, US)

Defferre, Gaston (1910–) French politician and journalist

deficient lacking a part; not to be confused with defective

definite, **definitive** definite means without doubt; definitive means final, conclusive and authoritative

deflection(US), **deflexion** (UK)

Defoe, Daniel (1659–1731) British author

De Forest, Lee (1873–1961) American inventor, principally in the field of electronics

defuse, **diffuse** defuse means to make harmless; diffuse means to disperse and spread out

Degas, Edgar (Hilaire Germaine) (1834–1917) French Impressionist artist

de Gasperi, Alcide (1881–1954) properly, Gasperi, Alcide de; Prime Minister of Italy 1945–53

de Gaulle, Charles (André Joseph Marie) (1890–1970) President of France 1944–6, 1959–69

de haut en bas (Fr.) with contempt

De Havilland Aircraft Co. named after Sir Geoffrey de Havilland (1882–1965), industrialist and engineer

Deighton, West Yorkshire, pronounced dee-tun

Deirdre of the Sorrows *not* Deidre; play by J. M. Synge

déjà vu

de jure (Lat.) according to law; *see also de facto*

Dekker, Thomas (*c.* 1570–*c.* 1640) English playwright

de Klerk, F(rederik) W(illem) (1936–) President of South Africa 1989–

de Kooning, Willem (1904–) Dutch-born American painter

Del. Delaware

Delacroix, (Ferdinand Victor) Eugène (1789–1863) French painter

de la Madrid (Hurtado), Miguel (1935–) President of Mexico 1982–8

de la Mare, Walter (1873–1956) English novelist and poet

Delaney, Shelagh (1939–) English dramatist

de Larosière (de Champfeu), Jacques (Martin Henri) (1929–) former chairman of the International Monetary Fund, president of the European Bank for Reconstruction and Development (1993–)

De La Rue British security printing firm

de la Tour, Frances (1944–) British actress

de La Tour, Georges (1593–1652) properly, La Tour, Georges de; French painter

De Laurentiis, Dino (1919–) Italian film producer

delectable

Deledda, Grazia (1871–1936) Italian novelist; Nobel Prize for Literature 1926

De Leeuw, Ton (1926–) Dutch composer

deleterious

delftware (no cap.)

Delibes, Léo (1836–91) French composer

Delilah

Delius, Frederick (1862–1934) British composer

de los Angeles, Victoria (1923–) Spanish soprano

Delta Air Lines US airline

De Lucchi, Michele (1951–) Italian architect

Delvaux, Paul (1897–) Belgian surrealist painter

demagogue/demagog (alt. US)

de mal en pis, de pis en pis (Fr.) both mean from bad to worse

de Maupassant, Guy (Henri René Albert) (1850–93) properly, Maupassant, Guy de; French writer of short stories and novels

dementia praecox schizophrenia

demerara sugar

Demerol (cap.)

Demeter Greek goddess of agriculture and fertility; Roman equivalent is Ceres

De Mille, Cecil B(lount) (1881–1959) American film producer and director, noted for epics

demimonde (US)/ ***demi-monde*** (UK, Fr.) term loosely applied to prostitutes, kept women or anyone else living on the wrong side of respectability

demise does not mean decline; it means death

de mortuis nil nisi bonum (Lat.) say nothing but good of the dead

Demosthenes (384–322 BC) Athenian orator and statesman

de nada (Sp.) it's nothing; think nothing of it

Deng Xiaoping (Pinyin)/**Teng Hsiao-ping** (1904–) Chinese elder statesman, member of the Politburo, architect of modernization programme

De Niro, Robert (1943–) American film actor

dénouement

deodorant

Deo gratias (Lat.) thanks to God

De Palma, Brian (1941–) American film director

dependant, dependent The first refers to a person; the second to a situation

depositary, depository The first refers to a person or body; the second to a place; *see also* ADR

de profundis (Lat.) from the depths; a heartfelt cry

De Quincy, Thomas (1785–1859) English writer

Derain, André (1880–1954) French artist

de rigueur (Fr.) according to etiquette or fashion; note two u's

derisive, derisory The first means conveying ridicule or contempt; the second, inviting ridicule or contempt

DERV/derv diesel-engined road vehicles

desalination *not* desalinization

Descartes, René (1595–1650) French mathematician and philosopher, propounder of the maxim *Cogito, ergo sum* (I think, therefore I am)

descendible

déshabillé/dishabille (Fr.) untidily or only partly dressed

desiccate *not* -ss-; to dry, as in desiccated coconut

De Sica, Vittorio (1902–74) Italian film actor and director

Des Moines pronounced duh moyne; capital of Iowa

de Soto, Hernando (*c.* 1496–1542) Spanish explorer, discovered Mississippi River

despatch (alt.)/**dispatch** (pref.)
desperate
Des Plaines pronounced dess plainz; city and river in Illinois
destructible
detestable
detritus
de trop (Fr.) excessive
Deukmejian, George (1928–) Governor of California 1983–91
deus ex machina in drama, a character who, or event that, arrives late in the action and provides a solution
Deuteronomy the last book of the Pentateuch in the Old Testament
Deutsche Mark (two words) abbr. DM; main unit of currency of Germany, comprising 100 pfennigs
Deutsches Museum, Munich
de Valera, Éamon (1882–1975) US-born Prime Minister of Ireland 1919–21, 1932–48, 1957–9, and President 1959–73
devilry/deviltry
Devil's Island/Île du Diable (Fr.), French Guiana, site of infamous prison
Devils Playground (no apos.) desert in California
Devils Tower National Monument, Wyoming (no apos.)
Devon It is the Earl of Devon, but the Duke of Devonshire
De Voto, Bernard (Augustine) (1897–1955) American historian and biographer
dextrous (UK, pref.), **dexterous** (US, pref.)
de Young, M. H., Memorial Museum, San Francisco, California
De Zoete & Bevan British stockbroking firm
dhow Arab boat
diaeresis (UK)/**dieresis** (US) two marks put above a vowel to indicate that it is pronounced separately, as in Brontë and naïve; *pl.* **diaereses**
Diaghilev, Sergei (Pavlovich) (1872–1929) Russian ballet impresario; founder of Ballet Russe
Dial 'M' for Murder note quotation marks around M; drama by Frederick Knott and film by Alfred Hitchcock

dialysis

Diana Roman goddess of the moon and the hunt; identified with the Greek goddess Artemis

diaphragm

diarrhea (US)/**diarrhoea** (UK)

Dickins & Jones London fashion store

Dickinson, Emily (Elizabeth) (1830–86) American poet

Diderot, Denis (1713–84) French encyclopaedist and philosopher

Didrikson, Mildred (1913–56) nickname 'Babe'; American golfer and athlete

Diefenbaker, John George (1895–1979) Prime Minister of Canada 1957–63

Dien Bien Phu battle in 1954 that led the French to pull out of Indo-China (later Vietnam)

Dieppe French port

diesel *not* deisel

dietitian

Dietrich, Marlene (1904–92) born Maria Magdalene von Losch; German-born actress and singer

Dieu et mon droit (Lat.) God and my right, motto of British royal family

different to The persistent belief that different to is somehow ungrammatical and to be avoided at all costs is without foundation. Different from is, to be sure, the normal construction, but there is no grammatical reason to insist on it. Different than is principally a US expression, and is equally unobjectionable in terms of its grammar, though it is likely to offend British idiom

diffuse to spread out; not to be confused with defuse

digestible

dignitary *not* -tory

dike/dyke

dilapidated, **dilapidation**

dilatory *not* -tary

dildos

dilemma refers to a situation involving two courses of action, both unsatisfactory. A person who cannot decide what he wants for breakfast is not in a dilemma.

dilettante a lover of, or dabbler in, the fine arts; most often used with a hint of condescension; *pl.* dilettantes or dilettanti

diligence, **diligent**

dilly-dally

DiMaggio, Joe (Joseph Paul), (1914–) American baseball player

Diners' Club

Dinesen, Isak pen name of Baroness Karen Blixen (1885–1962), Danish writer

dingo, *pl.* **dingoes**

Dinkins, David (1927–) American politician, Mayor of New York 1989–

Diogenes (*c.* 412–323 BC) Greek philosopher

Dionysius the Elder (*c.* 430–367 BC) tyrant of Syracuse, who suspended the famous sword above the head of Damocles

Dionysus/Dionysos *not* -ius; Greek god of wine and revelry; corresponding to the Roman god Bacchus; adj. is **Dionysian** or **Dionysiac**

diphtheria *not* dipth-; pronounced diff-, *not* dipth-. A similar spelling and pronunciation error is often made with diphthong

dirigible

dirigisme (Fr.) dominance of the economy by the state; adjective is ***dirigiste***

dirndl Alpine dress with full skirt

disassemble, **dissemble** The first means to take to pieces; the second to disguise or conceal.

disastrous *not* -erous

disc (UK)/**disk** (US) *except* that in the US disc is the more frequent spelling for phonograph albums, and in the UK disk is used for computer materials

discernible

discomfit means to thwart or baffle; not to be confused with discomfort

discothèque

discreet, discrete The first means with propriety, circumspect; the second means in separate parts, discontinuous

dishevelled (UK)/**disheveled** (US)
disintegrate
disinter exhume
disinterested, uninterested The first means neutral; the second not caring
dismissible
Disneyland, Disney World Disneyland is in Anaheim, California. Disney World is near Orlando, Florida. The European version is Euro Disneyland
dispatch (pref.)/**despatch** (alt.)
dispensable
disposable
Disprin (cap.)
Disraeli, Benjamin, Earl of Beaconsfield (1804–81) British Prime Minister 1868, 1874–80. The family name was spelled d'Israeli by his father, Isaac (1766–1848)
dissatisfy, dissatisfied, dissatisfaction
dissect, dissection
dissemble, disassemble The first means to disguise or conceal; the second to take to pieces.
dissent but **dissension**
dissertation
dissimilar
dissipate
dissociate (pref.)/**disassociate** (alt)
dissolvable
***distrait*, distraught** The first means lost in thought; the second deeply agitated
diurnal happening during the daytime, opposite of nocturnal
dived (UK, US)/**dove** (alt. US)
divergences *not* -cies
Divina Commedia, La Dante's 'Divine Comedy'
divvy to divide, especially equally, as with a shared jackpot
Dixie states that fought for the Confederacy in the American Civil War, now used loosely as a synonym for the South
Djakarta use Jakarta
Djibouti formerly French Somaliland and, briefly, French Terri-

tory of the Afars and Issas; officially now the Republic of Djibouti or Jumhouriya Djibouti; the capital is also called Djibouti

DNA deoxyribonucleic acid

Dniester river, Moldova

Dobbs Ferry, New York state (no apos.)

Dobermann pinscher (UK)/**Doberman pinscher** (US) breed of dog named after Ludwig Dobermann, a German breeder

Döblin, Alfred (1878–1957) German-born French novelist

Doctor Zhivago novel by Boris Pasternak (1957)

Dodecanese chain of twelve Greek islands, including Rhodes and Kos

Dodgson, Charles Lutwidge (1832–98) real name of Lewis Carroll

Dodoma capital of Tanzania

Dodsworth novel by Sinclair Lewis (1929)

doggerel

dogsbody

doily, *pl.* **doilies**

Dolgellau, Gwynedd, Wales, pronounced doll-geth-lee

Dollfuss, Engelbert (1892–1934) Austrian Chancellor 1932–4, assassinated by Austrian Nazis

doll's house (UK)/**dollhouse** (US)

dolor (US)/**dolour** (UK), but **dolorous** (UK, US)

Domenichino (1581–1641) Italian painter

Domesday Book *not* Doomsday; pronounced doomz-day; census of England carried out in 1086, during the reign of William the Conqueror

Dominica small Caribbean island state, capital Roseau. not to be confused with Dominican Republic, also a Caribbean island state, capital Santo Domingo

dominoes

Donatello (Donato di Niccolò di Betto Bardi) (*c.* 1386–1466), Italian sculptor

Donatism a heresy

Donegal Irish county, but Marquess of Donegall

Don Giovanni opera by Mozart (1787)

Dönitz, Karl (1891–1980) German admiral and briefly President of the German Reich at the time of Hitler's suicide, 1945

Donizetti, (Domenico) Gaetano (Maria) (1797–1848) Italian composer

Donleavy, J(ames) P(atrick) (1926–) American-born Irish writer

Donne, John (*c.* 1571–1631) pronounced dun; English poet

doorjamb

doppelgänger (Ger.) a person's ghostly double

Doppler effect the change that occurs in sound waves as the source and the observer move closer together; named after Christian Johann Doppler (1803–53), Austrian physicist

dormouse, *pl.* **dormice**

Dorneywood, Buckinghamshire, country house used as official residence by any Minister chosen by the Prime Minister

dos and don'ts *not* do's

Dos Passos, John (Roderigo) (1896–1970) American writer

Dostoevsky/Dostoyevski, Fyodor/Feodor Mikhailovich (1821–81) Russian novelist

Doublebois, Cornwall, pronounced double-boyze

Douglas-Home, Alec (Alexander Frederick), Baron Home of the Hirsel (1903–) pronounced hume; British Prime Minister 1963–4; brother of **William Douglas-Home** (1912–92), playwright

Douglass, Frederick (1817–95) born Frederick Augustus Washington Bailey; escaped American slave who became leading abolitionist and statesman

Dounreay nuclear power station, Caithness, Scotland

douse, dowse The first means to drench; the second, to search for water

Douwe Egberts Koninklijke Tabaksfabriek-Koffiebranderijen-Theehandel NV full name of Dutch coffee and tea company; literally, Douwe Egberts Royal Tobacco Factory-Coffee Roasters-Tea Traders Limited

dovecot (UK)/**dovecote** (US) In both countries the second syllable is pronounced as spelled

Dovorian, Old former student of Dover College

Dowding, Hugh Caswall Tremenheere, Baron (1882–1970) British air chief marshal

Dow Jones industrial average (no hyphen, last two words no caps.)

Down's syndrome congenital subnormality, formerly referred to as mongolism; named after Dr J. L. H. Down (1828–96), British physician

D'Oyly Carte, Richard (1844–1901) British light opera impresario

D.Phil. the form used at some British universities, notably Oxford, instead of Ph.D.

DPP (UK) Director of Public Prosecutions

draft (US, UK)/**draught** (UK) In the US the first spelling is used for all meanings. In the UK draft applies only to military conscription, preliminary plans, rough sketches and money orders; draught applies to beer, chill winds, ships' displacement and working horses. A draftsman draws up documents; a draughtsman makes drawings.

DRAM dynamic random access memory, computer chips

dramatis personae cast of characters

Dreiser, Theodore (1871–1945) American writer

Drexel Burnham Lambert (no commas) defunct US investment bank

Dreyfus, Alfred (1859–1935) French officer whose wrongful imprisonment on Devil's Island became a *cause célèbre*

Dreyfuss, Richard (1949–) American film actor

Driberg, Tom (Thomas Edward Neil), Baron Bradwell (1905–76) British politician and journalist

drier (UK), **dryer** (US) machines for drying clothes and hair

droit de/du seigneur feudal lord's supposed right to spend the first night with a vassal's bride

drosophila fruit fly

Drottningholm Court Theatre, Stockholm

drunken driving *not* drunk driving

drunkenness

DTI (UK) Department of Trade and Industry

dual, duel Dual means twofold, while a duel is a fight between two parties

Duarte, José Napoleón (1925–90) President of El Salvador 1972, 1980–82, 1984–9

du Barry, Marie Jeanne Bécu, Comtesse (1743–93) mistress of Louis XV, beheaded during French Revolution

Dubček, Alexander (1921–92) First Secretary of Communist Party (i.e., head of state) in Czechoslovakia 1968–9, whose reforms led to the Soviet invasion of the country in 1968

dubiety state of being dubious

Dubonnet fortified sweet wine

Duchamp, Marcel (1887–1968) French painter

dudgeon feeling of resentment

duenna/dueña (Sp.) governess or chaperon

duffel bag, **duffel coat** after Belgian town Duffel

Dufy, Raoul (1877–1953) French painter

Duisburg, Germany, pronounced doos-boork, *not* dwee-burg

Dukakis, Michael (Stanley) (1933–) US presidential candidate 1988, Governor of Massachusetts 1975–79, 1983–90

Dumas, Alexandre (1802–70), called Dumas *père*; French novelist and dramatist (*The Count of Monte Cristo*, *The Three Musketeers*)

Dumas, Alexandre (1824–95), called Dumas *fils*; French novelist and dramatist, best-known for *La Dame aux Camélias*

du Maurier, Dame Daphne (1907–89) English writer

Dumbarton town in Strathclyde, Scotland; *see also* Dunbarton

Dumbarton Oaks, Washington, DC

dumbfound (UK, alt. US)/**dumfound** (US, alt. UK)

dumdum bullet named after Dum-Dum, India

Dumfries & Galloway region of Scotland

Dummkopf (Ger.) *not* dumb- ; a stupid person

Dum spiro, spero (Lat.) While I breathe, there's hope

Dum vita est, spes est (Lat.) Where there is life, there is hope

Dun and Bradstreet Corporation *not* Dunn; US financial services and information company

Dunaway, Faye (1941–) American film actress

Dunbarton former Scottish county, now part of Strathclyde; *see also* Dumbarton

Dunkirk/Dunkerque (Fr.) French port

Dun Laoghaire pronounced dun leery; Irish port near Dublin

Duns Scotus, Johannes (*c.* 1270–1308) Scottish philosopher and theologian

duomo (It.) cathedral; *pl.* ***duomi***

Du Pont formally, E.I. du Pont de Nemours; US chemicals company

du Pré, Jacqueline (1945–87) British cellist whose career was destroyed by multiple sclerosis

Dürer, Albrecht (1471–1528) German artist and engraver

duress

Durkheim, Émile (1858–1917) French sociologist

Durrell, Gerald (Malcolm) (1925–) British zoologist and author, and brother of **Lawrence (George) Durrell** (1912–90), British novelist and poet

durum a type of wheat

Dushanbe capital of Tadzhikistan

Düsseldorf capital of North Rhine-Westphalia, Germany

Dutch Courtesan*, *The a comedy by John Marston (1605)

Dutchess County, New York

Dutch Guiana former name of Surinam

Duvalier, François (1907–71) known as Papa Doc, former President of Haiti

Dvořák, Antonin (1841–1904) pronounced dvor-zhak; Czech composer

dwarfs *not* dwarves

dyeing, **dying** The first means adding colour; the second becoming dead

Dyfed Welsh county formed from the former counties of Pembrokeshire, Cardiganshire and Carmarthenshire

Dylan, Bob (1941–) born Robert Allen Zimmerman, American singer and songwriter

dysentery

dyslexia

dystrophy

each When each precedes the noun or pronoun to which it refers, the verb should be singular: 'Each of us was . . . ' When it follows the noun or pronoun the verb should be plural: 'They each were . . . '

each and every is hopelessly tautological

Eagels, Jeanne (1894–1929) American actress

Eanes, António dos Santos Ramalho (1935–) President of Portugal 1976–86

Earhart, Amelia (1898–1937) pronounced air'-hart; American aviator who disappeared during round-the-world flight

Earls Court, London (no apos.)

earring note -rr-

EAS Electronic Article Surveillance, anti-theft system of marking products with a tag that sets off an alarm

East Bridgford, Nottinghamshire

East Chester, New York, and **Eastchester**, New York (separate places)

eau-de-vie *pl.* **eaux-de-vie**

Eaudyke, Lincolnshire pronounced oo'-dike

Ebbets Field, New York baseball stadium

Ebbw Vale/Glynebwy (Wel.), Gwent, Wales, pronounced eb'-ba vale

Eboracum Roman name for York

EC *see* European Community

Ecclesiastes book in the Old Testament; abbr. Eccles.

Ecclesiasticus book in the Old Testament Apocrypha; abbr. Ecclus.

ECG electrocardiogram

ECGD Export Credits Guarantee Department (UK); *not* Exports Credit

éclat brilliant display or effect, notable success, renown

Eco, Umberto (1929–) Italian academic and novelist

economic, economical For the sense of cheap, thrifty, not expensive, use economical; for every other meaning use economic

ecstasy

ECU European Currency Unit; notional unit of currency used by European countries within the European Monetary System to coordinate their exchange rates

Ecuadoreans

Eddy, Mary Baker (Glover) (1821–1910) American founder of the Christian Science Church, formally the Church of Christ, Scientist

Eddystone Lighthouse, **Eddystone Rocks** off Plymouth in the English Channel

edema (US), **oedema** (UK) swelling of body tissue as a result of abnormal retention of fluid

Eden, (Robert) Anthony, Earl of Avon (1897–1977) British Prime Minister 1955–7

Edensor, Derbyshire, pronounced enn'-zer

Edgbaston district of Birmingham (UK), site of famous cricket ground

Edgware Road, street and Underground station in central London (W2)

Edmonton capital of Alberta, Canada

Edmund Hall, St, Oxford, not to be confused with St Edmund's House, Cambridge

Edmund Ironside (*c.* 980–1016) English king

Education, Department for *not* of

Edwards, (Arthur) Trystan (1884–1973) British architect and town planner

Eduskunta Parliament of Finland

EEC European Economic Community, the Common Market; *see also* European Community

EEG electroencephalogram

eerie odd or frightening

effect, affect As a verb, effect means to accomplish ('The prisoners effected an escape'), while affect means to influence ('Smoking may affect your health') or to adopt a pose or manner ('He affected ignorance'). As a noun, effect is almost always the desired word (as in 'personal effects' and 'the damaging effects of war'); affect as a noun has a narrow psychological meaning.

EFTA *see* European Free Trade Association

e.g. *exempli gratia* (Lat.), for example

eggplant (US), **aubergine** (UK, Fr.)

Eglin Air Force Base, Florida

Ehrenburg, Ilya Grigoryevich (1891–1967) Russian novelist, essayist, short-story and travel writer, and poet

Eichendorff, Joseph Freiherr von (1798–1857) German poet, novelist and critic

Eichmann, Adolf (1906–62) notorious Nazi war criminal, head of Gestapo; captured by US Forces in 1945, recaptured in Argentina in 1960 by Israeli agents; tried, condemned and executed in Israel

Eifel Mountains, in Germany

Eiffel Tower/Tour Eiffel (Fr.), Paris

Eigg pronounced egg; small island in Inner Hebrides, Scotland

Eilean pronounced ell-'en; common name among Scottish islands (e.g., Eilean Dubh, Eilean More)

Eileithyia Greek goddess of childbirth

Eindhoven, Netherlands

Einstein, Albert (1879–1955) German mathematical physicist

Eisenbahn (Ger.) railway

Eisenhower, Dwight D(avid) (1890–1969) nickname 'Ike'; US general and President 1953–61

Eisenstein, Sergei (Mikhailovich) (1898–1948) Russian film director

eisteddfod Welsh festival and competition in music and literature; *pl.* **eisteddfods/eisteddfodau** (Wel.)

either If the noun or pronoun nearest the verb is singular, use a singular verb. If the noun or pronoun is plural, use a plural verb. Thus you should write 'Either the chairman or his deputy is going to speak first', but 'Either the chairman or the directors are going to speak first'

eke means to add to something in a meagre way or with difficulty, *not* to gain a narrow victory. A hungry person might eke out a supply of food, but a football team does not eke out a victory.

El Alamein/Al Alamein Egyptian village that gave its name to two battles in World War II

El Cerrito, California, suburb of San Francisco

El Dorado legendary city of gold

Electra in Greek mythology, the daughter of Agamemnon and Clytemnestra, and the subject of plays by Sophocles, Euripides and Aeschylus. Electra was also the name of one of the Pleiades, the daughters of Atlas and Pleione, who were transformed into stars. An Electra complex is an unnatural attachment to a father by a daughter.

electrolyte solution that conducts electricity

elegy a mournful poem, not to be confused with a **eulogy**, a tribute to the dead. The poem by Thomas Gray is 'Elegy Written in a Country Churchyard' (1751)

elephantiasis condition of abnormal swelling caused by disease affecting lymph nodes

Elgar, Sir Edward (1857–1934) English composer

Elgin Marbles, British Museum, pronounced with a hard *g*, *not* el-jin

Elham, Kent pronounced eel'um

Elien: signature of the Bishop of Ely

Eli Lilly *not* Lilley; US pharmaceuticals company

Eliot, George pen name of Mary Ann (later, Marian) Evans (1819–1880), English author

Eliot, T(homas) S(tearns) (1888–1965) American-born British poet, critic and playwright; Nobel Prize for Literature 1948

Elizabeth II (1926–) Queen of the United Kingdom 1952–
In the UK her formal title is Elizabeth the Second, by the Grace of God, of the United Kingdom of Great Britain and Northern Ireland and of Her Other Realms and Territories,

Queen, Head of the Commonwealth, Defender of the Faith. The title varies somewhat in other Commonwealth countries.

Ellesmere Port, Cheshire

Ellice Islands formerly Tuvalu; Pacific island group

Elliott, Denholm (Mitchell) (1922–92) British actor

Elliott, John (Dorman) (1941–) Australian businessman

Ellis Island site of former immigration centre in New York Bay

Ellough, Suffolk, pronounced el'-lo

El Salvador formally Republic of El Salvador/República de El Salvador (Sp.) Central American country, capital San Salvador. The people are Salvadorans

Elstree town and film studio in Hertfordshire

Élysée Palace, Paris *not* the; official home of French presidents

Elysium, Elysian Fields in Greek mythology, paradise

embalmment note -mm-

embarcadero (Sp.) wharf

embargoes

embarrass, embarrassment The French spelling is *embarras*, as in *embarras de richesses* (an embarrassment of riches) and *embarras du choix* (an embarrassment of choice)

Emerson, Ralph Waldo (1803–82) American poet and essayist

émigré an emigrant, particularly a political refugee

Emilia-Romagna a region of Italy, capital Bologna

Emmanuel College, Cambridge

Emmental a type of cheese

Empedocles (*c.* 495–*c.* 435 BC) Greek philosopher and poet

emphysema

empower *not* en-; to authorize

EMS *see* European Monetary System

encomium a lavish tribute or eulogy; *pl.* **encomiums**

encumbrance *not* -erance

encyclopaedia (UK)/**encyclopedia** (US)

Encyclopaedia Britannica

endemic, epidemic An epidemic is a rapid spread of a disease or other problem. When a disease or problem is of long standing or found only in a particular place or among a particular people, it is endemic

endorse *not* in-

Endymion in Greek mythology, a young man loved by the moon and condemned to eternal sleep

enfant terrible (Fr.) troublesome young person; anyone of embarrassingly indiscreet or unruly behaviour

Engels, Friedrich (1820–95) German socialist, collaborator with Karl Marx and co-author of the *Communist Manifesto*

Englischer Garten, Munich

en masse (Fr.)

Enniskillen, County Fermanagh, Northern Ireland, site of IRA bombing, November 1987; the army regiment is the Inniskilling Dragoons

ennoble

ennui

enormity wickedness, outrageousness; not to be confused with immensity

en passant (Fr.) in passing; also a chess move

enquiry (alt.)/**inquiry** (pref.) In the UK a formal investigation is always an inquiry, while either spelling is acceptable in other contexts

enrol, enrolment (UK, alt. US)/**enroll, enrollment** (US) and **enrolled, enrolling** (UK, US)

ENSA Entertainments National Service Association, British army entertainments division

entelechy in Aristotelian philosophy, the act of changing from potential to actual; in vitalism, the force that directs the actions of a living being

Entente Cordiale term first used to describe long-standing amity between the UK and France, then applied to a series of agreements between the two countries beginning in 1904. When applied to other treaties or understandings it is *entente cordiale*

Entertaining Mr Sloane *not* Sloan; comedy by Joe Orton (1964)

enthral (UK, alt. US)/**enthrall** (US) and **enthralled, enthralling** (UK, US)

entomology the study of insects

entr'acte a performance or interval between two acts

entrecôte tenderloin

entrepôt a trading place or storehouse

entrepreneur, **entrepreneurial**

enunciate, **enunciator**

envelop (vb) to wrap up

envelope (noun) a paper container for letters, anything that envelops

Environment, Department of the (UK) note the definite article

EOKA *Ethniki Organosis Kypriakou Agonos* (National Organization for Cypriot Struggle), a Greek Cypriot underground movement that sought to end British rule and unite Cyprus with Greece

eon (US)/**aeon** (UK)

epaulet (US)/**epaulette** (UK, alt. US)/***épaulette*** (Fr.) decoration worn on shoulder of uniform

EPCOT Environmental Prototype Community of Tomorrow, at Disney World, Florida

épée thin, flexible sword used in fencing

ephemera, *pl.* **ephemeras/ephemerae**

epicene of uncertain sex

Epicoene, or The Silent Woman comedy by Ben Jonson (1609)

epicurean person devoted to the pursuit of pleasure; when capitalized, refers to the philosophy of Epicurus

epiglottis

epilepsy

Epiphany in the Christian calendar, 6 January, the twelfth day of Christmas

'Epipsychidion' poem by Shelley (1821)

epistemology the theory of knowledge

E pluribus unum (Lat.) out of many, one; the motto on the official seal of the US

epsilon (E,) fifth letter of Greek alphabet

equally as is always wrong; a thing is equally good or, simply, as good as another

Equatorial Guinea formerly Spanish Guinea; west African country, capital Malabo

equerry royal attendant

equivocator

Equus play by Peter Shaffer (1973)

Erasmus, Desiderius (1466–1536) Dutch philosopher

Eratosthenes (*c.* 276–*c.* 194 BC) Greek mathematician, astronomer and geographer, calculated the Earth's circumference

Erdélyi, Arthur (1908–77) Hungarian-born British mathematician

Erevan capital of Armenia

Erewhon (1872) and ***Erewhon Revisited*** (1901) satirical novels by Samuel Butler. Erewhon is an anagram of nowhere

Erhard, Ludwig (1897–1977) Chancellor of West Germany 1963–6

Ericson/Ericsson/Eriksson, Leif (*c.* 10th c.) Norse explorer, discovered Vinland, possibly North America

Ericsson Swedish electrical group; formally, L. M. Ericsson; note -ss-

Erie, Pennsylvania; **Lake Erie; Erie Lackawanna Railway**

Erin go bragh Ireland for ever, an Irish motto

ERM *see* Exchange Rate Mechanism

ERNIE (UK) Electronic Random Number Indicator Equipment; the device that selects the winners of premium bond draws

Eros Greek god of love, son of Aphrodite

escudo unit of currency in Portugal and Cape Verde

escutcheon a shield bearing a coat of arms

Eskimo, *pl.* **Eskimos** (cap.) The preferred term is Inuit (*sing.* and *pl.*).

esophagus (US)/**oesophagus** (UK)

especial, special Especial means to a high degree, while special means for a particular purpose. A special meal may be especially delicious

Esperanto language devised by L. L. Zamenhof in 1887

esthetic (US)/**aesthetic** (UK)

ETA Euzkadi ta Azkatasuna (Basque Nation and Liberty), Basque separatist organization; also, estimated time of arrival

et al. *et alibi* (Lat.), and elsewhere; *et alii* (Lat.), and others; note full point after al only

et cetera (Lat.) abbr. etc.; and so forth; *not* pronounced ek-cetera
Eternal City, the Rome
Etherege, Sir George (*c.* 1635–91) English playwright
Etna, Mount in Sicily; highest active volcano in Europe
Etobicoke, greater Toronto, Ontario
'Et tu, Brute?' (Lat.), 'You too, Brutus?' Julius Caesar's dying words, in Shakespeare's *Julius Caesar* (III, i, 77)
etymology the study of the origin and development of words
eucalyptus, *pl.* **eucalyptuses/eucalypti**
Euclidean
Eumenides in Greek mythology, another name for the Furies
eunuch
euonymus any tree or shrub of the genus *Euonymus*
euphemism a mild expression substituted for one thought to be too direct or unpleasant
euphuism and **euphuistic** describe a pretentiously elevated style of writing, after John Lyly's *Euphues: the Anatomy of Wit* (1578)
Euratom European Atomic Energy Community
Euripides (*c.* 484–406 BC) Greek dramatist
European Community abbr. EC; formed in 1967 with a formal merger between the European Economic Community, the European Coal and Steel Community and the European Atomic Energy Community; members are Belgium, Denmark, France, Germany, Greece, Ireland, Italy, Luxembourg, The Netherlands, Portugal, Spain and the United Kingdom. The EC is governed by the European Commission, the European Parliament and the Council of Ministers. In addition, the various heads of state meet periodically as the European Council.
European Court of Human Rights, Strasbourg, deals with issues of civil liberties arising out of the European Convention on Human Rights; it has no connection with the EC or UN; *see also* Council of Europe
European Court of Justice, Luxembourg, an EC institution dealing exclusively with disputes involving member states
European Economic Community abbr. EEC; the Common

Market; an organization of European states aiming to create free trade among members and a common external tariff; now part of the EC

European Free Trade Association abbr. EFTA; a trade association of non-members of the European Community: Austria, Iceland, Norway, Sweden and Switzerland; Finland is an associate member.

European Monetary System abbr. EMS; a system within the EC designed to coordinate policies on stabilizing and harmonizing currencies. All members of the EC belong to the EMS; *see also* Exchange Rate Mechanism

European Organization for Nuclear Research formerly the European Council for Nuclear Research; more commonly called CERN (Conseil Européen de Recherches Nucléaires)

Eurydice in Greek mythology, wife of Orpheus

Eustachian tube connects middle ear to nasopharynx

euthanasia

Evatt, Herbert Vere (1894–1965) Australian statesman

Ever Ready batteries

Everest, Mount highest mountain in the world: 29,028 ft/ 8,848 m

everyday (adj.), **every day** (noun) 'He was wearing everyday clothes', but 'We come here every day.' The same distinction applies to everybody, everyone and everything

exaggerate

exasperate

Excalibur *not* -ber; King Arthur's sword

ex cathedra (Lat.) with authority

excavator

exchangeable

Exchange Rate Mechanism abbr. ERM; an arrangement within the EMS to encourage exchange-rate stability between the currencies of the member nations by allowing them to rise or fall not more than 2.25 per cent against the other currencies in the group; *see also* European Monetary System

excisable

excitable

exhalation
exhaustible
exhilarate
exhort, exhortation
ex officio (Lat.) by virtue of one's office or position
Exon: signature of the Bishop of Exeter; *see also* Exxon
exonerate
exorbitant
exorcise
expatriate one who lives abroad; but compatriot
Expedition of Humphry Clinker, The, *not* Humphrey; novel by Smollett (1771)
ex post facto (Lat.) after the fact
expressible
extempore impromptu
extraneous *not* exter-
extravagant
extrovert *not* extra-
Exxon Corporation formerly Standard Oil of New Jersey
Eyadéma, General Étienne Gnassingbé (1937–) President of Togo 1967–
eyeing
Eyre & Spottiswoode British publisher
Eysenck, Hans (Jurgen) (1916–) psychologist and writer
Ezeiza Airport, Buenos Aires

FAA Federal Aviation Administration (US)

Faber and Faber *not* &

facia (UK) variant of fascia, used to refer specifically to the dashboard of a car and the board over a shop bearing the occupier's name

facsimile an exact copy

factious in the manner of factions; not to be confused with factitious or fractious

factitious artificial, not genuine

faeces (UK)/**feces** (US)

Faerie Queene, The epic poem by Spenser (1589–96)

Faeroe Islands/The Faeroes/Faeröerne (Dan.) Danish islands in north Atlantic between Scotland and Iceland

Fahd (ibn Abdul Aziz) (1923–) King of Saudi Arabia 1982–

Fahrenheit abbr. F; temperature scale named after German physicist Gabriel Daniel Fahrenheit (1686–1736), who introduced it; sets freezing point of water at 32 degrees and boiling point at 212 degrees. To convert Celsius (centigrade) to Fahrenheit, multiply the Celsius temperature by 1.8 and add 32, or use the table in the Appendix

faience a kind of glazed pottery

faint, feint The first means weak, pale or to lose consciousness; the second refers to a misleading movement, and in the UK is also used to describe pale printing, as in feint-ruled paper

fairway *not* fare-

fait accompli (Fr). an accomplished fact; *pl.* ***faits accomplis***

Falange political party in Spain; members are Falangists; *see also* Phalange

Falkland Islands/Islas Malvinas (Sp.) British Crown Colony in the south Atlantic; capital Port Stanley. The fighting between Britain and Argentina in 1982 is properly called the Falklands conflict (or something similar), since war was never declared

Fälldin, Thorbjörn (1926–) pronounced fell'-din; Swedish Prime Minister 1976–78, 1979–82

fallible

fandango lively Spanish dance; *pl.* **fandangoes/fandangos**

Faneuil Hall, Boston, Massachusetts

Fannie Mae (US) nickname for the Federal National Mortgage Association and the bonds it issues, but the US confectionery company is Fannie May; *see also* Freddie Mac

FAO Food and Agriculture (*not* Agricultural) Organization; a UN body

Farabundo Martí National Liberation Front Salvadoran revolutionary movement

Faraday, Michael (1791–1867) British chemist and physicist

Far from the Madding Crowd *not* Maddening; novel by Thomas Hardy (1874)

Farne Islands, off Northumberland

Faroe Islands use Faeroe

Farouk I (1920–65) ex-king of Egypt

Farquhar, George (1678–1707) *not* Farqua-; Irish playwright

farrago a confused mixture; *pl.* **farragoes** (US)/**farragos** (UK)

Farrar, Straus and Giroux *not* Strauss; US publisher

Farrell, James T(homas) (1904–79) American novelist

farther, **further** Although their meanings overlap, farther usually appears in contexts involving literal distance ('New York is farther from Sydney than from London') and further in contexts involving figurative distance ('I can take this play no further') or the idea of moreover or additionally ('a further point')

farthing coin in old British money worth one quarter of a penny; withdrawn in 1961

fascia *see also* facia

fascism, **fascist**

Fassbinder, Rainer Werner (1946–82) German film writer and director

Fastnacht (Ger.) Shrove Tuesday

Fates, the/Moerae (Grk)/**Parcae** (Lat.) in Greek mythology, the three daughters of Nyx: Clotho, Lachesis and Atropos

Faubourg St-Honoré, Rue du, Paris

Faulkbourne, Essex, pronounced fah'-burn

Faulkner, William (Harrison) (1897–1962) American novelist; Nobel Prize for Literature 1949

fauna, **flora** The first means animals; the second plants

Fauré, Gabriel (Urbain) (1845–1924) French composer

faute de mieux (Fr.) for lack of anything better

fauvism derived from French word meaning wild beast, a short-lived but influential school of expressionist art in France whose proponents, known as Les Fauves, included Matisse, Rouault, Derain, Dufy, Braque and Vlaminck

faux bonhomme (Fr.) a person whose superficial good nature conceals a darker or more sinister side

faux pas (Fr.) an error or blunder; *pl.* the same

favela (Port.) a Brazilian shantytown

favor (US)/**favour** (UK)

Fawkes, Guy (1570–1606) Catholic rebel who helped organize unsuccessful Gunpowder Plot. Guy Fawkes' Day, which marks the date of his capture (not his execution), is 5 November

faze to disturb or worry; not to be confused with phase

FBI Federal Bureau of Investigation (US)

FCC Federal Communications Commission; authority responsible for regulating US television and radio

FDIC (US) Federal Deposit Insurance Corporation; authority that steps in when US banks fail

Fe *ferrum* (Lat.) iron

feasible

feces (US)/**faeces** (UK)

feijoada (Port.) pronounced fay-zhwa'-duh; Brazilian national dish, made up of various meats combined with sauces, black beans and orange segments

Feininger, Lyonel (Charles Adrian) (1871–1956) American artist; note unusual spelling of first name

feint rule on paper (UK); *see also* faint, feint

feisty (US) excitable

feldspar

Felixstowe town and port in Suffolk

Fellini, Federico (1920–) Italian film director

Ferlinghetti, Lawrence (1920–) American poet and writer

Fermanagh pronounced fur-man'-na; county in Northern Ireland

Ferrara city in Emilia-Romagna, Italy

Ferrari car manufacturer

Ferraro, Geraldine (Anne) (1935–) former Congresswoman from New York; became the first female US vice-presidential candidate when she ran with Walter Mondale in the 1984 election

ferrule, ferule A ferrule is a metal cap or band used to strengthen a tool, as with the metal piece that attaches the brush to the handle of a paintbrush. A ferule is a ruler or stick used for punishment. In both cases it is generally better to substitute more readily understood terms

Ferruzzi Italian commodities business

fervid, fetid/foetid (alt.) Fervid means intense, while fetid means foul-smelling

fettuccine note -tt-, -cc-; type of pasta

fetus (US)/**foetus** (UK)

Feuchtwanger, Lion (1889–1958) German writer

feud a dispute of long standing

feu de joie (Fr.) ceremonial salute with gunfire; *pl.* ***feux de joie***

Feuerbach, Ludwig (Andreas) (1804–72) German philosopher

feuilleton section of French newspaper containing literary reviews, fiction serializations or other pieces of light journalism

fewer, less Use less with singular nouns (less money, less sugar), fewer with plural nouns (fewer houses, fewer cars)

Feydeau, Georges (1862–1921) French playwright, known for bedroom farces

FHA (US) Federal Housing Administration

fiancé (masc.)/**fiancée** (fem.)
Fianna Fáil pronounced fee-yan'-na foil; Irish political party
fiasco, *pl.* **fiascos**
Fiat Fabbrica Italiana Automobile Torino; Italian car manufacturer
fiber (US)/**fibre** (UK)
fiddle-de-dee
FIDE pronounced fee'-day; Féderation Internationale des Échecs, the world governing body of chess
Fidei Defensor (Lat.) Defender of the Faith
fidget, **fidgeting**, **fidgeted**, **fidgety**
Fiennes, Sir Ranulph (Twisleton-Wykeham-) (1944–) pronounced fines; English explorer
FIFA Féderation Internationale de Football Associations, the world governing body of association football (soccer)
fifth column enemy sympathizers working within their own country. The term comes from the Spanish Civil War when General Mola boasted that he had four columns of soldiers marching on Madrid and a fifth column of sympathizers waiting in the city
Figheldean, Wiltshire pronounced fill'-deen
filament
filet mignon, but **fillet** for all other dishes and contexts
filial pertaining to a son or daughter
filibuster
filigree
Filipino (masc.)/**Filipina** (fem.) note -p-; a native of the Philippines (-pp-)
fille de joie (Fr.) a prostitute
Fillmore, Millard (1800–74) US President 1850–53
FIMBRA (UK) Financial Intermediaries, Managers and Brokers Association, financial regulatory body
finable liable to a fine
finagle to secure by cajoling; to use trickery
Financial Times Ordinary Share Index abbr. FT Index or FT30 Index; measures the performance of 30 leading shares on the London Stock Exchange

Financial Times-Stock Exchange 100-Share Index abbr. FT-SE Index; nickname Footsie; measures the performance of 100 leading shares on the London Stock Exchange

fin de siècle (Fr.) end of the 19th century; generally used to imply decadence

Fine Gael pronounced feen gayl; Irish political party

finial ornament on the pinnacle of a roof, gable, tower, etc.

finical, finicky Both words mean being fussy, over-precise

Finisterre, Cape westernmost point of Spanish mainland

Finnbogadóttir, Vigdís (1930–) President of Iceland 1980–

Finnegans Wake (no apos.) novel by James Joyce (1939)

fiord (pref.)/**fjord** (alt.)

Firbank, (Arthur Annesley) Ronald (1886–1926) English novelist

Firenze (It.)/**Florence**

first floor In the UK, the floor above the ground floor; in the US and many other countries, the ground floor

Fischer, (Robert James) Bobby (1943–) American chess genius; world champion 1972–5

Fischer-Dieskau, Dietrich (1925–) German baritone

fish, fishes Either is correct as a plural

Fisherman's Wharf, San Francisco, *not* men's

fission, fusion in physics, ways of producing nuclear energy: fission by splitting the nucleus of an atom; fusion by fusing two light nuclei into a single, heavier nucleus

fisticuffs

Fittipaldi, Emerson (1946–) Brazilian racing driver

FitzGerald, Edward (1809–83) English scholar and poet, translator of Omar Khayyám's *Rubáiyát*

Fitzgerald, F(rancis) Scott (Key) (1896–1940) American writer

Fitzgerald, Garret (Michael) (1926–) Irish Prime Minister 1981–7

Fitzwilliam Museum, Cambridge

fjord (alt.)/**fiord** (pref.)

fl. floruit (Lat.) flourished; used when the exact dates a person lived are not known, e.g., Caedmon (*fl.* seventh c.)

FL postal abbr. of Florida; traditional abbr. is **Fla.**

flabbergast, **flabbergasted**
flaccid limp
flagon drinking vessel
flair (noun), **flare** (noun, vb) Flair is a knack for doing something well. A flare is a sudden burst of flame, a brilliant but unsteady light, a signal light; as a verb flare means to widen gradually, to burst into anger or flame
flak anti-aircraft fire and, by extension, criticism or abuse
flaky *not* -ey
flamboyant
flamingo, *pl.* **flamingoes/flamingas**
flammable, **inflammable** Although inflammable means 'capable of being burned', it has so often been taken to mean the opposite that most authorities now suggest it be avoided, particularly in contexts that might one day involve urgency. Therefore it is generally better to use flammable for materials that will burn and nonflammable for those that will not
Flamsteed, John (1646–1719) first astronomer royal of England
flannel, **flannelled** (UK)/**flanneled** (US), **flannelette** (UK, US)
flare *see* flair, flare
Flaubert, Gustave (1821–80) French novelist
flaunt, **flout** Flaunt means to show off; flout to disregard
flautist person who plays a flute
Fledermaus, Die operetta by Johann Strauss the younger (1874)
fledgeling (UK)/**fledgling** (US)
Fleming, Sir Alexander (1881–1955) Scottish bacteriologist, discoverer of penicillin; shared Nobel Prize for Physiology or Medicine 1945
Flemings and Walloons The first are natives of Flanders, the northern, Flemish-speaking part of Belgium; the second are natives of Wallonia, the southern, French-speaking part
fleur-de-lis, *pl.* **fleurs-de-lis**
flexible
flibbertigibbet a scatterbrain
floccinaucinihilipilification the act of estimating as worthless; often cited as the longest word in English

Flodden Field, Battle of (1513) battle in which the Scottish forces of James IV were routed by the English

flora, **fauna** The first means plants; the second animals

florescent, **fluorescent** The first means in flower; the second radiating light

floruit (Lat.) abbr. *fl.*; flourished; used when the exact dates a person lived are not known, e.g., Caedmon (*fl.* seventh c.)

flotation *not* float-

flotilla

flotsam and jetsam Flotsam describes wreckage of a ship and its goods floating at sea. Jetsam applies to goods that have been thrown overboard (jettisoned). Historically flotsam went to the Crown and jetsam to the lord of the manor on whose land it washed up

flounder, **founder** Flounder means to struggle, founder means to sink, break down or fail. A drowning person flounders; ships founder

flourish

flout, **flaunt** The first means to disregard; the second to show off

flugelhorn (UK)/**fleugelhorn** or **flügelhorn** (US) brass musical instrument

flummox

flunkey, **flunkeys** (UK, alt. US) /**flunky**, **flunkies** (US, alt. UK)

fluorescent light *see also* florescent

fluoridate, **fluoridation**

fluoroscope

FMLN Farabundo Martí National Liberation Front, Salvadoran guerrilla group

Fo, Dario (1926–) Italian playwright

fo'c'sle forecastle

focused, **focusing**, **focuses**

foehn (US, alt. UK)/**föhn** (UK) pronounced fern; a type of warm mountain wind

foetus (UK)/**fetus** (US)

Fogg Art Museum, Cambridge, Massachusetts

Fogg, Phileas *not* Phogg, *not* Phineas; character in Jules Verne's *Around the World in Eighty Days*

fogy (pref.)/**fogey** (alt.) an old-fashioned person; *pl.* **fogies/fogeys**

föhn *see* foehn

foie gras fattened goose liver

folie à deux (Fr.) delusion shared by two people

Folies-Bergère Parisian music hall

Folketing Danish parliament

fondue

Fontainebleau magnificent château, town and forest on the Seine near Paris. The hotel of the same name in Miami, Florida, is pronounced fountain blue

Fonteyn (de Arias), Dame Margot (1919–91) born Margaret Hookham; English prima ballerina

Foochow/Fuzhou (Pinyin) pronounced foo-jo'; capital of Fujian Province, China

forbade (pref.)/**forbad** (alt.) pronounced for-bad'; past tense of forbid

forbear, forebear Forbear is a verb meaning to avoid or refrain from; forebear is a noun and means ancestor

force majeure (Fr.) an uncontrollable event

forcible

Ford, Ford Madox (1873–1939) born Ford Hermann Hueffer; English writer, grandson of Ford Madox Brown (1821–93), the artist

forebear *see* forbear, forebear

forego, forgo The first means to precede; the second to do without

Forester, C(ecil) S(cott) (1899–1966) English writer, chiefly remembered for his naval tales involving Horatio Hornblower; not to be confused with E. M. Forster

forever (UK, US)/**for ever** (UK) In the UK forever means constantly ('He is forever pestering me'), and for ever means for eternity ('I'll love you for ever'). In the US forever is used for both meanings

foreword introduction to a book written by someone other than the author

forgather (pref.)/**foregather** (alt.) The need for the word is doubtful; it is generally enough to say that people gather

formaldehyde

Formentera, Balearic Islands, Spain

Formosa former name of Taiwan

Fornebu Airport, Oslo

Forster, E(dward) M(organ) (1879–1970) English novelist

forsythia

forte abbr. *f.*; in music, loud; also a person's strong point

fortissimo abbr. *ff.*; in music, very loud

fortississimo abbr. *fff.*; as loud as possible

Fort-Lamy former name of N'djaména, capital of Chad

FORTRAN Formula Translation, a computer language

Fort Sumter, Charleston, South Carolina, site of first action in American Civil War

fortuitous means by chance; it is not a synonym for fortunate. A fortuitous event may be fortunate, but, equally, it may not

For Whom the Bell Tolls *not* Bells Toll; novel by Ernest Hemingway (1940)

Foucault pendulum pronounced foo-ko'; devised by French physicist Jean Bernard Léon Foucault (1819–68)

founder, **flounder** Founder means to sink, break down or fail, whereas flounder means only to struggle. A drowning person flounders; ships founder

foundry *not* -ery

Fouquet, Jean (*c.* 1420–*c.* 1480) French painter

Fouquet, Nicolas, Vicomte de Melun et du Vaux and Marquis de Belle-Isle (1615–80) French statesman; superintendent of finance under Mazarin

Four Horsemen of the Apocalypse represent Conquest, Slaughter, Famine and Death

fourth estate the press. The other three are the Lords, the Commons and the Church of England

Fowey, Cornwall, pronounced foy

Fowler's common name for *A Dictionary of Modern English Usage* by H. W. Fowler, first published 1926

Fox, George (1624–91) English religious reformer, founder of the Society of Friends, or Quakers

Foxe, John (1516–87) English clergyman and writer, most remembered for the book commonly known as *Foxe's Book of Martyrs*

fractious disorderly; not to be confused with factious or factitious

Fragonard, Jean Honoré (1732–1806) French painter and engraver

France is divided into 22 regions: Alsace, Aquitaine, Auvergne, Basse-Normandie, Bretagne (Brittany), Bourgogne (Burgundy), Centre, Champagne-Ardennes, Corse (Corsica), Franche-Comté, Haute-Normandie, Île de France, Languedoc-Roussillon, Limousin, Lorraine, Midi-Pyrénées, Nord-Pas-de-Calais, Pays de la Loire, Picardie (Picardy), Poitou-Charentes, Provence-Alpes-Côte d'Azur, Rhône-Alpes

France, Anatole pen name of Jacques Anatole François Thibault (1844–1924), French writer and editor

Francis of Assisi, St (1182–1226) born Giovanni Francesco Bernardone; founder of Franciscan order of monks

Franck, César Auguste (1822–90) Belgian-born French composer

Franco (y Bahamonde), Francisco (1892–1975) Spanish general and dictator 1937–75; called *Caudillo* (leader) in Spain, General Franco elsewhere

Francome, John (1952–) British jockey, trainer and novelist

Frankenstein is the scientist, not the monster. The full title of the novel, by Mary Wollstonecraft Shelley (1797–1851), is *Frankenstein, or the Modern Prometheus* (1818)

Frankfurt am Main, western Germany, not to be confused with **Frankfurt an der Oder**, eastern Germany, on the border with Poland. The towns in Indiana, Kentucky, Michigan, Ohio and several other US states are all **Frankfort**

Frankfurter, Felix (1882–1965) American jurist

Franz Josef II (1906–89) Prince of Liechtenstein 1938–89; handed over executive powers to his son, Prince Hans Adam II, in 1984

frappé (Fr.) iced; artificially chilled

Fraser, Peter (1884–1950) Scottish-born Prime Minister of New Zealand 1940–49

Frau (Ger.) married woman; as a title, Mrs; *pl.* ***Frauen***

Fräulein (Ger.) *sing.* and *pl.*; unmarried woman/women

Frayn, Michael (1933–) English writer and playwright

Frazer-Nash British sports car

FRCS Fellow of the Royal College of Surgeons

Freddie Mac nickname of US Federal Home Loan Mortgage Corporation; *see also* Fannie Mae

Frederick II (1712–86) King of Prussia 1740–86; known as Frederick the Great

Fredericksburg, Virginia, site of battle in American Civil War; *see also* Frederiksberg

Fredericton capital of New Brunswick, Canada

Frederiksberg suburb of Copenhagen

Freefone (cap.) free telephone service of British Telecom

Freemason, **Freemasonry**, **Mason** (caps.)

freesia flowering plant

Freiberg, Saxony, Germany

Freiburg (im Breisgau) ancient university town in Baden, Germany; *see also* Fribourg

Fremantle, Western Australia

French Guiana an overseas region of France on the South American mainland; capital Cayenne

French Somaliland former name of Djibouti

Freud, Lucian (1922–) German-born British painter

Freud, Sigmund (1856–1939) Austrian neurologist and founder of psychoanalysis

FRIBA Fellow of the Royal Institute of British Architects

Fribourg (Fr.)/**Freiburg** (Ger.), Switzerland

fricassee, *pl.* **fricassees**

FRICS Fellow of the Royal Institution of Chartered Surveyors

Friedman, Milton (1912–) American economist; Nobel Prize for Economics 1976

Friedrich, Götz (1930–) German opera director

Friedrichshafen, Germany

Friesian, **Frisian** Friesian is a breed of cattle; Frisian is a Germanic language

Friesland, **Frisian Islands** Friesland is a region of The Netherlands; the Frisian Islands form an island chain lying off, and politically divided between, The Netherlands, Denmark and Germany

frieze

Friml, (Charles) Rudolf (1879–1972) Czech-born American pianist and composer of light operas

Frisbee (cap.)

Frisian *see* Friesian/Frisian

Friulia-Venezia Giulia region of Italy; capital Trieste

Frobisher, Sir Martin (*c.* 1535–94) English explorer, sought the Northwest Passage

fromage (Fr.) cheese

front bench (noun), **frontbench** (adj.) (UK) A Member of Parliament who holds a senior office in the Government or Opposition sits on the front bench, but is a frontbench spokesman; *see also* back bench

frontispiece illustration facing the title page of a book

frowsty, **frowzy** The first means musty or stale; the second, untidy or dingy

Frühstück (Ger.) breakfast

FTC (US) Federal Trade Commission

FT Index *see* Financial Times Ordinary Share Index

Fuad I (1868–1936) King of Egypt 1923–36

fuchsia

Fuhlsbuttel Airport, Hamburg

Führer (pref.)/**Fuehrer** (alt.) (Ger.) leader

Fujiyama means 'Mount Fuji', so Mount Fujiyama is redundant; use either Fujiyama or Mount Fuji. The Japanese also call it Fujisan and Fuki-no-Yama

Fulbright scholarships US exchange programme for students and teachers, named after Senator (James) William Fulbright (1905–   )

fulfil, **fulfilment** (UK)/**fulfill**, **fulfillment** (US) but **fulfilled**, **fulfilling** (UK, US)

fulsome means odiously insincere. Fulsome praise, properly used, isn't a lavish tribute; it is unctuous toadying.

furor (US)/**furore** (UK)

further, **farther** Although their meanings overlap, farther usually appears in contexts involving literal distance ('New York is farther from Sydney than from London') and further in contexts involving figurative distance ('I can take this plan no further') or the idea of moreover or additionally ('a further point')

Furtwängler, Wilhelm (1886–1954) German conductor

fusion, **fission** in physics, ways of producing nuclear energy: fusion by fusing two light nuclei into a single, heavier nucleus; fission by splitting the nucleus of an atom

Fussell, Paul (1924–) American academic and writer

future plans and similar locutions are almost always redundant. If a person makes plans, it would follow that they are for the future

Fuzhou (Pinyin)/**Foochow** pronounced foo-jo'; capital of Fujian Province, China

G

g gram
GA postal abbr. of US state of Georgia; traditional abbr. is **Ga**
gabardine type of cloth
gaberdine long cloak
Gaborone capital of Botswana
Gabrieli, Andrea (*c.* 1510–86) Italian composer
Gabrieli, Giovanni (1557–1612) Italian composer, nephew and pupil of above
Gaddafi/Qaddafi, Muammar al- (1942–) Libyan head of state 1969– . He has no official title or position
Gadsden Purchase (1853) US purchase of large parts of Arizona and New Mexico from Mexico
Gaea/Gaia/Ge in Greek mythology, the Earth personified and, later, goddess of the Earth, mother of the Titans, Furies and Cyclops
Gaeltacht any region of Ireland where Gaelic is the vernacular
Gagarin, Yuri (Alekseyevich) (1934–68) Soviet cosmonaut, first man in space (1961)
gage a pledge or a challenge; *see also* gauge
gaiety
gaijin (Jap.) literally, 'outsider'; foreigner
gaillardia any flowering plant of the genus *Gaillardia*; sometimes called basketflower
Gainsborough, Thomas (1727–88) English landscape and portrait painter
Gaitskell, Hugh (Todd Naylor) (1906–63) British politician
Galahad, Sir the purest and noblest knight in the Arthurian legend

Galant *not*-ll-; car manufactured by Mitsubishi

Galápagos Islands/Archipiélago de Colón (Sp.) islands belonging to Ecuador

Galeries Lafayette Paris department store

Galeries St-Hubert, Brussels

Galileo Galileo Galilei (1564–1642), Italian astronomer and mathematician

Gallaudet College, Washington, DC

gallimaufry a jumble; *pl.* **gallimaufries**

Gallipoli/Gelibolu (Turk.) a peninsula on the European side of Turkey and site of World War I campaign

gallivant to wander

Gallup poll a public-opinion poll, named after its deviser, George Horace Gallup (1901–84)

Galsworthy, John (1867–1933) English novelist and playwright; Nobel Prize for Literature 1932

Gama, Vasco da (*c.* 1469–1524) Portuguese explorer; led first expedition to reach India by sea round the Cape of Good Hope

gambit an opening move that involves some strategic sacrifice or concession, *not* a simple synonym for tactic or ploy

gamut the whole series or extent of something

gamy *not* -ey

Gandhi, Indira (1917–84) Prime Minister of India 1966–77, 1980–84

Gandhi, Mohandas Karamchand (1869–1948) Indian leader; called Mahatma, or 'great soul'

ganef/gonof (Yidd.) thief, disreputable person

Gang of Four Chinese political faction accused of treasonable actions after the death of Mao Tse-tung. The four were Jiang Qing (Mao's widow), Zhang Chunqiao, Wang Hongwen and Yeo Wenyuan. In British political parlance, Gang of Four refers to the founding members of the Social Democratic Party: David Owen, Shirley Williams, Roy Jenkins and William Rodgers

gangrene *not* -green

Gannett Company pronounced guh-nett'; US newspaper group

Gannett Peak pronounced gan'-utt; a mountain in Wyoming

gantlet (US) section of railway track where two lines overlap; also alt. for gauntlet

Ganymede fourth moon of Jupiter; in Greek mythology, the young Trojan made cupbearer to the gods

García (Pérez), Alan (1949–) President of Peru 1985–90

García Lorca, Federico (1899–1936) Spanish poet and playwright

García Márquez, Gabriel (1928–) Colombian novelist; Nobel Prize for Literature 1982

Garda Siochána (Ir.) Civic Guard, formal name of the police force in the Republic of Ireland, usually shortened to Garda; a garda is a member of the force; *pl.* **gardai**

Gardner, Erle Stanley (1889–1970) American writer of detective fiction

Garibaldi, Giuseppe (1807–82) Italian leader, played important role in unification of Italy

garish gaudy

Garmisch-Partenkirchen, Germany, skiing resort

Garonne French river

Garrick, David (1717–79) English actor, playwright and theatrical manager

garrote (US)/**garrotte**(UK) to strangle, especially with an iron collar or length of cord or wire

gas, **gases**, **gaseous**, **gassed**, **gassing**, **gasify**, **gasification**

gasoline *not* -lene

Gasperi, Alcide de (1881–1954) Prime Minister of Italy 1945–53

Gasthaus (Ger.) an inn or guesthouse; *pl.* ***Gasthäuser*** (umlaut)

Gasthof (Ger.) hotel; *pl.* ***Gasthöfe*** (umlaut)

gastronome a connoisseur of food

gateau/gâteau cake; *pl.* **gateaus/gâteaux**

GATT General Agreement on Tariffs and Trade; UN agency that attempts to regulate world trade

Gaudier-Brzeska, Henri (1891–1915) French sculptor

gauge *not* guage; standard measure or measuring device

Gauguin, (Eugène Henri) Paul (1848–1903) French painter

Gauloise French brand of cigarettes
gauntlet a form of punishment or severe criticism, as in 'run the gauntlet'; to challenge, as in 'throw down the gauntlet'; *see also* gantlet
Gautama, Siddhartha Buddha
Gauthier-Villars French publisher
gauzy
Gaviria (Trujillo), César (1947–) President of Colombia 1990–
Gawain, Sir one of the Arthurian knights
Gay-Lussac, Joseph Louis (1778–1850) French chemist and physicist
Gaza Strip an area of Sinai administered by Israel since its capture from Egypt during war in 1967
gazetteer
gazpacho a cold Spanish soup
GCE General Certificate of Education (UK); replaced by GCSE
GCHQ Government Communications Headquarters, base for British intelligence-gathering operations, Cheltenham, Gloucestershire
GCSE General Certificate of Secondary Education (UK)
Gdańsk, Poland, formerly Danzig
GDP, GNP GDP, gross domestic product, is everything produced by a nation during a given period, except earnings from overseas. GNP, gross national product, is the total worth of everything produced by a nation during a given period, including earnings from overseas
GDR German Democratic Republic (East Germany); *see also* Germany
Geelong, Victoria, Australia
geezer (UK) slang for an old man; *see also* geyser
Geffrye Museum, London
gefilte fish (Yidd.) chopped fish dish
Gehrig, (Henry Louis) Lou (1903–41) American baseball player
Geiger counter measures radioactivity; devised by German physicist Hans Geiger (1882–1945)

Geisenheimer wine
Gelsenkirchen, Germany
gemütlich (Ger.) agreeable, comfortable, good-natured
Gemütlichkeit (Ger.) congeniality, friendliness
gendarmes are not policemen, but soldiers performing police duties. French policemen are just that – policemen
genealogy
General Agreement on Tariffs and Trade abbr. GATT; UN body set up to promote world trade
generalissimo, *pl.* **generalissimos** but ***generalísimo*** (Sp.),
General Strike (caps.) national strike in the UK, 4–12 May 1926
Genet, Jean (1910–86) French novelist and playwright
Geneva/Genève (Fr.)/**Genf** (Ger.)/**Ginevra** (It.), Switzerland
Geneva, Lake/Genfersee (Ger.)/**Léman, Lac** (Fr.)
Geneva Convention (1864, revised 1950, 1978) international agreement on the conduct of war and treatment of wounded and captured soldiers
Geneviève, Sainte (*c.* 422–*c.* 512) patron saint of Paris
Genghis Khan (*c.* 1162–1227) Mongol conqueror
genie, *pl.* **genii**
Genova (It.)/**Genoa**
Genscher, Hans-Dietrich (1927–) (West) German politician, Foreign Minister 1974–92
gentilhomme (Fr.) gentleman or nobleman; *pl. gentilshommes*
Gentleman's Magazine, The UK periodical 1731–1914
Gentlemen's Quarterly *not* -man's US magazine, now called GQ
genuflection (US)/**genuflexion** (UK)
genus, species The second is a subgroup of the first. The convention is to capitalize the genus but not the species. People are of the genus *Homo* and the species *sapiens*: *Homo sapiens*; *pls.* **genera, species**
George Town former name of Penang; also, capital of Cayman Islands
Georgetown district and university in Washington, DC; also, capital of Guyana

Georgia former republic of Soviet Union, now an independent state, capital Tbilisi

Gephardt, Richard Andrew (1941–   ) American politician

geranium

gerbil *not* jer-

Géricault, Jean Louis André Théodore (1791–1824) French painter

germane *not*-main; relevant

German shepherd breed of dog; commonly called Alsatian in UK

Germany was partitioned into East Germany (Deutsche Demokratische Republik), with its capital in East Berlin, and West Germany (Bundesrepublik Deutschland), with its capital at Bonn, in 1949. The two Germanys (*not* -ies) were reunited on 3 October 1990. The 16 states, or *Länder*, are Baden-Württemberg, Bavaria, Berlin, Brandenburg, Bremen, Hamburg, Hesse, Lower Saxony, Mecklenburg-West Pomerania, North Rhine-Westphalia, Rhineland Palatinate, Saarland, Saxony, Saxony-Anhalt, Schleswig-Holstein and Thuringia

gerrymander to distort or redraw to one's advantage, particularly political boundaries; not to be confused with jerrybuilt

Gestapo *Geheime Staatspolizei* (Ger.), German secret police during Third Reich

Gethsemane olive grove outside Jerusalem where Jesus was betrayed

gettable note -tt-

Getty, J(ean) Paul (1892–1976) *not* John; US oil man and art benefactor. His son, Jean Paul Getty II (1932–   ), is also often wrongly given as John

Gettysburg, Pennsylvania, site of decisive (but not final) battle of American Civil War (July 1863)

geyser rhymes with sneezer in the UK, with miser in the US

gewgaw worthless bauble

Ghana West African state; capital Accra. A citizen is a Ghanaian

gherkin

ghettos *not* ghettoes

ghillie use gillie

Ghirardelli Square, San Francisco

ghiribizzoso musical term for whimsical playing

Ghirlandaio, Il Domenico di Tommaso Bigordi (1449–94), Florentine painter

Giacometti, Alberto (1901–66) Swiss sculptor and painter

Giannini, A(madeo) P(eter) (1870–1949) American banker, founded Bank of America (originally Bank of Italy)

Giant's Causeway, County Antrim, Northern Ireland, *not* Giants'

gibe (pref.), **jibe** (alt.), to ridicule. Not to be confused with gybe (US jibe), a nautical term

Gibbon, Edward (1737–94) English historian

Gibbons, Grinling (1648–1721) *not* Grindling; Dutch-born English sculptor and woodcarver

Gibbons, Orlando (1583–1625) English composer

Gide, André (Paul Guillaume) (1869–1951) French writer

Gielgud, Sir (Arthur) John (1904–) English actor, director and producer

giga- prefix meaning one billion (1,000,000,000)

Gigha, Strathclyde, pronounced gee'-a; small Scottish island

gigolo, *pl.* **gigolos**

Gilcrux, Cumbria, pronounced gill'-crooz

gild the lily The line from Shakespeare's *King John* is 'To gild refined gold, to paint the lily'

Gilgamesh Epic Babylonian epic poem

Gillette razors

gillie (Scot.) hunting or fishing assistant

Gillray, James (1757–1815) British caricaturist

Gimbel Brothers former New York department store; commonly referred to as Gimbels (no apos.)

gingivitis *not* -us; inflammation of the gums

ginkgo *not* gingko; Asian tree; *pl.* ginkgoes

Gioconda, La alt. name for the *Mona Lisa*; also a play by Gabriele d'Annunzio (1898) and an opera by Amilcare Ponchielli (1876)

Giorgione, Il Giorgio Barbarelli da Castelfranco (1478–1510); Italian painter

Giotto (di Bondone) (*c.* 1266–1337) Italian painter and architect

Giraudoux, (Hippolyte) Jean (1882–1944) French playwright and diplomat

giro (UK) *not* gyro; Post Office system for transferring money; colloquially, the name for dole money, or unemployment benefit

Giscard d'Estaing, Valéry (1926–   ) President of France 1974–81

gismo (UK)/**gizmo** (US), *pl.* **gismos** (UK)/**gizmos** (US)

giveable

gladiolus, *pl.* **gladioli**

Gladstone, William Ewart (1809–98) British Liberal politician and four times Prime Minister

Glamis, Tayside, pronounced glahmz

glamour, **glamorous**, **glamorize**

glandular fever (UK), **mononucleosis** (US)

glasnost (Russ.) literally, publicity; the effort to make Soviet government and life more open

glassful, *pl.* **glassfuls**

Glaston, Leicestershire, pronounced glay'-stun

Glaswegian of or from Glasgow

Glazunov, Aleksander (Konstantinovich) (1865–1936) Russian composer

GLC Greater London Council

Glencoe mountain pass in Highland region in Scotland, site of 1692 massacre of MacDonalds by the Campbells

Glendower, Owen/Glyndwr, Owain (Wel.) (*c.* 1354–1416) Welsh chieftain

Glenlivet a whisky

Gloria in excelsis Deo (Lat.) Glory be to God on high

Glorious Revolution (1688–9) the removal of James II as king and his replacement by William of Orange and James's daughter Mary, who ruled as William III and Mary II

Glorious Twelfth (UK) 12 August, first day of grouse-hunting season

Gloucestershire pronounced gloss'-ter-sher; abbr. Glos.; English county

Gluck, Christoph Willibald von (1714–87) German composer

Glyndebourne, East Sussex

GMB (UK) formally the General, Municipal, Boilermakers and Allied Trades Union

GmbH *Gesellschaft mit beschränkter Haftung* (Ger.), limited liability company, equivalent to Ltd or PLC (UK) and Inc. (US)

GMT Greenwich Mean Time

gneiss pronounced nice; a kind of rock, similar to granite

gnocchi small dumplings

GNP, GDP GNP, gross national product, is the total worth of everything produced by a nation during a given period, including earnings from overseas. GDP, gross domestic product, is everything produced by a nation during a given period, except earnings from overseas

gobbledegook (UK)/**gobbledygook** (US)

Gobelin tapestry

Gobi Desert

go-cart (US)/**go-kart** (UK)

Godard, Jean-Luc (1930–) French film director

Goddard, Robert Hutchings (1882–1945) American physicist and rocket scientist

Goderich, Frederick John Robinson, Viscount (1782–1859) British statesman, Prime Minister 1827–8; later became first Earl of Ripon

godsend, **godforsaken**, **godhead** (no caps.), but **God-awful**, **God-fearing** and **Godspeed** (caps.)

Godthaab (Dan.) pronounced gott'-hop; former name of the capital of Greenland, now called Nuuk

Godunov, Boris Fyodorovich (1552–1605) tyrannical Russian tsar 1598–1605; subject of play by Pushkin and opera by Moussorgsky

Godwin Austen (not Austin, no hyphen) more commonly called K2, the highest mountain in the Karakoram range: 28,250 ft/8,511 m

Goebbels, (Paul) Joseph (1897–1945) German Nazi propaganda chief and administrator

Goering/Göring, Hermann (1893–1946) German Nazi field

marshal, established the Gestapo and concentration camps; second in command to Hitler

Goethe, Johann Wolfgang von (1749–1832) German poet and dramatist

Gogol, Nikolai (Vasilievich) (1809–52) Russian novelist and playwright

Golders Green, London (no apos.)

Gollancz, Sir Victor (1893–1967) British author, philanthropist and publisher after whom the publishing firm is named

Gomorrah city in ancient Palestine

Gomulka, Władysław (1905–82) First Secretary of Polish Communist Party (i.e. head of state) 1956–71

Goneril one of Lear's daughters in Shakespeare's *King Lear*

gonof/ganef (Yidd.) thief, disreputable person

gonorrhea (US)/**gonorrhoea** (UK)

Gonville and Caius College, Cambridge, normally referred to as just Caius (pronounced keys)

González (Marquez), Felipe (1942–) Spanish Prime Minister 1982–

goodbye (one word)

Good-natur'd Man, The comedy by Oliver Goldsmith (1768)

good will/goodwill Either form is acceptable in general senses, but it is always one word when referring to the reputation and trading value of a business

Good Woman of Setzuan, The play by Bertolt Brecht (1941)

GOP Grand Old Party; nickname of Republican Party in the US

Gorbachev, Mikhail (Sergeyevich) (1931–) General Secretary of the Communist Party of the Soviet Union 1985–91, President of the Supreme Soviet of the USSR 1988–91, President of the USSR 1990–91

Gordian knot a complex problem. According to legend, King Gordius of Phrygia tied the knot and it was said that anyone who could undo it would rule Asia; Alexander the Great cut it with his sword. 'To cut the Gordian knot' is to solve a difficult problem by a decisive action.

Gordonstoun School private school in the Grampian region of Scotland, but Gordonstown, Grampian, Scotland

gorgeous
gorgheggio musical term for a trill
Gorgons in Greek mythology, three creatures (Medusa, Stheno and Euryale) so ugly that anyone gazing at them turned to stone
Gorgonzola an Italian cheese called after a village of the same name
gorilla
Göring, Hermann use Goering
Gorky, Maxim pseudonym of Aleksei Maksimovich Peshkov (1868–1936), Russian writer. The Russian city named after him has reverted to its original name of Nizhny Novgorod
gospodin Russian for 'sir'
Göteborg/Gothenburg (Ger.) second largest city in Sweden
Götterdämmerung (Ger.) 'Twilight of the Gods', last part of Wagner's *Ring* cycle; figuratively, a complete downfall
gouache pronounced goo-ash; a kind of opaque watercolour paint mixed with a gluelike preparation; a picture painted in this way or with such a pigment
Gould, Bryan (Charles) (1939–) British politician
Gould, Elliott (1938–) note -ll-, -tt-; born Elliot Goldstein; American film actor
gourmand A word to be employed carefully: some dictionaries define it only as a person who likes to eat well, but many others equate it with gluttony. Unless you mean to convey a pejorative sense, it would be better to use gourmet, gastronome, epicure or some other word
goy (Yidd.) a gentile; *pl.* **goyim**
Goya (y Lucientes), Francisco (José de) (1746–1828) Spanish artist
gracias (Sp.) thank you
Gradgrind a cold, emotionless person, after a character in Dickens's *Hard Times*
Graeae in Greek mythology, three sisters who guard the Gorgons
Graf, Steffi (1969–) German tennis player
graffiti is plural; one defacement is a **graffito**

Graham, (William Franklin) Billy (1918–) American evangelist

Grahame, Kenneth (1858–1932) British writer

gram/gramme (alt. UK) abbr. g; basic metric unit of mass; equivalent to about 1/28 or 0.035 ounce

Gramm-Rudman-Hollings Act (US) Generally referred to as the Gramm-Rudman Act, this law is intended to limit and phase out the US budget deficit. A common misconception is that it requires a certain reduced level of spending to be achieved each year. In fact, it requires only that a reduced level of spending be *forecast* for the pending fiscal year. Whether that forecast is subsequently achieved is not within the scope of the law

gramophone *not* grama-

Granada city in Spain; British television network; *see also* Grenada

Grand Coulee Dam on the Columbia River, Washington state

grandad (UK)/**granddad** (US)

granddaughter, **grandfather**, **grandmother**, **grandson**

Grand Guignol high drama constructed around a sensational theme. The term comes from the Théâtre de Grand Guignol in Paris, where such plays were in vogue in the last years of the 19th century

grandiloquence *not* -eloquence; inflated speech

grand jury in US law, a jury of up to twenty-three people empowered to decide whether there is enough evidence for a case to proceed against an accused person

Grasmere, Cumbria, site of Dove Cottage, home of the poet Wordsworth

gratia Dei (Lat.) by God's grace

Gray, Thomas (1716–71) English poet

Gray's Inn and **Gray's Inn Road**, London (apos.)

grazie (It.) thank you

Great Hautbois, Norfolk, pronounced hob'-iss

Great Smoky Mountains National Park, North Carolina-Tennessee

Greco, El Domenikos Theotokopoulos (1541–1614); Cretan-born Spanish painter

Greeley, Horace (1811–72) American politician and journalist, founder of the *New York Tribune* (1841). The expression 'Go west, young man' is usually attributed to him, probably wrongly

Greene, Graham (1904–91) prolific British writer

Greene, Nathanael (1742–86) note -ael; American Revolutionary War general

Greenhalgh, Lancashire, pronounced green'-halsh

Green Paper, **White Paper** A Green Paper is a consultative document, outlining Government proposals for discussion. A White Paper outlines the Government's planned legislation

Greenstreet, Sydney (1879–1954) British character actor

Grenada small island state in the Caribbean; capital St George's

Grenadines, The island chain in the Caribbean

Grendel monster in *Beowulf*

Gresham's Law 'bad money drives out good', attributed to Sir Thomas Gresham (1519–79)

Greuze, Jean Baptiste (1725–1805) French painter

Grey, Lady Jane (1537–54) Queen of England for 10 days in 1553

Grey Friars Franciscans

Greyfriars College, Oxford

Greysouthen, Cumbria, pronounced gray'-soon

Greywell, Hampshire, pronounced gruel

Grieg, Edvard (Hagerup) (1843–1907) Norwegian composer

grievous *not* -ious

griffin (pref.)/**gryphon** (alt.) winged creature with an eagle's head and wings, and a lion's body

grille decorative screen or grating

Grimethorpe, South Yorkshire, pronounced grim'-thorp

Grimm, Brothers Jacob Ludwig Carl Grimm (1785–1863) and Wilhelm Carl Grimm (1786–1859), German writers and philologists

Grimond, Jo(seph), Baron (1913–) British politician, leader of Liberal Party 1956–67 and May–July 1976

grisly, **grizzly** The first means horrifying while the second means grey-haired and is also a type of bear; *see also* gristly

Grisons/Graubünden (Ger.) a Swiss canton

gristly full of gristle; *see also* grisly

Grobbelaar, Bruce (David) (1957–) South African-born British soccer player

groggy

Gromyko, Andrei (Andreyevich) (1909–89) Soviet statesman, Foreign Minister 1957–85, President of Supreme Soviet 1985–8

grosbeak a species of finch

groschen Austrian coin and monetary unit worth 1/100 of a schilling

gros rouge (Fr.) ordinary red table wine

gross domestic product, **gross national product** *see* GDP, GNP

Grosse Pointe, Michigan

Grossmith, George (1847–1912) British comedian and entertainer, and with his brother, **Weedon Grossmith** (1852–1919), co-author of *The Diary of a Nobody*

Grosz, George (1893–1959) German-born American artist

Grósz, Karoly (1930–) Communist Party leader and Prime Minister of Hungary 1987–8

grotto, *pl.* **grottoes**

Group of Seven sometimes called G7; seven leading industrial nations that meet periodically to discuss economic and trading matters: Canada, France, Germany, Italy, Japan, the UK and US

groveled, **groveling** (US)/**grovelled**, **grovelling** (UK)

grueling (US)/**gruelling** (UK)

gruesome

Gruinard Bay, Highland Region, Scotland, pronounced grin'-yard

Grünewald, Mathias (*c.* 1480–1528) born Mathis Gothardt or Nithardt; German Gothic artist and architect

Gruyère cheese The Swiss town from which it takes its name is Gruyères

gryphon use griffin

GT Gran Turismo

Guadalajara cities in Spain and Mexico

Guadalupe name of mountains in Texas and New Mexico, a river in Texas, and towns or cities in California, Spain, Brazil, Peru and the Azores. The city in Mexico once called Guadalupe Hidalgo is now Gustavo A. Madero City

Guadeloupe overseas department of France in the Caribbean

Guangdong (Pinyin)/**Kwantung** Chinese province

Guangzhou (Pinyin)/**Canton** capital of Guangdong Province

Guantánamo Bay, Cuba, site of US naval base

guarantee, **guaranty** In the UK guarantee is generally used for all senses. In the US guarantee is often reserved for the verb ('I guarantee to help you') and guaranty for the noun ('This TV is still under guaranty'), though most dictionaries allow a wide overlap of definitions. If in doubt, use guarantee

Guatemala Central American republic; capital Guatemala City

Guayaquil, Santiago de largest city in Ecuador

Guernica (y Luno) pronounced gher-nee'-ka; Spanish town near Bilboa, ancient capital of the Basques. Its bombing by German aircraft on 27 April 1937, during the Spanish Civil War, was the subject of a painting by Picasso

guerrilla note -rr-

gueuze rich Belgian beer

Guevara (de la Serna), Ernesto (1928–67) nickname 'Che'; Argentine-born revolutionary, murdered by Bolivian troops

Guggenheim Museum, New York; formally, Solomon R. Guggenheim Museum; Guggenheim Fellowships are awarded by the John S. Guggenheim Memorial Foundation

Guiana British Guiana is now Guyana; Dutch Guiana is now Surinam

Guildford, Surrey, but the Earl of Guilford (no middle *d*)

Guildhall, London *not the* Guildhall

Guillaume de Machaut (*c.* 1300–77) French poet and musician

guillemet pronounced gee-yuh-meh'; quotation marks « » used in French, Spanish and other languages

guillemot pronounced gill'-a-mot; a sea-bird

Guillén, Nicolás (1902–89) Cuban poet

guillotine

guinea (UK) historically, the sum of one pound and one shilling (now £1.05), and a gold coin of that value

Guinea, Republic of formerly French Guinea; West African country; capital Conakry

Guinea-Bissau, Republic of formerly Portuguese Guinea; West African country; capital Bissau

Guinevere wife of King Arthur

Guinness, Sir Alec (1914–) note -nn-, -ss; British actor

***Guinness Book of Records*, Guinness Mahon** (UK merchant bank), **Guinness Peat** (UK financial services group), **Guinness stout** all -nn-, -ss

Guisborough, Cleveland, pronounced gizz'-burr-a

Guizhou (Pinyin)/**Kweichow** Chinese province

Gujarat Indian state; capital Gandhinagar

GUM pronounced gay-oo-em; *Gosudarstvennyi Universal'nyi Magazin* (Russ., Government Universal Store), Moscow department store

gunny sack

Gunpowder Plot conspiracy among group of English Catholics to blow up Houses of Parliament in 1605

gunwale *not* -whale; pronounced gunnel and sometimes so spelled; the topmost edge of the side of a ship

Guomindang *see* Kuomintang

Gurdjieff, Georgei Ivanovitch (*c.* 1874–1949) Russian mystic

Gurkha a Nepalese soldier in the British army

guten Abend*, *guten Morgen*, *guten Tag*, *gute Nacht (Ger.) respectively, good evening, good morning, good day and good night

Gutenberg, Johann (*c.* 1400–68) born Johannes Gensfleisch; German credited with the invention of movable type

gutta-percha hard, rubbery substance produced from the latex of various tropical trees

guttural *not* -er-

Guyana formerly British Guiana; South American country; capital, Georgetown

Guy's Hospital, London, named after Thomas Guy (*c.* 1645–1724), its founder

Gwent county of Wales, formerly Monmouthshire, county town Cwmbran

Gwyn, Nell (1650–87) born Eleanor Gwynne; actress and mistress of Charles II of England

Gwynedd pronounced gwin'-neth; county of Wales, comprising the former counties of Anglesey, Caernarvonshire, Merioneth and part of Denbighshire; county town Caernarfon

Gyllenhammar, Pehr (Gustaf) (1935–) Swedish businessman

gymkhana

gynaecology (UK)/**gynecology** (US)

gypsy, *pl.* **gypsies**; also, **gypsy moth**

H

ha hectare

Häagen-Dazs brand of ice cream

Haakon VII (1872–1957) King of Norway 1905–57

Haarlem, The Netherlands, but **Harlem**, New York

Haas, Ernst (1921–86) Austrian-born photographer

Haas-Lilienthal House, San Francisco, California

habeas corpus (Lat.) deliver the body; writ requiring that a person be brought before a court. Its purpose is to ensure that prisoners are not unlawfully detained

Habgood, Most Rev. Dr John (Stapylton) (1927–) Archbishop of York 1983–

habitué (masc.)/***habituée*** (fem)

Habsburg(s) (UK, Ger.)/**Hapsburg(s)** (US) Austrian imperial family

Hades god of the dead

Haeckel, Ernst (Heinrich Philipp August) (1834–1919) German naturalist

haematology, **haematoma**, **haematemesis** (UK)/**hematology**, **hematoma**, **hematemesis** (US)

haemoglobin, **haemophilia** (UK)/ **hemoglobin**, **hemophilia** (US)

haemorrhage (UK)/**hemorrhage** (US)

haemorrhoids (UK)/**hemorrhoids** (US)

Haggai (*fl.* sixth c. BC) a Hebrew prophet; also the book of his prophecies in the Old Testament

Haggard, Sir H(enry) Rider (1856–1925) English author of adventure stories

haggis Scottish dish

Hague, The (cap. T)/**Den Haag** (Dut.)/ **'s-Gravenhage** (roughly pronounced skrah'-ven-hogga) (Dut.). Although Amsterdam is the constitutional capital of The Netherlands, The Hague is the *de facto* capital and seat of government

Haifa, Israel, pronounced hi'-fuh

hail, hale Hail describes a greeting, salute, frozen raindrops or a downpour. Hale means robust and healthy or to drag forcibly. The main expressions are 'hail-fellow-well-met', 'hale and hearty' and 'haled into court'.

Haile Selassie (1892–1975) born Tafari Makonnen; later Ras (Prince) Tafari, then Emperor of Ethiopia 1930–36, 1941–74; *see also* Rastafarianism

Hainault, London, pronounced hay'-nawt

hairbrained is wrong; it's **hare-brained**

hairbreadth/hair's breadth

Haiti republic in West Indies on the island of Hispaniola, which it shares with the Dominican Republic; capital Port-au-Prince

Haitink, Bernard (1929–) Dutch conductor; music director at the Royal Opera House, Covent Garden

Hakluyt, Richard (*c.* 1553–1616) pronounced hak'-loot; English geographer

halberd a combined spear and battleaxe, carried by a halberdier

halcyon calm, peaceful

hale, hail Hale means robust and healthy or to drag forcibly. Hail describes a greeting, salute, frozen raindrops or a downpour. The main expressions are 'hale and hearty', 'haled into court' and 'hail-fellow-well-met'.

Haleakala National Park, Maui, Hawaii

half a crown (UK) former coin worth two shillings and sixpence, equivalent to 12½ pence in UK decimal currency

halfpenny/ha'penny pronounced hape'-nee

halfpennyworth/ha'p'orth pronounced hay-peth

halibut *not* halli-

halitosis bad breath

hallelujah

Hallé Orchestra, Manchester, founded by Sir Charles Hallé (1819–95)

Halley, Edmond (1655–1742) *not* Edmund; pronounced hal'-ee, not hayley or hawley; English astronomer and mathematician; predicted the return of the comet named after him

hallo (UK)/**hello** (US)

Hallowe'en 31 October

halo, *pl.* **haloes** (UK)/**halos** (US)

Hamelin/Hameln (Ger.) city in Germany, source of the legend of the Pied Piper of Hamelin

Hamlisch, Marvin (1944–) American composer

Hammarskjöld, Dag (Hjalmar Agne Carl) (1905–61) Swedish statesman, Secretary-General of the United Nations 1953–61; Nobel Peace Prize 1961 (posthumous)

Hammerstein, Oscar (1895–1960) pronounced hammer-stine; American dramatist and lyric-writer, well known for his collaborations with Jerome Kern and, later, Richard Rodgers

Hammett, (Samuel) Dashiell (1894–1961) American writer of crime novels

Hammurabi (*fl.* 18th c. BC) Babylonian king, codifier of laws

Hampton Court Palace, *not* just Hampton Court, is the title of the building in outer London

Hamtramck pronounced ham-tramm'-ick; suburb of Detroit

Handel, George Frideric (1685–1759) born Georg Friedrich Händel; German composer long resident in Britain

handicraft, **handiwork** *not* handy-

Handl, Jacob (1550–91) Austrian composer

Handschrift (Ger.) manuscript

Haneda Airport, Tokyo

hangar *not* -er; building where aircraft are stored

hanged, **hung** People are hanged; objects are hung

Hangchow/Hangzhou (Pinyin) Chinese city

Hanover/Hannover (Ger.) capital of Lower Saxony, Germany

Hansard formally, *The Official Report of Parliamentary Debates*; daily verbatim transcript of debates in UK Parliament, named after the printer Luke Hansard (1752–1828)

Hansen's disease alt. name for leprosy

hansom cab
Hants (no full point) abbreviation of Hampshire
Hanuka (US)/**Hanukkah** (UK) Jewish festival of lights, celebrating the rededication of the Temple in 165 BC by Judas Maccabaeus
haole (Haw.) in Hawaii, a non-Polynesian person
Happisburgh, Norfolk, pronounced hayz'-burr-a
Hapsburg(s) (US)/**Habsburgs** (UK, Ger.) Austrian imperial dynasty
hara-kiri *not* hari-kari. The term usually used by the Japanese is *seppuku*
Harald V (1937–) King of Norway 1991–
Harare capital of Zimbabwe, formerly called Salisbury
harass, harassment *not* -rr-. The correct pronunciation is hăr'-uss, though some dictionaries in the UK and most in the US accept huh-rass' as an alternative
harbor (US)/**harbour** (UK)
Harcourt Brace Jovanovich (no commas) US publisher
Hardenhuish, Wiltshire, pronounced har'-nish
Hardie, (James) Keir (1856–1915) British socialist politician, one of the founding fathers of the Labour Party
hardiness *not* hardy-
Harding, Warren G(amaliel) (1865–1923) US President 1921–3
Hardwicke, Sir Cedric (Webster) (1893–1964) British actor
hare-brained It has nothing to do with hair
Hare Krishna religious movement
harelip *not* hair-
Haresceugh, Cumbria, pronounced hare'-skewf
Harewood House, West Yorkshire, and the Earl of Harewood are both pronounced har'-wood, but the nearby village is pronounced hair'-wood
Hargreaves, James (*c.* 1720–78) English inventor of the spinning jenny
Haringey London borough; *see also* Harringay
hark, but **hearken**
Harland and Wolff Belfast shipyard

Harley Street, London
HarperCollins Publishers, formerly Harper & Row
Harpers & Queen UK fashion magazine
Harper's Bazaar US fashion magazine
Harpers Ferry, West Virginia (no apos.) site of 1859 rebellion led by John Brown
Harper's Magazine US magazine
Harraden, Beatrice (1864–1936) English novelist
harridan bad-tempered old woman
Harriman, (William) Averell (1891–1986) American politician and diplomat
Harringay a district of the London borough of Haringey, and a British Rail station
Harrisons & Crosfield *not* Cross-; British trading company
Harrods (no apos.) London department store
Harte, Bret (1836–1902) born Francis Brett Harte; American writer and editor
hartebeest African antelope
Hartsfield Airport, Atlanta, Georgia; formally, Hartsfield Atlanta International Airport
harum-scarum
Harz Mountains, Germany, *not* Hartz
Hasid, *pl.* **Hasidim**; **Hasidic** (adj.) Jewish sect
Haslemere, Surrey, pronounced hay'-zul-mere
Hassan II (1929–) King of Morocco 1961–
Hasselblad cameras made by Victor Hasselblad AB of Göteborg, Sweden
Haulgh, Greater Manchester, pronounced hoff
Hauptmann, Gerhart (1862–1946) German novelist, poet and playwright; Nobel Prize for Literature 1912
Hausfrau (Ger.) housewife; *pl.* ***Hausfrauen***
Haussmann, Boulevard, Paris, named after Baron Georges Eugène Haussmann (1809–91), who led the rebuilding of the city
haute couture (Fr.) high fashion
Havana/Habana (Sp.) capital of Cuba
Havel, Václav (1936–) Czech playwright and reformist politician, President 1990–92

Havering-atte-Bower, Essex, pronounced hay-vring att-ee bau-er

Hawaii formerly, the Sandwich Islands; became the 50th state of the US in 1959; comprising eight main islands (Hawaii, Kahoolawe, Kauai, Lanai, Maui, Molokai, Niihau and Oahu) and many islets; adj., Hawaiian; official postal abbreviation, HI

Haw-Haw, Lord nickname of William Joyce (1906–46), an American who made propaganda broadcasts for the Germans in World War II

Hawke, Bob (Robert James Lee) (1929–) Australian trade union leader and politician; Prime Minister of Australia 1983–91

Hawker Siddeley (no hyphen) British aviation company

Hawksmoor, Nicholas (1661–1736) English architect

Haworth, West Yorkshire, pronounced how'-worth; home of the Brontës

hawthorn thorny tree or shrub

Hawthorne, Nathaniel (1804–64) American writer

Haydn, Franz Joseph (1732–1809) Austrian composer

Hayes, Rutherford B(irchard) (1778–1830) US President 1877–81

Hazlitt, William (1778–1830) English essayist and critic

hazy

headmaster, **headmistress**, but **head teacher**

Healey, Denis (Winston) (1917–) British politician

'hear, hear!' is the exclamation of parliamentarians, *not* 'here, here!'

Hébert, Jacques René (1757–94) French revolutionary and journalist

Hebrew, **Yiddish** The words are not interchangeable

Hebrides group of islands off west coast of Scotland; adj. Hebridean; also called Western Isles

hectare abbr. ha; 10,000 sq m; equivalent to 2.47 acres

hecto- prefix meaning 100

Hecuba in Greek mythology, wife of Priam, King of Troy, and mother of Hector, Paris and Cassandra

Hedda Gabler *not* -bb-; play by Henrik Ibsen (1890)

Heep, Uriah character in Dickens's *David Copperfield*

Hegel, Georg Wilhelm Friedrich (1770–1831) German philosopher

hegira/*hijrah* (Arab.) the flight by Muhammad from Mecca to Medina on 16 July 622, used as the starting point for the Muslim era

Heian former name of Kyoto, Japan

Heidegger, Martin (1889–1976) German philosopher

Heidelberg ancient university city in Baden-Württemberg, Germany

Heidsieck champagne

heifer *not* -ff-; a young cow

Heifetz, Jascha (1901–87) Russian-born American violinist

Heineken Dutch beer

Heinemann (Ltd), (William) British publisher

heinous pronounced hay'-nuss; wicked

heir apparent, heir presumptive The first inherits no matter what; the second inherits only if a nearer relation is not born first

Heisman Trophy US football award to outstanding college player of the year

Helena pronounced hel'-enn-a; capital of Montana

Helensburgh, Strathclyde, Scotland

Hellespont former name of Dardanelles

Hellinikon Airport, Athens

Hellman, Lillian (1905–84) American playwright

hello (US)/**hallo** (UK)

helmeted

Héloïse (1101–64) lover of Pierre Abelard; but the poem by Alexander Pope is 'Eloisa to Abelard' (1717)

Helsingør (Dan.)/**Elsinore** port in Denmark, setting for Shakespeare's *Hamlet*

Helsinki Agreement an accord on human rights signed by 35 countries in 1975

Helvétius, Claude Adrien (1715–71) French philosopher

hematology, **hematoma** (US)/**haematology**, **haematoma** (UK)

Hemel Hempstead, Hertfordshire

Hemingway, Ernest (Miller) (1898–1961) American writer

hemoglobin (US)/**haemoglobin** (UK)

hemophilia (US)/**haemophilia** (UK)

hemorrhage (US)/**haemorrhage** (UK)

hemorrhoids (US)/**haemorrhoids** (UK)

Henderson, Sir Denys (1933–) British business executive

Hendrix, Jimi (1942–70) born Johnny Allen Hendrix; American rock musician and composer

Hennessy cognac

Henry, O. pen name of William Sydney Porter (1862–1910), American short story writer

hepatitis

Hephaestus Greek god of fire and metal-working, analogous to Roman god Vulcan

Hepplewhite 18th-century style of furniture, named after English cabinetmaker George Hepplewhite (d. 1786)

Hera Greek goddess and wife of Zeus, identified with the Roman goddess Juno

Heracles Greek demi-god

herbaceous

Hercegovina (Serbo-Croat)/**Herzegovina** region of Bosnia-Hercegovina, a former republic of Yugoslavia

Herculaneum Roman city destroyed with Pompeii during eruption of Vesuvius in AD 79

Hercules Roman name of Greek demi-god Heracles

Hereford & Worcester use &, *not* and; county of England

Heriot-Watt University, Edinburgh

Hermannsson, Steingrímur (1928–) Prime Minister of Iceland 1983–7, 1988–91

hermaphrodite plant or animal having both male and female sexual organs. The name comes from the Greek god Hermaphroditus

hermeneutics (*sing.*) the science of interpretation, especially of biblical texts

Hermes in Greek mythology, the messenger to the gods, and god of science, commerce and oratory, thieves and travellers, and guide to souls of the dead; identified with the Roman god Mercury

Hermon, Sir John (1928–) Chief Constable of the Royal Ulster Constabulary 1980–89

Hero and Leander two lovers in Greek legend: Hero drowned herself in despair after her lover, Leander, drowned while swimming across the Hellespont to see her

heroin, **heroine** The first is a drug; the second a female hero

herpetology the study of reptiles

Herrick, Robert (1591–1674) English poet

Herschel, Sir William (1738–1822) born Friedrich Wilhelm Herschel; German-born English astronomer, discoverer of Uranus and two satellites of Saturn

Herstmonceux, East Sussex, preferred pronunciation is hurst'-mon-so, though hurst'-mon-soo is also acceptable; site of Royal Observatory 1948–90

Hertzog, James Barry Munnik (1866–1942) South African Prime Minister 1924–39

Herzegovina/Hercegovina (Serbo-Croat) region of Bosnia-Hercegovina, a former republic of Yugoslavia

Heseltine, Michael (Ray Dibdin) (1933–) British politician

Hess, Rudolf (1894–1987) German politician

Hesse, Hermann (1877–1972) German novelist and poet

heterogeneous made of unrelated parts; dissimilar

heureusement (Fr.) happily

Heveningham Hall, Suffolk, pronounced hen'-ing-um

HEW (US) Department of Health, Education and Welfare

Hewlett-Packard US computer company

heyday

Heyerdahl, Thor (1914–) Norwegian anthropologist

Heyrod, Greater Manchester, pronounced hair'-ud

Heysham, Lancashire, pronounced hee'-shum; site of nuclear power station

HI postal abbr. of Hawaii

Hialeah pronounced hei'-a-lee-a; city and race course near Miami, Florida

Hiawatha, The Song of epic poem by Henry Wadsworth

Longfellow (1855)

hiccup (pref.)/**hiccough** (alt.)

hic et nunc (Lat.) here and now

Hicpochee, Lake, Florida

hierarchy, **hierarchies**, **hierarchical**

hieroglyphics

higgledy-piggledy

high dudgeon

highfalutin *not* -faluting or -falutin'

high-flier (US)/**high-flyer** (UK)

high jinks (two words) *not* jinx

Highlands, Scottish The general area is called the Highlands, but the specific governmental region is Highland (sing.)

high street Unless you are talking about a specific high street, there is no reason to capitalize it

hijack *not* highjack

Hilary a term at Oxford and some other universities, and a session of the High Court of Justice, beginning in January

Hillary, Sir Edmund (Percival) (1919–) New Zealand explorer and mountaineer, first person to scale Everest (1953)

Hilliard, Nicholas (*c.* 1547–1619) English court goldsmith and painter of miniatures

Himmler, Heinrich (1900–45) German Nazi leader

Hinckley, Leicestershire, but **Hinkley Point Power Station**, Somerset

Hindenburg, Paul (Ludwig Hans Anton von Beneckendorf und) von (1847–1934) German general; President of the Weimar Republic 1925–34. The dirigible that exploded at Lakehurst, New Jersey, in 1937 was also the *Hindenburg*

Hindi, **Hindu**, **Hindustani** Hindi is the main language of India; Hindu describes a follower of Hinduism, the main religious and social system of India; Hindustani is the main dialect of Western Hindi used throughout most of India

hindrance *not* -erance

Hindu Kush mountain range in Afghanistan

Hinkley Point Power Station, Somerset, but **Hinckley**, Leicestershire

hippie *not* -ppy

Hippocrates (*c.* 460–*c.* 377 BC) Greek physician, considered the 'father of medicine'

hippopotamus, *pl.* **hippopotamuses**

hireable

Hirshhorn Museum, Washington, DC; note -hh-; part of the Smithsonian Institution

HIS, **HJS** *hic iacet sepultus/sepulta, hic jacet sepultus* (Lat.) here lies buried; often seen on English gravestones

Hispaniola Caribbean island shared by Haiti and Dominican Republic

historic, **historical** Historic is something that makes history; historical describes something that is based on history; e.g., a historic occasion, but a historical novel

hitchhike, **hitchhiker**

Hitchin, Hertfordshire

Hittites ancient people of Asia Minor

HIV Human Immunodeficiency Virus, virus associated with AIDS

Hizbollah Islamic fundamentalist group

Hnatyshyn, Ramon John (1934–) Canadian politician

hoard, **horde** The first is a cache; the second, a swarm of people

hoary *not* -ey; grey, aged

Hobbema, Meindert (1638–1709) Dutch artist

Hobbes, Thomas (1588–1679) English philosopher

Hobby Airport, Houston, Texas

hobo, *pl.* **hoboes**

Hoboken, New Jersey

Hobson's Choice taking what is offered or nothing at all, i.e. having no choice

Hochhuth, Rolf (1931–) German playwright

Ho Chi Minh City, Vietnam, formerly Saigon; named after the Vietnamese revolutionary Ho Chi Minh (1890–1969)

Hodder & Stoughton Ltd British publisher

hodgepodge (US)/**hotchpotch** (UK)

Hodgkin, Howard (1932–) English artist

Hodgkin's disease a cancer of the lymphatic system, named after the English doctor Thomas Hodgkin (1798–1866)

Hoek van Holland Dutch spelling of Hook of Holland

Hoffman, Dustin (1937–) American actor

Hoffmann, Ernest Theodor 'Amadeus' (1776–1822) German author and artist, several of whose stories inspired Offenbach's opera *Tales of Hoffmann*

Hoffmann-La Roche Swiss pharmaceuticals company

Hofheinz Pavilion, Houston, Texas

Hofstadter, Richard (1916–70) American historian

Hofstadter, Robert (1915–) American scientist and academic; Nobel Prize for Physics 1961

Hogmanay (Scot.) New Year's Eve

Hohenzollern German royal family and a former province of Prussia

hoi polloi (Grk.) *not* preceded by 'the'; the common people, the masses

Hokkaido Japanese island; capital Sapporo

Hokusai, Katsushika (1760–1849) Japanese artist and wood engraver

Holbein, Hans, the Elder (*c.* 1460–1524) German painter and father of **Hans Holbein the Younger** (1497–1543), court painter to Henry VIII

Holborn, London, pronounced ho'-bern

Holden-Brown, Sir Derrick (1923–) British businessman

Holiday, Billie (1915–59) born Eleanor Fagan Holiday; American singer

Holinshed, Raphael (d. *c.* 1580) English historian, known for *The Chronicles of England, Scotland and Ireland* (1577)

Holkeri, Harri (Hermanni) (1937–) Prime Minister of Finland 1987–90

hollandaise sauce

Holman-Hunt, William (1827–1910) English painter

Holmegaard Danish crystal

Holmes, Oliver Wendell (1809–94) physician, professor at Harvard, poet, essayist and novelist, and father of **Oliver Wendell Holmes** (1841–1935), the most respected jurist of his day, an Associate Justice of the US Supreme Court 1902–32

Holmes à Court, (Michael) Robert (Hamilton) (1937–90) Australian businessman

Holyhead, Gwynedd, Wales pronounced holly-; port for ferries to Ireland

Holyoake, Sir Keith Jacka (1904–83) Prime Minister of New Zealand 1957, 1960–72

Holyroodhouse, Palace of, Edinburgh; pronounced holly-

Home Counties the counties immediately around London, usually taken to mean Berkshire, Buckinghamshire, Essex, Hertfordshire, Kent, Surrey, and East and West Sussex

Home of the Hirsel, Baron, Home is pronounced hume; title of Alec Douglas-Home (1903–), British Prime Minister 1963–4

homely In the UK it means comfortable and appealing; in the US it means unattractive and unappealing

homey

homogeneous, **homogenous** Homogeneous means consistent and uniform; homogenous is almost always restricted to biological contexts and describes organisms that are similar in structure because of a common ancestry

homonym, homophone A homonym is a word that sounds and is spelled the same as another but has a different meaning. A homophone is a word that sounds the same as another but is spelled differently and has a different meaning and origin

Honecker, Erich (1912–) chairman of East German Communist Party (i.e., head of state) 1977–89

Honegger, Arthur (1892–1955) Swiss-French composer

Hong Kong/Hongkong Hong Kong is the more common spelling, but either is correct

Hongkong and Shanghai Banking Corporation The company now styles itself HongkongBank (one word), and follows this curious practice for some, but not all, of its subsidiaries (e.g., HongkongBank of Australia, but Hongkong Bank of Canada). I would suggest for the sake of consistency writing Hongkong Bank as two words in every instance

Honiara capital of the Solomon Islands

Honi soit qui mal y pense (Fr.) usually translated as 'Evil to him who evil thinks', but more accurately 'Shame to him . . . '; motto of the Order of the Garter (UK)

honnête homme (Fr.) an honest man

honor, **honorable** (US)/**honour**, **honourable** (UK)

honorarium, *pl.* **honorariums**, *not* -ia

honorificabilitudinatibus nonce word in Shakespeare's *Love's Labour's Lost*

Honshu main island of Japan, site of Tokyo and Yokohama

Hooch/Hoogh, Pieter de (*c.* 1629–*c.* 1684) pronounced hoke for either spelling; Dutch painter

Hoogovens Groep Dutch steel manufacturer

Hook of Holland/Hoek van Holland (Dut.)

Hoover, Herbert (Clark) (1874–1964) US President 1929–33

hopefully Much ink has been expended arguing whether the word is acceptable when used in an absolute sense, as in 'Hopefully the sun will shine tomorrow.' Many usage authorities argue that that sentence should be recast as 'It is to be hoped that the sun will shine tomorrow' or something similar. However, other authorities say that such a stand is pedantic and inconsistent, since no one objects to other -ly words, such as apparently, sadly, thankfully and mercifully, being used absolutely. I side with the second group, but you should be aware that the use of hopefully in an absolute sense is still widely, and often hotly, objected to and may result in censure

Hopi North American Indian people; *pl.* **Hopis**

Hopkins, Gerard Manley (1844–89) British poet and Jesuit priest. His poetry was published posthumously

Hopkins, Johns (1795–1873) *not* John; American financier who endowed now-famous hospital and university, both in Baltimore, named after him

Hoppner, John (1758–1810) British portrait painter

Horace, properly Quintus Horatius Flaccus (65–8 BC) Roman poet and satirist

Horae Greek goddesses who presided over the weather and seasons

horde, **hoard** The first is a swarm of people; the second a cache

Hornsby, Rogers (1896–1963) *not* Roger; American baseball player and manager

Horowitz, Vladimir (1904–89) Russian-born American concert pianist

hors de combat (Fr.) out of action

hors-d'oeuvre an appetizer; *pl.* **hors-d'oeuvres**

'Horst Wessel Lied' Nazi song

hosanna a shout of praise

Hosokawa, Morihiro (1938–), Japanese Prime Minister (1993–)

hotchpotch (UK)/ **hodgepodge** (US)

Hôtel des Invalides, Paris, site of Napoleon's tomb

hôtel de ville (Fr.) town hall

Housman, A(lfred) E(dward) (1859–1936) *not* House-; English poet, and brother of Laurence (1865–1959), a noted artist, novelist and playwright

Houston pronounced hew'-stun, *not* hoo'-stun; largest city in Texas, named after Samuel Houston (1793–1863). Note that Houston Street in New York City is pronounced how'-stun

Houyhnhnms pronounced win'-ums; in Swift's *Gulliver's Travels* a race of horses with the finer qualities of humans

Hovenweep National Monument, Utah

hovercraft (no cap.) The name is no longer a trade mark, though there is still a company, the British Hovercraft Corporation

Howards End (no apos.) a novel by E. M. Forster (1910)

Howard's Way BBC TV series

Howells, William Dean (1837–1920) American critic, editor and writer

Howerd, Frankie (1921–92) born Francis Alex Howard; British actor

howitzer a cannon

Hoxha, Enver (1908–85) pronounced hod'-juh; head of state of Albania as Prime Minister 1944–54 and First Secretary of Communist Party in Albania 1954–85

Hrvatska Croatian name for Croatia

Hua Guofeng (Pinyin)/**Hua Kuo-feng** (1920–) Chinese Prime Minister 1976–80 and Communist Party chairman 1976–81

Huanghe (Pinyin)/**Hwang-Ho/Yellow River**

HUD (US) Department of Housing and Urban Development

hudibrastic in a mock-heroic manner

Hudson Bay, **Hudson Strait**, **Hudson River**, but **Hudson's Bay Company** all named after the English explorer Henry Hudson (d. 1611)

Huguenot 16th–17th-century French Protestants

hullabaloo

Human Immunodeficiency Virus abbr. HIV; virus associated with AIDS

humerus bone in the arm between the elbow and the shoulder; *pl.* **humeri**

humor (US)/**humour** (UK), but **humorous, humorist, humoresque** (UK, US)

Humperdinck, Engelbert (1854–1921) German composer; stage name of British popular singer, born Arnold (Gerry) Dorsey (1935–   )

Humphry Clinker, The Expedition of, *not* Humphrey; a novel by Tobias Smollett (1771)

Humshaugh, Northumberland, pronounced humz'-hoff

humus *not* humous; broken-down plant material in soil

Hundred Years/Years' War (1337–1453) series of wars in which France wrested back all its territory from England except Calais

Hungary/Magyarország (Hung.)

Hunstanton, Norfolk, pronounced 'Hunston'

Hunt, William Holman (1827–1910) English painter

Huntingdonshire former county of England

hurdy-gurdy musical instrument activated by a crank

hurly-burly

Husák, Gustáv (1913–   ) Czechoslovakian politician

Husbands Bosworth, Leicestershire

Hussein (ibn Talal) (1935–   ) King of Jordan 1952–

Huston, Anjelica (1952–   ) American actress, daughter of John Huston; not Angelica

Huston, John Marcellus (1906–87) American-born Irish film director, son of Canadian-born American actor **Walter Huston** (1884–1950)

Hutchison Whampoa *not* -inson; Hong Kong company

Huxley, Aldous (Leonard) (1894–1963) English novelist and essayist; brother of **Sir Julian (Sorell) Huxley** (1887–1975), a leading biologist and writer, and first Director-General of UNESCO (1946–8). Their grandfather, **T(homas) H(enry) Huxley** (1825–95), was a leading scientist, essayist and champion of Charles Darwin

Hu Yaobang (1915–89) Chairman of the Chinese Communist Party 1981–2 and General Secretary 1981–7

Huygens, Christiaan (1629–95) note -aa- in first name; Dutch astronomer, mathematician and physicist

Huysmans, Joris Karl (1848–1907) French novelist

Huyton, Merseyside, pronounced hie'-tun

Hwang-Ho/Huanghe (Pinyin)/**Yellow River**

hyacinth flower

Hyannis, **Hyannis Port**, but **West Hyannisport**, Cape Cod, Massachusetts

Hyderabad capital of Andhra Pradesh, India. There is also a city in Pakistan of the same name, which is sometimes spelled Haidarabad

Hydra in Greek mythology, a many-headed monster

hydrangea

hydrography the study and mapping of oceans, rivers and lakes

hyena

Hygeia Greek goddess of health

hygiene, **hygienic**

hymen *not* -man; vaginal membrane, named after Hymen, the Greek god of marriage

Hynes, John B., Auditorium, Boston, Massachusetts

hyperbole

hypertension high blood pressure

hypochondria

hypocrite, **hypocrisy**

hypotenuse on a right-angled triangle the side opposite the right angle

hypothermia lack of body warmth

hypothesis, *pl.* **hypotheses**

hysterectomy

Hywel pronounced howl; Welsh forename

I

IA postal abbr. of Iowa; traditional abbr. is **Ia**

Iacocca, Lee A(nthony) (1924–) born Lido Anthony Iacocca; American businessman

IATA International Air Transport Association

IBA (UK) Independent Broadcasting Authority

Ibadan, Nigeria

ibex a mountain goat; *pl.* **ibexes**

ibid. *ibidem* (Lat.) in the same place; used in reference notes to indicate that a source is the same as the one in the previous note; *see also* op. cit.

-ible/-able There are no reliable rules for when a word ends in -ible and when in -able; *see* Appendix for a list of some of the more frequently confused spellings

ibn Abdul Aziz, Saud (1902–69) son of Abdul Aziz ibn Saud and King of Saudi Arabia 1953–64, succeeded by his brothers **Feisal ibn Abdul Aziz** (1904–75, reigned 1964–75), **Khalid ibn Abdul Aziz** (1913–82, reigned 1975–82) and **Fahd ibn Abdul Aziz** (1923– , reign 1982–)

ibn Saud, Abdul Aziz (1880–1953) King of Saudi Arabia 1932–53; *see also* ibn Abdul Aziz

Ibsen, Henrik (Johan) (1828–1906) Norwegian playwright

Ibstock Johnsen *not* Johnson; British company

ICBM intercontinental ballistic missile

iceberg

Iceni British tribe that revolted against Rome under the leadership of Boudicca in first century AD

Ich dien (Ger.) I serve; motto of the Princes of Wales

ichthyology the study of fishes
ichthyosaur/ichthyosaurus prehistoric marine reptile
ici on parle français French spoken here
Icknield Way prehistoric track running from Salisbury Plain to the Wash
I, Claudius note comma; novel by Robert Graves (1934)
icon *not* ikon
Ictinus (*fl.* fifth c. BC) Greek architect, co-designer (with Callicrates) of the Parthenon
ID postal abbr. of Idaho; traditional abbr. is **Id.** or **Ida.**
ideally
idée fixe (Fr.) obsession, fixation; *pl.* ***idées fixes***
Identikit (cap.)
ideology, ideological, ideologue
ides of March 15 March, the day on which Julius Caesar was assassinated. In the Roman calendar the ides was the 15th of March, May, July and October, and the 13th of all other months
idiosyncrasy *not* -cy
idyll poem or prose depicting rural bliss
i.e. *id est* (Lat.) that is (to say); used to introduce an elaboration, as in 'He is pusillanimous, i.e. lacking in courage.'
igneous rock
ignominy, ignominious
ignotum per ignotius (Lat.) the unknown by the even less known; an explanation more confusing than what it is meant to explain
Iguaçu/Iguassu Falls/Cantaratas del Iguazú (Sp.)/**Saltos do Iğuaçu** (Port.) waterfall on the Argentina-Brazil border
iguanodon *not* -ana-; dinosaur
IJsselmeer, The Netherlands note caps.; freshwater lake created by damming part of the Zuider Zee
ikon use icon
IL postal abbr. of Illinois
ILEA Inner London Education Authority, abolished 1990
Île de France region of France that includes Paris
ileum, Ilium, ilium The ileum is part of the small intestine,

Ilium is the Latin name for Troy, and the ilium is part of the pelvis

Iliad epic poem attributed to Homer

ilk (Scot.) same. 'Of that ilk' means the owner and the property have the same name; e.g., McFarlan of that ilk means McFarlan of McFarlan. Most authorities condemn it as a synonym for 'type' or 'kind'

Ill. Illinois

illegitimate, illegitimize

illuminati (always plural) enlightened people

illustrator *not* -er

imbroglio a predicament, a complicated situation; *pl.* **imbroglios**

immanent, imminent The first means inherent; the second impending; neither should be confused with eminent, which means outstanding

immaterial

immeasurable

immoral, amoral Immoral applies to things that are evil; amoral to matters in which questions of morality do not arise or are disregarded

Immortels, Les *not* -als; nickname of members of the Académie française

immovable, immovability

immutable

impala *not* -ll-

impassable, impassible The first means impossible to negotiate; the second impervious to pain

impazientemente (It.) in music, to perform in an impatient manner

impelled, impelling

imperative

imperceptible

impermeable

impertinent *not* in-

implacable incapable of being placated

imply, infer Imply means suggest; infer means deduce. A speaker implies, a listener infers

impostor *not* -er

impractical, impracticable, unpractical Impractical and unpractical both mean a thing can be done but is not worth doing. Impracticable means it cannot be done

impresario

impressible

impressionable

imprimatur official authorization

improvable

improvvisata (It.) note -vv-; in music, improvisation

impugn to criticize or attack

impunity freedom or safety from punishment

IN postal abbr. of Indiana

in absentia (Lat.) while absent

inadmissible

inadvertent

inadvisable

inamorata (fem.), **inamorato** (masc.) lover; *pl.* **inamorati**; note Italian has -nn-: *innamorata, innamorato*

inasmuch (one word)

in camera behind closed doors; not in open court

incessant

inchoate undeveloped, just starting out

incidentally *not* -tly

incisor

incognito

incombustible cannot be burned

incommodious

incommunicado/***incomunicado*** (Sp.) unable or unwilling to communicate

incomparable

incompatible

incomprehensible

incongruous, incongruity

incorrigible

incubus an evil spirit that has intercourse with sleeping women; a nightmare; anything that oppresses like a nightmare; *see also* succubus

incunabulum a book printed at an early date, esp. before 1501; early stages of development of something; *pl.* **incunabula**

in curia (Lat.) in open court

Ind. Indiana

Ind Coope Ind rhymes with sinned; English brewer

indefatigable tireless, beyond fatigue

indefeasible permanent, cannot be made void

indefensible

indelible

Independence Day (US) 4 July, marks the signing of the Declaration of Independence (1776)

indescribable

indexes/indices

Index Librorum Prohibitorum catalogue of books forbidden to Roman Catholics by their Church; not to be confused with Index Expurgatorius, a catalogue of books in which only certain passages are forbidden

indict, indite both pronounced indite. The first means to accuse formally of a crime; the second to set down in writing

indigenous

indigent

indigestible

indiscreet, indiscrete The first means lacking discretion; the second not composed of separate parts

indispensable

indivisible

indomitable

indubitable, indubitably

Industrial Workers of the World abbr. IWW; a radical US trade union movement (1905–25), often called Wobblies, particularly by detractors

inebriate, inebriety

inedible

ineffaceable indelible

inefficacious a longer way of saying ineffective

ineligible

ineluctable unavoidable, inevitable

inequable, inequitable The first means not even or uniform; the second unfair
ineradicable
inevitable
in excelsis (Lat.) to the highest degree
inexcusable
inexplicable
inexpressible
in extenso (Lat.) at full length
inextinguishable
in extremis (Lat.) in dire circumstances; at the point of death
infallible
infer, inferable, inferred, inferring *see also* imply, infer
infinitesimal *not* -ss-; exceedingly tiny
infinitude
in flagrante delicto (Lat.) in the act of committing an offence
inflammable, flammable, nonflammable Although inflammable means 'capable of being burned', it has so often been taken to mean the opposite that most authorities now suggest it be avoided, particularly in contexts that might one day involve urgency. Therefore it is generally better to use flammable for materials that will burn and nonflammable for those that will not
inflammation, inflammatory *not* im-; note -mm-
inflatable
inflection (US)/**inflexion** (UK)
inflexible
infra dig (no full points) *infra dignitatem* (Lat.), beneath one's dignity
infuse
Inge, William (1913–73) American playwright, not to be confused with the next entry
Inge, William Ralph (1860–1954) English theologian
ingenious, ingenuous The first means to be clever or inventive; the second means innocent, unsophisticated, guileless
ingénue
Ingres, Jean Auguste Dominique (1780–1867) pronounced an'gruh; French painter

inhere, inherent
inherit, inheritance, inheritable
inimical harmful, antagonistic
inimitable cannot be imitated or equalled
iniquitous wicked
initialed, initialing (pref. US)/**initialled, initialling** (UK, alt. US)
Inkatha predominantly Zulu political and cultural organization in South Africa, properly known as the Inkatha Freedom Party
in loco citato (Lat.) abbr. loc. cit.; in the place cited
in loco parentis (Lat.) in place of the parent
in medias res (Lat.) in the middle of things
in memoriam *not* -um
innamorata (It., fem.), ***innamorato*** (It., masc.) a lover or the state of being in love; *see also* inamorata
Inness, George (1825–94) American landscape painter of the Hudson River school
innocuous
Inns of Court, London: Gray's Inn, Lincoln's Inn, Inner Temple and Middle Temple
innuendo, *pl.* **innuendoes**
inoculate note -n-
inquiry (pref.)/**enquiry** (alt.) In the UK a formal investigation is always an inquiry, while either spelling is acceptable in other contexts
inquisitive
inscrutable
inshallah if Allah wills it
insidious, invidious Insidious means the stealthy spread of something undesirable; invidious means likely to cause offence, especially by an injustice
insignia, *pl.* **insignia** Some dictionaries insist on insigne for the singular
in situ (Lat.) in place
in so far (UK)/**insofar** (US), but **inasmuch, insomuch** (UK, US)

insouciance, insouciant lack of concern; carefree
install (UK, US), **installment** (US)/**instalment** (UK), **installation** (UK, US)
instantaneous
instil (UK)/**instill** (US), but **instilling**, **instilled** (UK, US)
Institut de France *not* -tute; umbrella organization for the five French academies: Académie des Beaux-Arts, Académie Française, Académie des Inscriptions et Belles-Lettres, Académie des Sciences, and the Académie des Sciences Morales et Politiques
Institute for Fiscal Studies (UK) *not* of
Institution of Professionals, Managers and Specialists (UK) formerly the Institution of Professional Civil Servants (trade union)
insuperable
insuppressible
insurer
intangible
intelligentsia the intellectual élite of a society
intelligible
Intelsat International Telecommunications Satellite
in tenebris (Lat.) in the dark, in doubt
inter alia (Lat.) among other things
InterCity train service operated by British Rail
intermezzo in music, a short piece between longer pieces or movements; also used to refer to a short piece for a solo *pl.* **intermezzi/intermezzos**
interminable
intermit, **intermittent**, **intermitted**, **intermitting**
international courts The International Court of Justice, or World Court, in The Hague is an offspring of the UN and deals with disputes between UN member states. The European Court of Justice, in Luxembourg, is an EC institution dealing exclusively with disputes involving EC member states. The European Court of Human Rights, in Strasbourg, deals with issues of civil liberties arising out of the European Convention on Human Rights. It has no connection with the UN or EC

interpellate, **interpolate** Interpellate means to interrupt or question formally; interpolate means to insert

interregnum note -rr-; period between reigns; *pl.* **interregnums**

interrelated note -rr-

intifada Palestinian uprising against Israeli military occupation of West Bank and Gaza

in toto (Lat.) in total

intransigence, intransigent

intransitive verbs those that do not require a direct object, as sleep in the sentence 'He sleeps all night'; *see also* transitive

intrauterine device abbr. IUD

intra vires (Lat.) within one's powers

in utero (Lat.) in the uterus

in vacuo (Lat.) in a vacuum; in empty space

Inveraray, Strathclyde, Scotland

Inverness-shire former Scottish county, now part of Highland Region

Investors in Industry UK investment group, familiarly known as 3i

invidious, insidious Invidious means likely to cause offence, especially by an injustice; insidious describes the stealthy spread of something undesirable

in vino veritas (Lat.) in wine there is truth

in vitro (Lat.) literally 'in glass', i.e. in a test-tube, as with *in vitro* fertilization

in vivo (Lat.) in a living organism

IPMS (UK) Institution of Professionals, Managers and Specialists (trade union)

ipsissima verba (Lat.) the very words

ipso facto (Lat.) by that very fact

IQ intelligence quotient

Iraqi, **Iraqis**

Ireland, **Republic of/Éire** (Gaelic) consists of the following provinces (and their counties): Connacht (Galway, Leitrim, Mayo, Roscommon, Sligo), Leinster (Carlow, Dublin, Kildare, Kilkenny, Laois, Longford, Louth, Meath, Offaly,

Westmeath, Wexford, Wicklow), Munster (Clare, Cork, Kerry, Limerick, Tipperary, Waterford), Ulster (Cavan, Donegal, Monaghan)

Ireshopeburn, Co. Durham, pronounced is'-hop-burn

Irgun Zvai Leumi Jewish guerrilla organization whose aim was to establish a state in Israel

iridescence, **iridescent** having the colours of the rainbow; changing colour with position

Iroquois North American Indian group consisting of Cayuga, Mohawk, Oneida, Onondaga, Seneca and Tuscaroras peoples; *pl.* **Iroquois**

Irrawaddy principal river in Myanmar

irreconcilable

irrefragable, **irrefrangible** The first means indisputable; the second indestructible

irregardless is wrong; use regardless

irrelevance, **irrelevant**

irreparable

irreplaceable

irrepressible

irresistible

irreversible

IRS (US) Internal Revenue Service, the federal tax authority

Isaiah abbr. Isa.; book of the Old Testament

ISBN International Standard Book Number

Ischia volcanic island in the Bay of Naples

-ise/-ize In the UK whether verbs end -ise or -ize (e.g., recognize/recognise, authorise/authorize) is usually a matter of preference or house style. Many leading publishers and publications use -ize endings, as does this dictionary. If you follow the -ize system, remember that there are some verbs that can end only -ise, of which the following are the main ones: advertise, advise, apprise, chastise, circumcise, comprise, compromise, demise, despise, devise, disguise, excise, exercise, franchise, improvise, incise, merchandise, premise, reprise, supervise, surmise, surprise, televise

Iseult/Isolde/Isolt/Ysolt in Arthurian legend, an Irish princess who falls tragically in love with Tristan, the nephew of a Cornish king; Wagner's opera is *Tristan und Isolde*

Isherwood, Christopher (William Bradshaw) (1904–86) English writer

Ishiguro, Kazuo (1954–) Japanese-born British novelist

Ishikawajima-Harima Heavy Industries Japanese industrial company

Isidore of Seville, St (*c.* 560–636) Spanish scholar and ecclesiastic

Islam the religion of Muslims

Islay, Strathclyde, Scotland pronounced eye'-la

Isleworth, London pronounced eye'-zul-worth

isosceles triangle one with two equal sides

Isozaki, **Arata** (1931–) Japanese architect

Issigonis, **Sir Alec** (1906–88) Turkish-born British car designer

Italy is divided into 20 regions: Abruzzi, Basilicata, Calabria, Campania, Emilia-Romagna, Friuli-Venezia Giulia, Lazio (Latium), Liguria, Lombardia (Lombardy), Marche (Marches), Molise, Piemonte (Piedmont), Puglia (Apulia), Sardegna (Sardinia), Sicilia (Sicily), Trentino-Alto Adige, Toscana (Tuscany), Umbria, Valle d'Aosta, Veneto

Itoh, C. Japanese trading company

IUD intrauterine device

Ivy League group of eight colleges in northeastern US noted for high academic standards: Brown, Columbia, Cornell, Dartmouth, Harvard, Princeton, University of Pennsylvania, Yale

Iwerne Courtney, Dorset, pronounced ewe'-urn

IWW Industrial Workers of the World, called Wobblies

Izmir, Turkey, formerly Smyrna

Izvestiya/Izvestia Russian newspaper

J

ja, *jawohl* (Ger.) yes

'Jabberwocky' poem by Lewis Carroll in *Through the Looking Glass* (1872) and (no caps.) any kind of nonsense writing

jacana tropical bird

jacaranda tropical tree

jackal

jackanapes a cocky person

Jackson, Andrew (1767–1845) nickname 'Old Hickory'; US President 1829–37

Jackson, Thomas Jonathan (1824–63) nickname 'Stonewall'; Confederate general during American Civil War

Jacobean, **Jacobin**, **Jacobite** Jacobean describes the period of the reign of James I of England (1603–25). Jacobins were radical republicans during the French Revolution, among them Robespierre, Danton and Marat. Jacobites were supporters of James II of England and his heirs following the Glorious Revolution

Jacobi, Derek (George) (1938–) English actor

Jacobs Suchard Swiss chocolate company

jactitation of marriage note -ctit-; falsely claiming to be someone's wife or husband

Jacuzzi (cap.) whirlpool bath

Jaeger clothing

jai alai also called pelota, a fast-paced ball game popular in Spain and Latin America

Jakarta generally preferred to Djakarta as the spelling for the Indonesian capital; formerly Batavia

jalopy
jalousie slatted shutter
jamb *not* jam; a door-post or similar
Janáček, Leoš (1854–1928) Czech composer
Jane Eyre novel by Charlotte Brontë (1847)
Janus Roman god of the gate of Heaven, depicted as having two faces – one at the front of his head and one at the back – because every door or gate looks two ways, and god of beginnings and of the first month, January
Japan Air Lines *not* Airlines
Jaques *not* Jacques, for the character in Shakespeare's *As You Like It*
jardinière ornamental pot or stand for plants; a garnish of mixed vegetables
Jarratt, Sir Alexander (Anthony) (1924–) *not* -ett; British business executive
Jaruzelski, General Wojciech (Witold) (1923–) pronounced voits'-yek yah-roo-zel'-ski; Polish general, Prime Minister 1981–5; head of state 1985–9, President 1989–90
Järvefelt, Göran (1947–89) Swedish opera director
Jarvik 7 artificial heart
JAT *Jugoslovenski Aerotransport* Yugoslav national airline
javelin
Jayawardene, Junius Richard (1906–) President of Sri Lanka 1978–89
Jedda/Jidda Saudi Arabia
jeep/Jeep Use jeep generally for Army vehicles and four-wheel-drive rough-terrain cars, but Jeep specifically for the brand-name of cars produced by the American company Chrysler
Jeffreys, George, Baron (1648–89) 'hanging' judge, infamous for severity of punishments handed down after Monmouth's rebellion (1685)
Jehovah's Witness
jejune insubstantial
Jekyll and Hyde The full title of the book by Robert Louis Stevenson is *The Strange Case of Dr Jekyll and Mr Hyde* (1886)
Jellicoe, John Rushworth, Earl (1859–1935) British admiral,

First Sea Lord 1916–17, Admiral of the Fleet 1919, and Governor-General of New Zealand 1920–24

Jell-O (US) brand of gelatin dessert

Jenkins' Ear, War of (1739–48) war between Britain and Spain over trade with South America, ostensibly provoked by incident in which Spanish sailors boarded a British vessel in the Caribbean and cut off the ear of the captain, Robert Jenkins, but this was seven years before the hostilities began

je ne sais pas (Fr.) I don't know

je ne sais quoi (Fr.) I don't know what, applied to the indescribable

jeopardy, jeopardize

jeremiad elaborate lamentation

jeroboam wine bottle variously defined as containing 10–12 imperial qt/12½–15 US qt/13 l, or the equivalent of four ordinary wine bottles

jerry-build, jerry-built shoddily constructed; not to be confused with gerrymander

Jervaulx Abbey, North Yorkshire, pronounced jur'-voe

jetsam, flotsam flotsam describes wreckage of a ship and its goods floating at sea. Jetsam applies to goods that have been thrown overboard (jettisoned). Historically flotsam went to the Crown and jetsam to the lord of the manor on whose land it washed up

jettison

Jeu de Paume, Musée du; Paris

jeune fille (Fr.) a girl

jewellery (UK)/**jewelry** (US)

jew's harp (no caps.)

Jhabvala, Ruth Prawer (1927–) German-born British novelist and screenwriter

Jiang Zemin (1926–) General Secretary of the Chinese Communist Party 1989–

jibe (US) to be in agreement (slang); a nautical term describing the act of changing course; *see also* gibe, gybe

Jibuti use Djibouti

jihad a Muslim holy war

Jilin (Pinyin)/**Kirin** Chinese province; capital Changchun

Jinnah, Mohammed Ali (1876–1948) founder of Pakistan, Governor-General 1947–8

Joan of Arc, St/Jeanne d'Arc (Fr.) (1412–31) French military leader and martyr, tried for heresy and sorcery and burned by the English at Rouen

Jobs, Steven Paul (1955–) *not* -ph-; American computer wunderkind, co-founder of Apple Computer Inc. and NeXT Inc.

jodhpurs riding breeches, named after Jodhpur, city in Rajasthan, India

Jodrell Bank, Cheshire, site of observatory; formally, Nuffield Radio-Astronomy Laboratories, operated by the University of Manchester

Johannesburg, South Africa, but **Johannisberg**, Germany; the German wine is *Johannisberger*

John B. Hynes Auditorium, Boston, Massachusetts

John o' Groat's site of legendary house in Highland region on the coast of Scotland traditionally given as northernmost point on British mainland

Johns Hopkins University and **Johns Hopkins Medical Center**, Baltimore, Maryland; *not* John

Johnson, Andrew (1808–75) US President 1865–9

Johnson, Lyndon B(aines) (1908–73) US President 1963–9

Johnson, Nunnally (1897–1977) American screenwriter, film director and producer

Johnson, Samuel (1709–84) English lexicographer, critic and poet

joie de vivre (Fr.) state of being carefree, full of joy of living

Joliet/Jolliet, Louis (1645–1700) French-Canadian explorer

Joliet, Illinois

Joliette County, Quebec

Joneses *not* Jones', for 'keeping up with the'

Jones, Inigo (1573–1652) English architect and designer

Jones Lang Wootton UK property group

jonquil species of narcissus

Jonson, Ben(jamin) (1572–1637) English poet and dramatist

Jordaens, Jakob (1593–1678) Flemish painter
Josquin Des Prés (*c.* 1450–1521) French composer
joss stick
Jove alternative name for Roman god Jupiter
Juan Carlos I (1938–) King of Spain (1975–)
Juárez, Benito Pablo (1806–72) Mexican President 1861–5, 1867–72. The Mexican city named after him is formally Ciudad Juárez
Judas Iscariot apostle who betrayed Jesus for 30 pieces of silver
judgement (UK)/**judgment** (US, UK legal)
juggernaut
Jugoslavia/Jugoslavija (Serbo-Croat) use Yugoslavia
Jugoslovenski Aerotransport abbr. JAT; national airline of Yugoslavia
jugular vein
Juilliard School of Music New York
jujitsu Japanese form of unarmed combat
Juliana, Louise Emma Marie Wilhelmina (1909–) Queen of The Netherlands 1948–80
julienne vegetables cut into strips and a soup containing such vegetables
Jung, Carl Gustav (1875–1961) Swiss psychiatrist
junk bonds financial slang term for securities rated below investment grade. Because they pose a higher risk of default (hence 'junk'), they carry a higher rate of interest
Juno Roman goddess, wife of Jupiter
Juno and the Paycock play by Sean O'Casey (1924)
junta pronounced hoon'-ta; government run by political or military clique after a *coup d'état*; also a Spanish, Italian or Latin American council
Jupiter supreme Roman god, also called Jove; also fifth planet from the Sun
just in time/*kanban* (Jap.) manufacturing system devised in Japan to avoid stockpiling, so raw materials are delivered 'just in time' to be made into finished products
Juvenal Decimus Junius Juvenalis (*c.* 60–*c.* 140) Roman poet
j'y suis, j'y reste (Fr.) here I am, here I stay

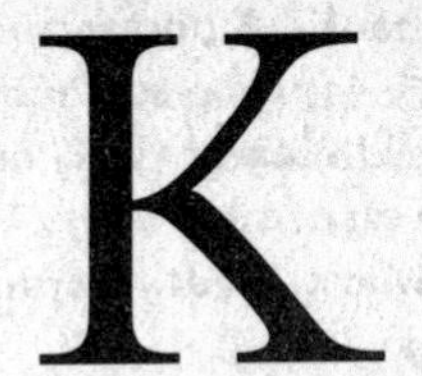

kabuki a form of Japanese theatre
Kabul capital of Afghanistan
Kádár, János (1912–89) Hungarian politician
kaffeeklatsch (Ger.) a gathering for coffee and conversation
Kafka, Franz (1883–1924) Czech-born Austrian novelist and short story writer
Kahn-Freud, Sir Otto (1900–79) German-born English lawyer and academic
Kaifu, Toshiki (1932–) Prime Minister of Japan 1989–91
Kaiser, Georg (1878–1945) German playwright
Kalamazoo, Michigan
Kalashnikov rifle
kaleidoscope
Kalgoorlie, Western Australia
Kali Hindu goddess
Kamchatka Peninsula, Russia
kamikaze
Kampuchea official name for Cambodia 1975–89
Kandinsky, Wassily/Vasily (1866–1944), Russian-born French artist
Kans. Kansas
Kansas City, Missouri, is older and much larger than Kansas City, Kansas, which is on the opposite side of the Missouri River
Kant, **Immanuel** (1724–1804) German philosopher
Kapuściński, Ryszard (1932–) Polish writer
Karachi former capital of Pakistan, now provincial capital of Sind

Karajan, Herbert von (1908–89) Austrian conductor, principal conductor of Berlin Philharmonic 1955–89

Karamanlis, Konstantinos (1907–) Prime Minister of Greece 1955–63, 1974–80; President 1980–85, 1990–

karat (US)/**carat** (UK) one twenty-fourth part of pure gold; *see also* carat; caret

Karl-Marx-Stadt, Germany (hyphens) now called Chemnitz again

Karlovy Vary Czech spa formerly known as Carlsbad/Karlsbad (Ger.)

Karlsruhe, Germany

Kármán, Theodor von (1881–1963) *not* -dore; Hungarian-born American physicist

Karolinska Institute, Stockholm

Karpov, Anatoly (Yevgenievich) (1951–) Russian chess player, world champion 1975–85

Kasavubu, Joseph (1917–69) President of the Congo (now Zaïre) 1960–65

Kaskaskia River, Illinois

Kasparov, Garry (Kimovich) (1963–) born Harry Weinstein; Russian chess player, youngest winner of world championship (1985)

Kassel Germany

Katharevusa/**Katharevousa** until 1976 the official written language of Greece

Katharina character in Shakespeare's *The Taming of the Shrew*

Katharine's Docks, St, London; note -ar-

Kathasaritsagara Sanskrit epic

Kathmandu/Katmandu capital of Nepal

Katrine, Loch, Central Region, Scotland, pronounced kat'-trin

Kattegat (Dan.)/**Kattegatt** the strait between Denmark and Sweden

Kaufingerstrasse, Munich

Kaufman, George S(imon) (1889–1961) American dramatist and writer

Kaufman, Gerald (Bernard) (1930–) British politician

Kazakhstan Central Asian republic, formerly part of Soviet Union, capital Alma Ata

Kazan, Elia (1909–) born Elia Kazanjoglous; Turkish-born American stage and film director and novelist

Kazantzakis, Nikos (1883–1957) Greek poet and novelist

KCB Knight Commander of the Order of the Bath; note second 'the'

KCMG Knight Commander of the Order of St Michael and St George

Kean, Edmund (*c.* 1787–1833) English actor

Kearsley, Greater Manchester, pronounced kurz'-lee

Keats House, Hampstead, London (no apos.)

Keble College, Oxford, pronounced keeble; named after John Keble (1792–1866)

kedgeree

keelhaul

keenness note -nn-; but **keenest**

Kefauver, (Carey) Estes (1903–63) American politician

Keighley, West Yorkshire, pronounced keath'-ley

Keisby, Lincolnshire, pronounced kaze'-bee

Kellogg-Briand Pact short-lived 1928 agreement renouncing war signed by 64 nations; named after Frank B. Kellogg, US Secretary of State, and Aristide Briand, French Foreign Minister

Kelmscott, Oxfordshire, pronounced kemz'-kott

Kemal, Mustafa *see* Atatürk

Keneally, Thomas (Michael) (1935–) Australian novelist

Kennedy, John Fitzgerald (1917–63) US President 1961–3

Kenyatta, Jomo (*c.* 1897–1978) born Kamau Ngengi; President of Kenya 1964–78

Kerensky, Alexander (Feodorovich) (1881–1970) Russian revolutionary, briefly Prime Minister 1917

kerfuffle disorder, commotion

Kerkyra (Grk)/**Corfu**

kerosene

Kerouac, Jack (1922–69) born Jean Louis Kerouac; American novelist, a spokesman for the 'beat generation'

kerb (UK)/**curb** (US) raised edging along street

Kern, Jerome (1885–1945) American composer

kewpie doll

Key, Francis Scott (1780–1843) American lawyer, author of 'The Star-Spangled Banner'

Keynes, John Maynard, Baron (1883–1946) pronounced Kainz; British economist

kg kilogram

KGB *Komitet Gosudarstvennoi Bezopasnosti* (Russ.) (Commission of State Security), the Soviet secret service. In earlier manifestations it was known successively as Cheka, GPU, NKVD and MVD

khaki, *pl.* **khakis**

Khamenei, Ayatollah Seyed Ali Leader of the Islamic Republic in Iran 1989–

Khartoum capital of Sudan

Khayyám, Omar Omar is not a first name, so alphabetically this Persian poet and mathematician (*c.* 1050–*c.* 1125) should be listed under O

Khomeini, Ayatollah Ruhollah (1908–89) Iranian religious and political leader, head of state 1979–89

Khrushchev, Nikita (Sergeyevich) (1894–1971) leader of the USSR as Secretary-General of the Communist Party 1953–64 and Prime Minister 1958–64

kibbutz Israeli communal settlement; *pl.* **kibbutzim**; not to be confused with kibitz

kibitz to watch at cards, to give unwanted advice; not to be confused with kibbutz

kibosh

kidnapped, kidnapper, kidnapping

Kierkegaard, Søren (Aabye) (1813–55) Danish philosopher

Kiev capital of Ukraine

Kigali capital of Rwanda

Kilauea active volcano on Mauna Loa, Hawaii

Kilimanjaro mountain in Tanzania, the highest point in Africa (19,340 ft/5,895 m); at the end of a line divide it Kilima-njaro

Killarney, Co. Kerry, Ireland

kilo- prefix meaning 1,000

kilogram/kilogramme (alt. UK) abbr. kg; 1,000 g; equivalent to 2.2046 lb

kilometer (US)/**kilometre** (UK) abbr. km; 1,000 metres; equivalent to 1,094 yd, 3,281 ft, 0.62137 mile; for conversion to miles, *see* table in Appendix

kiloton abbr. kT; an explosive force equal to 1,000 tons of TNT

kilowatt abbr. kW; 1,000 watts

Kimberley, South Africa

Kimberly-Clark US paper and forest products group

Kim Il Sung (1912–) North Korean soldier and statesman; head of state as Prime Minister 1948–72 and President 1972–

kimono, *pl.* **kimonos**

kind, kinds There should always be agreement between kind or kinds and its antecedents: 'These kind of mistakes' should be 'This kind of mistake' or 'These kinds of mistake'

Kindley Field main airport of Bermuda

King Abdulaziz International Airport, Jedda, Saudi Arabia

King, (William Lyon) Mackenzie (1874–1950) Prime Minister of Canada 1921–6, 1926–30, 1935–48

kings and queens of Britain *see* Appendix

King's Bromley, Staffordshire

Kings Canyon National Park, California (no apos.)

King's Cross, London railway station and district

King's Langley, Hertfordshire

Kings Norton, Leicestershire (no apos.)

Kingston upon Hull, Humberside (no hyphens) formal name of Hull

Kingston upon Thames, London (no hyphens)

King's Walden, Hertfordshire

Kings Worthy, Hampshire (no apos.)

Kinnock, Neil (Gordon) (1942–) British politician

Kinshasa formerly Léopoldville; capital of Zaïre

Kirin/Jilin (Pinyin) Chinese province

Kirkby, Merseyside, pronounced kur'-bee

Kirkcaldy, Fife, pronounced kur-caw-dee

Kirkcudbright, Dumfries & Galloway, Scotland, pronounced kur-koo'-bree

Kirgizstan/Kirghizstan/Kyrgyzstan Central Asian republic, formerly part of Soviet Union, capital Bishkek

Kirkpatrick, Jeane (1926–) American diplomat; US representative to the UN 1981–5

Kishinev capital of Moldova

Kissinger, Henry (Alfred) (1923–) German-born American academic and statesman; National Security Adviser 1969–73, Secretary of State 1973–7; Nobel Peace Prize 1973

Kitakyushu city on island of Kyushu, Japan

Kit-Cat Club 18th-century London club whose members included Addison, Steele and Congreve

Kitchener, Horatio Herbert, Earl (1850–1916) Irish-born British field marshal, best known for victory over Sudanese at Khartoum

kitemark (one word, no cap.) logo of the British Standards Institution indicating that a product has been approved as safe

kith and kin a cliché. Kith are friends and acquaintances; kin are relatives

Kitcat & Aitken British stockbroking firm, ceased business 1990

kitsch

Kitzbühel Austrian resort

Klee, Paul (1879–1940) Swiss painter

Klein, Calvin (Richard) (1942–) American fashion designer

Kleist, (Bernd) Heinrich (Wilhelm) von (1777–1811) German dramatist and poet

Kleenex a brand of paper handkerchiefs and other paper products

klieg light

Kline, Franz (1910–62) American painter

KLM *Koninklijke Luchtvaart Maatschappij*, national airline of The Netherlands

Klöckner-Werke German steel manufacturer

km kilometer (US)/kilometre (UK)

K Mart American retailer (no hyphen)

knead to manipulate a soft substance with the hands, as with clay or dough

kneel, **knelt**

Kneller, Sir Godfrey (1646–1723) German-born British portrait painter

Knesset Israeli parliament

knick-knack

Knightsbridge, London

knot speed of one nautical mile an hour. A ship does eight knots or it does eight nautical miles an hour, but not eight knots an hour

koalas are marsupials; koala bear is wrong

København Danish spelling of Copenhagen

Koblenz, Germany

Kohinoor/Koh-i-noor famous Indian diamond, now part of the British crown jewels

kohlrabi a vegetable; *pl.* **kohlrabis**

Koivisto, Mauno (Henrik) (1923–) Finnish banker and politician, President of Finland 1982–

Kokoschka, Oskar (1886–1980) Austrian-born British artist and writer

konditorei (Ger.) bakery

kookaburra Australian kingfisher

kopek/kopeck/copeck a coin worth 1/100th of a rouble in Soviet currency

Kopit, Arthur (1937–) American playwright

Koppel, Ted (1940–) American television journalist

Korchnoi, Viktor (1931–) Soviet-born Swiss chess player

Korea partitioned in 1948 into South Korea (officially the Republic of Korea), capital Seoul; and North Korea (officially the People's Democratic Republic of Korea), capital Pyongyang

Korean names are similar to Chinese in that the family name comes first; thus after the first reference Park Chung Hee becomes Mr Park. But Koreans tend not to hyphenate their given names, nor as a rule do they write the second given name without caps. as in the old Chinese system

Korsakoff's syndrome mental disorder, including loss of

memory, associated with chronic alcoholism or vitamin deficiencies

koruna abbr. kčs; basic unit of currency in Czech Republic and Slovakia, equal to 100 halers; *pl.* **koruny**

Kosciusko, Thaddeus/Kościuszko, Tadeusz Andrzej Bonawentura (Pol.) (1746–1817) Polish patriot and general; fought on the colonial side in the American Revolutionary War; defended Poland against Russia

Kosinski, Jerzy (Nikodem) (1933–91) Polish-born American novelist

Kosygin, Alexei (Nikolayevich) (1904–80) Soviet Prime Minister 1964–80

kowtow/kotow (alt. UK) act of submission

KPMG Peat Marwick, British accountancy firm

Krafft-Ebing, Richard, Baron von (1840–1902) *not* Ebb-; German psychiatrist

Kraków Poland use Cracow

Krapp's Last Tape one-act play by Samuel Beckett (1958)

Kreuger, Ivar (1880–1932) *not* Ivan; Swedish financier who perpetrated $500 million fraud on investors

Kristallnacht (Ger.) literally 'crystal night', so called because of broken glass on pavements during night of looting and destruction of Jewish businesses and synagogues in Germany and Austria, 9/10 November 1938

krona, *pl.* **kronor** (Swed.)/**króna**, *pl.* **krónur** (Ice.)/**krone**, *pl.* **kroner** (Dan., Nor.)

krugerrand note -rr-

Krung Thep (Thai)/**Bangkok**

KS postal abbr. of Kansas

kT kiloton

Kuala Lumpur capital of Malaysia

Kublai Khan (1216–94) Mongol emperor of China 1279–94; the unfinished poem by Coleridge was 'Kubla Khan'

kudos, meaning fame or glory, is singular: a person receives the kudos that is (*not* are) his due

Ku Klux Klan (no hyphens)

kulak entrepreneurial peasant in pre-revolutionary Russia

Kumagai Gumi Company Limited Japanese construction company

kumquat

Kuomintang/Guomindang (Pinyin) the Chinese Nationalist Party, founded by Sun Yat-sen. The syllable tang/dang contains the notion of party, so refer only to the Kuomintang, *not* Kuomintang Party

Kurosawa, Akira (1910–) Japanese film director

Kuwaiti, *pl.* **Kuwaitis**

Kuybyshev formerly Samara; Russian city

Kuznetsov, Anatoly (1930–79) born Alexander Vasilievich Kuznetsov; Russian novelist, using pen name A. Anatoli

kW kilowatt

KwaNdebele national state/non-independent black homeland in Transvaal, South Africa

kwashiorkor nutritional disorder in young children

KY postal abbr. of Kentucky; traditional abbr. is **Ky**

Kyd, Thomas (1558–94) English playwright

Kyzyl-Kum desert in Kazakhstan and Uzbekistan

L

LA postal abbr. of Louisiana; traditional abbr. is **La**

Labor Day US and Canadian holiday on the first Monday of September

labyrinth

lackadaisical *not* lacks-

Lackawanna, New York state

lacquer

lacrosse a sport, but **La Crosse**, Wisconsin

lacuna a missing part, a gap; *pl.* **lacunae/lacunas**

lacy *not* -cey

laddie *not* -dy

Ladies' Home Journal note apos.; US magazine

Lady Chatterley's Lover novel by D. H. Lawrence (1928)

Lafayette, Marie Joseph Paul Yves Roch Gilbert du Motier, Marquis de (1757–1834) French general who played a leading role in both the American and French revolutions

Laffitte, Jacques (1767–1844) French statesman

Lafite, Château celebrated wine from Bordeaux

Lafitte/Laffite, Jean (*c.* 1780- *c.* 1826) French pirate

La Follette, Robert (Marion) (1855–1925) American politician

Lag b'Omer Jewish holiday

lagniappe/lagnappe (US) pronounced lan-yap; a small, unexpected gift

Lagting upper house of Norwegian parliament, or Storting

La Guardia Airport, New York, pronounced la gwardia; named after Fiorello La Guardia (1882–1947), mayor of New York City

Laibach (Ger.)/**Ljubljana**, Slovenia

laissez-faire (Fr.) noninterference by government in trade and industry

Laius in Greek mythology, the King of Thebes and father of Oedipus

La Jolla, California, pronounced la hoy'-ya

Lake Wobegon fictional town in stories by Garrison Keillor

lama, **Lammas**, **llama** Lama describes a Buddhist monk from Tibet or Mongolia (his dwelling place is a lamasery). Lammas is a harvest festival formerly celebrated on 1 August in the UK. The llama is a wool-bearing animal from South America

lambaste *not* -bast; to criticize sharply

Lamborghini Italian sports car

lamb's-wool *not* lambswool

Lancelot/Launcelot Both spellings are used for the Arthurian knight, the first in a 13th-century French narrative and by Tennyson and Percy, the second in a 14th-century English poem and by Malory. The Royal Navy ship is HMS *Lancelot*

Lancing College, West Sussex, but **Lansing**, Michigan

Land-Rover (hyphen), but Range Rover (two words)

Land's End, Cornwall

Lange, David (Russell) (1942–) pronounced lohng'-ee; New Zealand Prime Minister 1984–9

languor, languorous

Langtry, Lillie (1853–1929) born Emilie Charlotte Le Breton; British actress. Her first name is often misspelled, presumably because of confusion with her nickname, 'The Jersey Lily'.

Languedoc-Roussillon region of of France. The dialect of Languedoc is written *langue d'oc* (pronounced lang'-dok), from the Old French word *oc* (yes) spoken there. This contrasts with the northern dialect *langue d'oïl* (pronounced lang'-do-el), from *oïl*, the traditional word for 'yes' there

lanyard *not*-iard; short rope or cord

Lanzhou (Pinyin)/**Lanchow** pronounced lan-joe'; Chinese city, capital of Gansu Province

Laois/Laoighis (Gaelic) pronounced lay'-ish; county in

Republic of Ireland, formerly called Leix (pronounced laix) and Queen's

Laomedon in Greek mythology, the founder of Troy

Lao-tzu/Lao-tze/Lao Zi (Pinyin) (*c.* 600–530 BC) Chinese philosopher, reputed founder of Taoism

laparotomy surgical incision into the abdominal wall

La Paz administrative capital and main city of Bolivia

lapis lazuli

Laphroaig whisky named after a village on the Scottish island of Islay

La Plata, Argentina, but **Rio de la Plata**

Lapp, Lappish, but **Lapland, Laplander** The correct name for the people is Sami

lapsus memoriae (Lat.) a lapse of memory

Lardner, Ring(gold) (Wilmer) (1885–1933) American writer

largess (pref.)/**largesse** (alt.) a gift or bounty

La Rochefoucauld, François, Duc de (1613–80) French author, noted for maxims

La Rochelle, France

Larousse French publisher of reference books

larrikin Australian term for a miscreant

larynx, *pl.* **larynges/larynxes**

lasagna (US, It. *sing.*)/**lasagne** (UK, It. *pl.*)

La Scala formally Teatro alla Scala; Milan opera house

laser acronym for light amplification by stimulated emission of radiation

Lasham, Hampshire, pronounced lass'-um

Laski, Harold (Joseph) (1893–1950) British political theorist

La Spezia, Italy

Lassen Peak volcanic mountain in northern California

lasso, *pl.* **lassos**

Lateran Treaty (1929) treaty between Italy and the Vatican by which the papacy recognized Italy as a state, and Italy recognized the Vatican City as a sovereign papal state and agreed other measures concerning the role of the Catholic Church in Italy; effective until 1985

latitude *not*-tt-

Latour, Château a wine from Bordeaux

La Tour, Georges de (1593–1652) French artist

Latter-Day Saints Mormons' name for themselves

Laugharne, Dyfed, Wales, pronounced larn

Launcelot/Lancelot Both spellings are used for the Arthurian knight, the first in a 14th-century English poem and by Malory, the second in a 13th-century French narrative and by Tennyson and Percy. The Royal Navy ship is HMS *Lancelot*

launderette (UK)/**Laundromat** (US trademark, cap.)

Lausanne, Switzerland

Law, Andrew Bonar (1858–1923) Canadian-born British Prime Minister for seven months in 1922–3

Lawrence, D(avid) H(erbert) (1885–1930) English novelist and poet

Lawrence, T(homas) E(dward) (1888–1935) British soldier and writer, known as Lawrence of Arabia

Lazarus, Emma (1849–87) American poet, remembered chiefly for 'The New Colossus', the poem inscribed on the Statue of Liberty

L-dopa drug used in the treatment of Parkinson's disease

Leacock, Stephen (Butler) (1869–1944) Canadian economist and humorist

lead, led The past tense of the verb to lead is led. When l-e-a-d is pronounced 'led', it applies only to the metallic element; *see also* LED

Leadbelly Huddie Leadbetter (1888–1949), American guitarist, and folk and blues singer

Leakey, **Louis (Seymour Bazett)** (1903–72) husband of **Mary Douglas Leakey** (1913–) and father of **Richard (Erskine Frere) Leakey** (1944–), all distinguished British archaeologists

Leamington Spa, Warwickshire, pronounced lem'-ing-tun; formally Royal Leamington Spa

Leatherstocking Tales*, *The series of novels by James Fenimore Cooper

Leavis, F(rank) R(aymond) (1895–1978) English critic and essayist

Leazes Park, **Castle Leazes**, Newcastle upon Tyne

lebensraum (Ger.) living space, the imperialist notion pursued by Hitler that Germans should be entitled to occupy neighbouring lands

Le Carré, John pen name of David John Moore Cornwell (1931–), British novelist

Le Corbusier pseudonym of Charles Édouard Jeanneret (1887–1965), Swiss architect and town planner

LED light-emitting diode

lederhosen leather shorts

Lee Kuan Yew (1923–) Prime Minister of Singapore 1959–91

Leeuwarden pronounced lay'-vord-un; capital of Friesland, The Netherlands

Leeuwenhoek, Anton van (1632–1723) pronounced lay'-vun-hook; Dutch naturalist associated with early microscopes

Leeuwin, **Cape**, Western Australia

Leeward Islands Formerly a British colony comprising the Caribbean islands of Anguilla, Antigua, the British Virgin Islands, Montserrat, Nevis and St Kitts, the name now applies to all those islands plus Guadeloupe, the US Virgin Islands and other smaller islands in the Lesser Antilles north of the Windward Islands

Le Fanu, Joseph (Sheridan) (1814–73) pronounced leff'-ann-oo; Irish writer

Léger, Fernand (1881–1955) French painter

legerdemain

Leghorn English name, now seldom used, for Livorno, Italy

legible, **legibility**

Légion d' honneur supreme French order of merit

Legionnaires' disease

legitimate, **legitimize** *not* -matize

Lehmann, Rosamond (1901–90) English novelist

Leibniz, (Gottfried Wilhelm), Baron von, (1646–1716) pronounced libe'-nits, *not* leeb-nits; German philosopher and mathematician

Leicester, **Leicestershire** abbr. Leics.

Leiden (Dut.)/**Leyden** (Eng. alt.), Netherlands, pronounced lie'-den; *see also* Leyden

Leif Ericson/Ericsson/Eriksson (*c.* 10th c.) Norse explorer, discovered Vinland, possibly North America

Leinster province of the Republic of Ireland comprising the counties of Carlow, Dublin, Kildare, Kilkenny, Laois, Longford, Louth, Meath, Offaly, Westmeath, Wexford and Wicklow

Leipzig, Germany, pronounced lipe'-zig

leitmotif/leitmotiv pronounced lite'-mo-teef; a recurring or dominant theme associated with a particular character or idea in a musical or literary work

Leitrim pronounced lee'-trim; Irish county

Lely, Sir Peter (1618–80) Dutch-born British painter

Léman, Lac French name for Lake Geneva

Le Mesurier, John (1912–83) English actor

Lemmon, Jack (1925–) American actor

lend, **loan** Loan as a verb ('The banks have been asked to loan Brazil $120 million') is frowned on by many authorities; use lend or lent, as appropriate

Lenin, Vladimir Ilyich (1870–1924) born Vladimir Ilyich Ulyanov; sometimes called Nikolai; Russian revolutionary and premier 1918–24

Leningrad Russia, formerly St Petersburg (1703–1914), then Petrograd (1914–24), then reverted to St Petersburg (1991)

lens *not* lense; *pl.* **lenses**

Leominster, Hereford & Worcester, pronounced lem'-ster

Leonardo da Vinci (1452–1519) Renaissance genius. A work by him is a Leonardo, not a da Vinci

Léopoldville former name of Kinshasa, Zaïre

leprechaun *not* lepra-

lèse-majesté (Fr.)/**lese-majesty** (alt. UK, US) literally, wounded majesty; treason or similar offence; insolence towards anyone to whom deference is due

Lesotho formerly Basutoland; independent kingdom surrounded by South Africa

less, **fewer** The simplest rule is to use less with singular nouns (less money, less sugar), fewer with plural nouns (fewer houses, fewer cars)

Lesseps, Ferdinand Marie, Vicomte de (1805–94) French engineer, planned, and was instrumental in building, the Suez Canal. On second reference **de Lesseps**

Lessing, Doris (May) (1919–) British novelist

Lessing, Gotthold Ephraim (1729–81) German critic, playwright and philosopher

Letzeburgesch the variety of German spoken in Luxembourg

leukaemia (UK)/**leukemia** (US)

leveraged buyout making a takeover of a company with money borrowed on the expectation of selling parts of the purchased company at a sufficient profit to pay for the cost of the acquisition

Leverrier, Urbain Jean Joseph (1811–77) French astronomer

Levittown note -tt-; name of towns in Pennsylvania and New York state

Levi's (apos.) trademark of denim trousers, or jeans, manufactured by Levi Strauss

Leviticus abbr. Lev.; book of the Old Testament

Lewis, Meriwether (1774–1809) *not* Merri-; American explorer and politician; co-led (with William Clark) exploration of American West known as Lewis and Clark Expedition

Lewis, (Percy) Wyndham (1884–1957) English writer and artist

Leycett, Staffordshire, pronounced lee'-set

Leyden jar pronounced lie'-den ; the Dutch town is now usually spelled Leiden

Lhasa capital of Tibet

Lhaso apso breed of dog

liaison *not* liason

Líakoura modern name of Mt Parnassus, Greek mountain sacred in mythology

Liaoning province of China; capital Shenyang

Liaotung Gulf, **Liaotung Peninsula**, China

libel, **slander** The first refers to written defamation; the second to spoken defamation

Liberal Democrats British political party, formerly called Social and Liberal Democratic Party

liberté*, *égalité*, *fraternité (Fr.) liberty, equality, fraternity; slogan of the French Revolution

Liberty formerly the National Council for Civil Liberties

Liberty, Statue of officially *Liberty Enlightening the World* (1886); designed by Frédéric Auguste Bartholdi

LIBOR pronounced lie'-bore; short for London interbank offered rate; benchmark interest rate for international loans based on the interest rates prevailing in the Eurodollar market in London

licence (UK noun)/**license** (UK vb) In the USA, license is used for all forms

Lichfield Cathedral

Lichfield, Patrick professional name of Thomas Patrick John Anson, fifth Earl of Lichfield, Viscount Anson and Baron Soberton (1939–), fashion photographer

Lichfield, Staffordshire

Lichtenstein, Roy (1923–) American painter

lickerish greedy or lascivious

licorice (US)/**liquorice** (UK)

Lie, Trygve (Halvdan) (1896–1968) Norwegian statesman, Secretary-General of the UN 1946–53

Liebfraumilch/*Liebfrauenmilch* (Ger.) pronounced leeb-; a white Rhine wine

Liechtenstein pronounced leek-ten-stine; a principality; capital Vaduz

light year the distance that light travels through empty space in one year (*c.* 5,878 billion miles/9,460 billion km)

likable (US)/**likeable** (UK)

likelihood

Lilienthal, Otto (1849–96) German inventor

Lilliput (cap.), but lilliputian (no cap.) for something small

Lilly, Eli *not* -ey; US pharmaceuticals company

Lilongwe capital of Malawi

lily, *pl.* **lilies**

Limassol, Cyprus

Limbourg a province of Belgium

Limburg a province of The Netherlands. The cheese is Limburg or Limburger

linage pronounced line'-uhj; number of written or printed lines; payment by the line; *see also* lineage

linchpin, but **lynch law**, **lynch gang**

lineage pronounced lin'-ee-uhj; ancestry

Linnaeus, Carolus (1707–78) born Carl von Linné, Swedish botanist who devised the system for classifying plants and animals

Linnean Society

Lipari Islands group of islands off Sicily, also known as Aeolian Islands

Lipchitz, Jacques (1891–1973) born Chaim Jacob Lipchitz; Lithuanian-born American sculptor

Li Peng (1928–) Chinese Prime Minister 1988–

Lippmann, Walter (1889–1974) influential US newspaper columnist and writer

liquefy, **liquefaction** *not* liqui-

liqueur a flavoured alcoholic spirit

liquorice (UK)/**licorice** (US) *see also* lickerish

lira, *pl.* **lire** abbr. L. The abbr. Lit is best avoided in general writing, as it is not widely known

lissome supple

Liszt, Franz (1811–86) Austrian composer

litchi Chinese tree and its fruit

literally means actually. It is best reserved for those infrequent occasions when an expression that is usually used metaphorically is meant to be taken at its word, e.g. 'He literally died laughing.'

literati *not* -tt-; literary elite, learned people

Littlehampton, West Sussex (one word)

livable (US)/**liveable** (UK)

Livingston, West Lothian, Scotland

Livingstone, David (1813–73) Scottish explorer and missionary

Livingstone, Ken (1945–) British politician

Livy (Titus Livius), (59 BC–AD 17) Roman historian

Ljubljana pronounced loob-lee-yah'-na; capital of Slovenia

Llandrindod Wells, Powys, Wales

Llandudno, Gwynedd, Wales

Llanfairpwllgwyngyllgogerychwyrndrobwyll-llantysilio-gogogoch, Gwynedd, Wales, usually shortened to Llanfair Pwllgwyngyll or Llanfair P.G.; village on Anglesey with the longest name in Britain

Lloyd George, David (1863–1945) (Earl Lloyd-George of Dwyfor) British Prime Minister 1916–22

Lloyd's of London (apos.) association of insurance underwriters

Lloyds Bank (UK, no apos.)

Lloyd Webber, Andrew (1948–) British composer of musicals, and brother of **Julian Lloyd Webber** (1951–), cellist

Llullaillaco mountain on border of Argentina and Chile

LME London Metal Exchange

loath, loathe The first means reluctant; the second to despise

loathsome disgusting or offensive

loc. cit. *loco citato* (Lat.) in the place cited

local residents Residents generally are local, so in most contexts the first word can be deleted.

Locke, John (1632–1704) English philosopher

locum tenens, *pl.* **locum tenentes**

lodestar (pref.)/**loadstar** (alt.)

lodestone (pref.)/**loadstone** (alt.)

Łódź, Poland, pronounced woodj

logarithm

Lomé Convention (1975) trading agreement between European Community and 46 Third World countries, so called because it was signed in Lomé, the capital of Togo

London Greater London comprises the City of London, the City of Westminster and 31 boroughs: Barking and Dagenham, Barnet, Bexley, Brent, Bromley, Camden, Croydon, Ealing, Enfield, Greenwich, Hackney, Hammersmith and Fulham, Haringey, Harrow, Havering, Hillingdon, Hounslow, Islington, Kensington and Chelsea, Kingston upon Thames, Lambeth, Lewisham, Merton, Newham, Redbridge,

Richmond upon Thames, Southwark, Sutton, Tower Hamlets, Waltham Forest, Wandsworth

London interbank offered rate *see* LIBOR

Longfellow, Henry Wadsworth (1807–82) American poet

Longleat House, Wiltshire, ancestral home of the Marquess of Bath

longueur note -ueu-; boring interval or section of a written or performed work

Lonrho international trading group; originally London and Rhodesian Mining and Land Co.

Lord's Cricket Ground, London

Lorenz, Konrad (Zacharias) (1903–89) Austrian zoologist

losable

Los Alamitos Race Course, Los Angeles

Los Angeles, Victoria de (1923–) Spanish opera singer

Loughborough, Leicestershire, pronounced luff'-burr-a

Louis, Joe (1914–81) pronounced loo'-iss, *not* loo'-ee; born Joseph Louis Barrow; nickname The Brown Bomber; American boxer, world heavyweight champion 1937–49

Louis Roederer champagne

Louisville, Kentucky, pronounced loo'-ee-ville

Lourenço Marques former name of Maputo, the capital of Mozambique

Louvain (Fr., Eng.)/**Leuven** (Fl.), Belgium

louver (US)/**louvre** (UK) opening with slats. These are the preferred spellings, although in each country the alternative spelling is accepted

Love's Labour's Lost comedy by Shakespeare (*c.* 1595)

LPG liquefied petroleum gas

luau a Hawaiian feast

Lubbers, Rudolph (Frans Marie) (1939–) Prime Minister of The Netherlands 1982–

Lubitsch, Ernst (1892–1947) German-born film director

lubricious (UK, alt. US)/**lubricous** (US, alt. UK)

Lubyanka Moscow prison

Lucretius, (Titus Lucretius Carus) (*c.* 99–55 BC) Roman poet and philosopher

Luddite (cap.) note -dd-. workers opposed to progress, reputedly derived from Ned Ludd, an 18th-century figure, and has no connection with the mythical British monarch King Lud

Ludgvan, Cornwall, pronounced lud'-jun

ludo (UK), **Parcheesi** (US)

Ludwigshafen, Germany

Lufthansa German airline

Luftwaffe German air force

luge type of sledge

luminesce, luminescence

lumpenproletariat bottom of the working class

Lumumba, Patrice (Hémery) (1925–61) first Prime Minister of the independent Congo (now Zaïre) 1960–61

Lusitania Cunard liner sunk off Ireland by the Germans 7 May 1915

Luxembourg/Luxemburg, Grand Duchy of/Grand-Duché de Luxembourg (Fr.)/**Gross-Herzogtum Luxemburg** (Ger.)

Luxemburg, Rosa (1871–1919) Polish-born German socialist

lux mundi (Lat.) light of the world

luxuriant, luxurious Luxuriant means profuse growth or ornate; luxurious means sumptuous or expensive

Lyly, John (*c.* 1555–1606) English playwright and novelist

Lymington, Hampshire, pronounced limm'-ing-tun

Lympne, Kent, pronounced limm

Lysistrata comedy by Aristophanes

Lytham St Annes (no punc.), Lancashire, pronounced lith'-um

Lytton, Edward George Earle Bulwer-Lytton, Baron (1803–73) British politician, poet and playwright

M

MA postal abbr. of Massachusetts; Master of Arts

Maas (Dut.)/**Meuse** river flowing through France, Belgium and The Netherlands

Mac, **Mc**, **M'** In the UK all such words are treated as if they were spelled Mac when determining alphabetical order; thus McGuire would precede Mason. In the US the alphabetical order of the letters is followed literally, and Mason would precede McGuire

macadam type of road surface, named after John McAdam (1756–1836), a Scottish engineer

macadamia nut

macaque monkey of the genus *Macaca*

macaronic verse type of poetry in which two or more languages are mingled

MacArthur, Charles (1895–1956) American playwright and screenwriter, and father of **James MacArthur** (1937–), actor

MacArthur, Douglas (1880–1964) American general

MacArthur Foundation, John D. and Catherine T. US charity

Macaulay, Thomas Babington, Baron (1800–59) British historian, essayist and politician

Maccabees Jewish dynasty of second and first centuries BC

McCarran International Airport, Las Vegas, Nevada

McCarthy, Eugene (Joseph) (1916–) American politician

McCarthy, Joseph (Raymond) (1909–57) US senator notorious for campaign against alleged Communists during Congressional hearings in 1950s

McCarthy, Kevin (1914–) American film actor
McCarthy, Mary (Therese) (1912–89) American novelist
Macarthys Pharmaceuticals (no apos.) UK drugs company
McClellan, George B(rinton) (1826–85) American general and politician
MacCorkindale, Simon (1952–) British actor
MacCormac, Richard (1938–) British architect
McCormick Place convention centre in Chicago
McCowen, Alec (1925–) British actor
McCrea, Joel (1905–90) American actor
McCullers, Carson (1917–67) American novelist and playwright
MacDonald, (James) Ramsay (1866–1938) British Prime Minister 1924, 1929–35
Macdonald, Sir John Alexander (1815–91) Canadian Prime Minister 1867–73, 1878–91
Macdonald, Ross pen name of Kenneth Millar (1915–), American author of detective fiction
McDonald's (apos.) fast-food chain
McDonnell Douglas aircraft manufacturer
Macdonnell Ranges, Northern Territory, Australia
McDowall, Roddy (1928–) British-born American actor
McEnroe, John (Patrick) (1959–) American tennis player
McEwan, Geraldine (1932–) British actress
Macgillicuddy's Reeks mountain range in County Kerry, Ireland
McGillis, Kelly (1958–) American movie actress
McGill University, Montreal
McGonagall, William (1830–1902) Scottish poet known for his bad verse
McGoohan, Patrick (1928–) American actor
McGovern, George (1922–) American politician
MacGraw, Ali (1938–) American actress
McGraw-Hill Publishing US publisher
MacGregor Scottish clan
MacGregor, Sir Ian (1912–) British-born American business executive

McGuigan, Barry (1961–) Irish boxer

Machiavelli, Niccolò di Bernardo dei (1469–1527) Florentine statesman and political theorist, best known for *Il Principe* (The Prince), 1513

Mach number ratio of the speed of an object to the speed of sound in the medium (usually air) through which the object is travelling: e.g. an aircraft travelling at twice the speed of sound is said to be going at Mach 2; named after Ernst Mach (1836–1916), an Austrian physicist

Machu Picchu, Peru, pronounced mah'-choo peek'-choo; site of ancient Incan city

McIntosh a variety of red apple; *see also* mackintosh

Macintosh computer

McKenna, Siobhan (1923–) Irish actress

McKenna, Virginia (1931–) British actress

Mackenzie, Sir (Edward Montague) Compton (1883–1972) British writer

MacKenzie, Kelvin (Calder) (1947–) British journalist and newspaper executive

McKern, Leo (Reginald) (1920–) British actor

Mackinac Island and **Straits of Mackinac**, but **Mackinaw City**, Michigan. All are pronounced mack'-in-aw; products associated with the area are spelled -aw: Mackinaw blanket, Mackinaw boat and the type of woollen coat called a mackinaw (no cap.)

McKinley, Mount, Alaska; highest peak in North America (20,320 ft/6,194 m)

McKinley, William (1843–1901) US President 1897–1901

mackintosh abbr. mac; common UK term for a raincoat, named after Charles Macintosh (1766–1843), Scottish chemist who patented a method for waterproofing cloth; *see also* McIntosh

Mackintosh, Charles Rennie (1868–1928) British architect, artist and designer

MacLaine, Shirley (1934–) born Shirley MacLean Beaty; American actress

MacLean, Alistair (1922–87) British writer of adventure novels

McLean, Virginia, greater Washington, DC, pronounced muk-lane'

Maclean's Canadian weekly news magazine

MacLehose & Sons Glasgow printers

MacLeish, Archibald (1892–1982) American poet

Macleod, Lake, Western Australia

Macmillan, Sir (Maurice) Harold, Earl of Stockton (1894–1986) British Prime Minister 1957–63

MacMurray, Fred (1907–91) American actor

MacNee, Patrick (1922–) British actor

MacNelly, Jeff(rey Kenneth) (1947–) American political cartoonist

MacNeice, Louis (1907–63) British poet and writer

Mâcon, France *not* -ç-; city and wine

Macon, Georgia

McShane, Ian (1942–) British actor

Macy's formally, R. H. Macy & Co; department store in New York

Madagascar formerly the Malagasy Republic; island republic off southeast coast of Africa; capital Antananarivo

mademoiselle *not* madam-; *pl.* **mesdemoiselles**; as titles, abbr. Mlle, Mlles

Madhya Pradesh Indian state

Madison Avenue generic term for the US advertising industry

Madrileño citizen of Madrid

maelstrom

Maeterlinck, Count Maurice (1862–1949) Belgian poet and dramatist; Nobel Prize for Literature 1911

Mafeking/Mafikeng The first is the historical spelling for the South African town, now in Bophuthatswana, made famous by a siege withstood by British soldiers during the Boer War; the second is the current spelling

Mafioso a member of the Mafia; *pl.* **Mafiosi**

Magdalen College, Oxford; **Magdalene College**, Cambridge Both are pronounced maudlin, but **Magdalen**, Norfolk, is pronounced as spelled. The New Testament figure is **Mary Magdalene**

Magellan, Ferdinand/Maghalhães, Fernão de (Port.) (*c.* 1480–1521) Portuguese explorer, led first expedition that circumnavigated the globe, though he was killed *en route*

Maggiore, Lake, Italy

Maginot Line line of defensive fortifications across northeastern France, breached by Germany in 1940

Magna Carta/Charta charter of rights signed by King John at Runnymede, Surrey, in 1215

magnum opus, ***opus magnum*** (Lat.) The first is an author's masterpiece; the second, a great work.

Magritte, René (Françoise Ghislain) (1898–1967) Belgian surrealist painter

Mahabharata Indian epic

maharaja, **maharanee** Indian prince, princess

Mahathir bin Mohamad, Dr (1925–) Prime Minister of Malaysia 1981–

Mahfouz, Naguib (1912–) Egyptian novelist; Nobel Prize for Literature 1988

mah-jong/mahjong/mah jongg Chinese game played with tiles

Mahler, Gustav (1860–1911) Austrian composer

mahogany

Mahomet use Mohammed (pref. US)/Muhammad (pref. UK) (*c.* 570–632), the founder of Islam

Maillol, Aristide (Joseph Bonaventure) (1861–1944) French sculptor

maître d'hôtel (Fr.) hotel manager or headwaiter; *pl.* ***maîtres d'hôtel***

Majlis Parliament of Iran

Makhachkala formerly Petrovsk; capital of Dagestan, Russia

Malabo formerly Santa Isabel; capital of Equatorial Guinea

Malagasy Republic former name of Madagascar

malarkey

Malawi formerly Nyasaland; African republic; capital Lilongwe

mal de mer (Fr.) seasickness

Maldives island republic in the Indian Ocean; capital Malé

maleficence, **malfeasance** Maleficence means propensity for causing hurt or harm, and is a back-formation from malefic. Malfeasance is a legal term describing wrongdoing

Malev national airline of Hungary

Mali formerly French Sudan; republic in western Africa; capital Bamako

Mallarmé, Stephane (1842–98) French poet

malleable pronounced mal'-ee-able

Mallorca (Sp.)/**Majorca**

malmsey a sweet wine; *pl.* **malmseys**

malodorous *not* -odour-

Malory, Sir Thomas (d. 1471) shadowy figure who was the author, or compiler, of *Le Morte d'Arthur*

Malvinas (Sp.)/**Falkland Islands**

Mamaroneck, New York

Mammon (cap.) wealth regarded as an object of worship

manacle *not* -icle; shackle

manageable, manageability

Managua capital of Nicaragua

Manassas, Virginia town near the site of two battles in the American Civil War, called Battles of Bull Run in the North and Battles of Manassas in the South

manatee the sea-cow, an aquatic mammal

Manaus, Brazil, formerly Manáos

Mancunian of or from Manchester

Mandalay, Myanmar

mandamus writ commanding a particular thing be done or public duty performed, handed down from a higher court to lower one or to a person or government office, respectively

mandatory, mandatary The first means compulsory; the second is a rarer word, which applies to one holding a mandate

Mandlikova, Hana (1962–   ) Czech tennis player

Manet, Édouard (1832–83) French artist

mango *pl.* **mangoes/mangos**

manhattan (no cap.) a cocktail

Manhattan *not* -en; island borough at the heart of New York City

Manhattan Project code name for the project to build the first atomic bomb

manifesto *pl.* **manifestoes** (US)/**manifestos** (UK)

manikin an anatomical model of the human body; *see also* mannequin

Manila capital of the Philippines

manila paper (no cap.) *not* -illa; a brown paper used for envelopes, wrapping paper, etc.

Mankiewicz, Joseph L(eo) (1909–) American screenwriter, film director and producer; father of **Tom Mankiewicz** (1942–), also a screenwriter

mannequin a person who models clothes; a dummy for displaying clothes; *see also* manikin

manner born, to the *not* manor; *Hamlet* (I, iv, 14)

Mannesmann Kienzle GmbH German manufacturing company

manoeuvre, **manoeuvrable**, **manoeuvrability** (UK)/**maneuver**, **maneuverable**, **maneuverability** (US)

manqué (Fr.) unsuccessful, would-be; always follows the noun it modifies

Mantegna, Andrea (1431–1506) Italian painter

mantel, **mantle** The first is a shelf over a fireplace; the second a cloak or cover

Manufacturers Hanover Corporation (no apos.) US bank

mao tai a strong Chinese liquor

Mao Tse-tung/Mao Zedong (Pinyin) (1893–1976) founder and Chairman of the People's Republic of China 1949–59, and Chairman of the Chinese Communist Party 1935–76

Mapplethorpe, Robert (1947–89) American photographer

Maputo formerly Lourenço Marques; capital of Mozambique

Maquis French resistance during World War II

Maracaibo city and lake in Venezuela

maraschino type of cherry and liqueur

Marat Sade in full: *The Persecution and Assassination of Marat as Performed by the Inmates of the Asylum of Charenton under the Direction of the Marquis de Sade*; play by Peter Weiss (1964)

Marazion, Cornwall

March, Fredric (1897–1975) *not* Frederick; born Frederick McIntyre Bickel; American actor

marchioness wife or widow of a marquis, or woman holding the title of marquess

Marconi, Guglielmo (1874–1937) Italian inventor of wireless telegraphy; Nobel Prize for Physics 1909.

margarine *not* -ger-

margarita a cocktail

Margaux, Château- a claret

Margrethe II (1940–) Queen of Denmark 1972–

Maria de' Medici (It.)/**Marie de Médicis** (Fr.) (1573–1642) Italian-born wife and Queen Consort of Henry IV of France

Marianas Trench site in Pacific Ocean where greatest depth (36,220 ft/11,040 m) has been measured. The nearby island chain is called either the Mariana (*not* -s) Islands or the Marianas

Marie Antoinette (Josèphe Jeanne) (1755–93) Austrian-born wife of Louis XVI and Queen of France (1774–93)

Marie Claire magazine

Marienbad (Ger.)/**Marianske Lazne** (Czech) Czech spa

Marignane Airport, Marseille

marionette/***marionnette*** (Fr.)

markka unit of Finnish currency

Marks & Spencer British retail group

Marlboro cigarettes *not* -borough

Marlborough, Wiltshire, England, pronounced 'Maulbruh'

Marlowe, Christopher (1564–93) English playwright

Marmara, Sea of

marmoset monkey of Central and South America

marquee large tent used for entertaining (UK); rooflike projection over an entrance, as on the front of a cinema or theatre (US)

Marrakesh, Morocco

Marriage-à-la-Mode note hyphens; a play by John Dryden (1672)

Marriott US hotels group

Marseille (Fr.)/**Marseilles** seaport in southern France. The French national anthem is **'La Marseillaise'**.

marshal *not* -all

Marshall Islands island state in the Pacific Ocean; capital Majuro

Marshalsea Prison, Southwark, London; debtors' prison, closed in the 19th century

Martial, properly Marcus Valerius Martialis (*c.* 40–*c.* 104) Roman poet and epigrammatist

Martin-in-the-Fields, St *not* Martin's; London church overlooking Trafalgar Square

Marubeni Corporation Japanese trading company

Marunouchi Tokyo financial district

Marylebone pronounced marry-luh-bun; road and district in London

Masaccio Tommaso Guidi/di Giovanni (1401–28), Italian painter

Masaryk, Thomas/Tomáš (Garrigue) (1850–1937) Czech statesman, first President of Czechoslovak Republic 1918–35, and father of **Jan Masaryk** (1886–1948), Czech diplomat, Foreign Minister 1940–48

Mascagni, Pietro (1863–1945) Italian composer

Masefield, John (1878–1967) English poet and novelist

Maserati Italian sports car

Mason-Dixon line the boundary line between the states of Maryland and Pennsylvania, surveyed by Charles Mason and Jeremiah Dixon in 1763–7, regarded as the dividing line between the North and the South

Massachusetts capital Boston; postal abbr. MA; traditional abbr. Mass.

Massapequa, **Massapequa Park**, **East Massapequa**, etc., New York state

masseur (masc.), **masseuse** (fem.)

masterful, **masterly** The first means imperious, domineering; the second adroit, expert

Matabeleland region of Zimbabwe

Mather, Cotton (1662–1728) American Puritan theologian

Matisse, Henri (Émile Benoît) (1869–1954) French artist

Mato Grosso formerly Matto Grosso; area of Brazil, now

forming two states: Mato Grosso, capital Cuiabá; Mato Grosso do Sul, capital Campo Grande

Matsuyama, Japan

Matthau, Walter (1920–) American actor

Maudsley Hospital, London *not* Maudes-

Maugham, W(illiam) Somerset (1874–1965) English author

Maundy Thursday *not* Maunday; the day before Good Friday

Maupassant, (Henri René Albert) Guy de (1850–93) French writer of short stories and novels

Mauretania ancient African country and name of two Cunard ships

Mauritania formally, Islamic Republic of Mauritania/République Islamique de Mauritanie (Fr.); capital Nouakchott

mausoleum

mauvaise honte (Fr.) needless embarrassment or shame

mauvais quart d'heure (Fr.) literally, 'a bad quarter-hour'; figuratively, a painful or dreaded experience of short duration

Maxwell Davies, Sir Peter (1934–) English composer

Mayakovski, Vladimir Vladimirovich (1893–1930) Russian poet

Mayall, Rik (1958–) British comedian

May Fair Hotel, London, but the district of London is **Mayfair**

mayonnaise

Mazarin, Jules, originally **Giulio Mazarini** (1602–61) Italian-born French prelate and statesman

Mazatlán, Mexico

mazel tov (Yidd.) good luck

Mazowiecki, Tadeusz (1927–) pronounced tah-day'-oosh mah-zho-vyet'-ski; Polish lawyer and politician, Prime Minister 1989–90

mazurka Polish dance

Mazzini, Giuseppe (1805–72) Italian republican and revolutionary

Mbabane capital of Swaziland

MD managing director (UK); postal abbr. of Maryland; *Medicinae Doctor* (Doctor of Medicine)

Md Maryland, mendelevium

ME postal abbr. of Maine; Marine Engineer; Mechanical Engineer; Middle English; Military Engineer; Mining Engineer; Most Excellent; myalgic encephalomyelitis, a type of chronic flu

ME (US)/**M.Ed** (UK) Master of Education

mea culpa (Lat.) my fault

mealy-mouthed

mean, median, midrange, mode In British usage, the mean is the sum of all the numbers in a sample divided by the number of numbers; it has the same meaning as average. The median is the middle number of an array of numbers arranged in order of magnitude. The midrange is the middle point between the smallest and largest numbers. And the mode is the most commonly occurring number in a sample of numbers. It should be noted that many American dictionaries give definitions that conflict with the above. Above all, it should be remembered that terms like mean and median are at best vaguely understood by most readers and should therefore be used sparingly in general writing.

measurable *not* - eable

Meccano (cap.) brand of bolt-together toy

Mecklenburg former state in Germany

Mecklenburgh Square, London

Medal of Honor, *not* Congressional Medal of Honor, is the correct name for the highest US military decoration

medallist

Medellín, Colombia

media is plural; the singular is **medium.** Television is a medium; newspapers and television are media. However, mediums is the correct plural for describing spiritualists

mediator

Medicaid (US) federal health-care insurance for the poor

Medicare (US) federal health-care insurance for the elderly

Medici leading family of Renaissance Florence, whose more noted members were **Cosimo de' Medici** (1389–1464), called Cosimo the Elder; **Lorenzo de' Medici** (1449–92), called Lorenzo the Magnificent; **Giovanni de' Medici** (1475–1521), later Pope Leo X; **Giulio de' Medici** (1478–1534), later Pope

Clement VII; the French spelling is normally used for **Catherine de Médicis** (1519–89), wife of Henry II of France; and **Marie de Médicis** (1573–1642), wife of Henry IV of France

medieval

mediocre

Meech Lake Accord (1987) Canadian constitutional agreement giving special recognition to Quebec as a 'distinct society' within Canada

Meekatharra, Western Australia

meerschaum soft, white clay-like mineral, used to make pipe bowls

meet, **mete** The first means suitable; the second to allot; thus one metes out punishment, but a fitting punishment is meet

mega- prefix meaning a million, or very large

megalomania *not* meglo-

Meigs Field formally, Merril (*not* -ll) C. Meigs Field, a Chicago airport

Meiji reign of the Emperor Mutsuhito (1867–1912), marking Japan's emergence as a modern industrial state

mein Herr, ***meine Dame*** (Ger.) form of address: sir, lady; *pl.* ***meine Herren***, ***meine Damen***

Meir, Golda (1898–1978) born Goldie Mabovich, later Goldie Myerson; Israeli Prime Minister 1969–74

Meissen porcelain porcelain made in German city of the same name

melamine (no cap.) type of plastic

Melanchthon, Philipp/Philip (1497–1560) born Philipp Schwarzerd; German professor of Greek (Melanchthon is Greek trans. of Schwarzerd), theologian, Luther's fellow worker and a leader of the Reformation

mêlée/melee (alt. US)

mellifluous sounding sweet

memento, *pl.* **mementos/mementoes**

memorabilia note this is a plural

Memorial Day US holiday commemorating the war dead, held on the last Monday in May; originally, and sometimes still, called Decoration Day

ménage à trois (Fr.) sexual relationship between three people living together, usually a married couple and the lover of one of them

menagerie

MENCAP formally, the Royal Society for Mentally Handicapped Adults and Children (UK charity)

Mencken, H(enry) L(ouis) (1880–1956) American writer, critic and editor

Mendel, Gregor Johann (1822–84) Austrian botanist whose work became the basis of modern genetics

Mendelssohn(-Bartholdy), (Jakob Ludwig) Felix (1809–47) German composer

Mendès-France, Pierre (1907–82) French Prime Minister 1954–5

Menem, Carlos (Saul) (1935–) President of Argentina 1989–

meningitis

Menninger Clinic, **Menninger Foundation**, Topeka, Kansas; large psychiatric hospital and training centre

menorah a seven-branched candelabrum used in Jewish worship

Menorca (Sp.)/**Minorca**

Menotti, Gian-Carlo (1911–) Italian-born American composer

Menuhin, Yehudi (1916–) American-born British violinist

meow (US)/**miaow** (UK)

MEP Member of the European Parliament

Mephistophelean/Mephistophelian evil; after Mephistopheles, the devil to whom Faust sold his soul

Mercalli scale measures intensity of earthquakes by subjective indication of damage at any one point

Mercedes-Benz (hyphen)

Mercia Anglo-Saxon kingdom roughly corresponding in area to the modern Midlands

meretricious vulgar, insincere; not to be confused with meritorious

meringue egg whites and sugar beaten until stiff, then baked

merino, *pl.* **merinos** sheep

meritocracy system of government based on merit

meritorious having merit, deserving praise or reward

Merrion Square, Dublin

Merthyr Tydfil, Mid Glamorgan, Wales

mesmerize

Messaggero, Il Italian newspaper

Messerschmitt, Willy (Wilhelm) (1898–1978) note -tt; German designer and producer of aircraft

Messiaen, Olivier (1908–92) French composer and organist, pronounced 'Messyon'

metamorphose (vb), **metamorphosis** (noun), *pl.* **metamorphoses**

metaphor, simile Both are figures of speech in which two things are compared. A simile likens one thing to another, dissimilar one: 'He ran like the wind', 'She took to racing as a duck takes to water'. A metaphor acts as if the two compared things are identical and substitutes one for the other, thus comparing the beginning of time to the beginning of a day produces the metaphor 'the dawn of time'

metathesis the transposition of sounds or letters in a word or between words; the latter commonly being called spoonerisms

mete, meet The first means to allot; the second suitable; thus one metes out punishment, but a fitting punishment is meet.

meteor, meteorite, meteoroid Meteors are the trails of light made by meteoroids – objects floating in space – falling through Earth's atmosphere. Meteorites are meteoroids that have survived the fall to Earth.

meter a device for measuring

meter (US)/**metre** (UK) poetic and musical rhythm; metric unit of length equivalent to 39.37 in., 1.1 yd

meticulous Several usage books, though fewer and fewer dictionaries, insist that the word does not mean merely very careful, but rather excessively so. Unless you mean to convey a pejorative tone, it is usually better to use scrupulous, careful or some other synonym

metonymy figure of speech in which a thing is described in terms of one of its attributes, as in calling the monarchy 'the crown'

metre (UK)/**meter** (US) metric unit of length equivalent to 39.37 in., 1.1 yd; poetic and musical rhythm

metric units *see* Appendix for list of main prefixes used with metric measurements

Metro-Goldwyn-Mayer abbr. MGM; Hollywood film studio, now part of MGM/UA Communications Company

metronome instrument for marking time

mettle courage or spirit

Meuse/Maas (Dut.) river in France, Belgium and The Netherlands

mezzanine

Mezzogiorno the southern, poorer half of Italy

mezzotint a method of engraving, and the engraving so produced

MGM Metro-Goldwyn-Mayer

MI postal abbr. of Michigan; Military Intelligence

miaow (UK)/**meow** (US)

Mich. Michaelmas; Michigan

Michaelmas abbr. Mich.; feast of St Michael, 29 September

Michelangelo (di Lodovico Buonarroti) (1475–1564) Italian architect, sculptor, painter, poet and military engineer

Michelin formally, Groupe Michelin, French tyre group

Michigan pronounced mish'-i-gan-, *not* mitch-; US state; capital Lansing; postal abbr. MI; traditional abbr. Mich.

mickey, take the make fun of

Mickey Finn (US) slang for a drink that has been doctored to incapacitate the drinker; sometimes shortened to mickey ('I slipped him a mickey'.)

micro- prefix meaning one-millionth, or very small

Micronesia, Federated States of comprises Kosrae, Ponape, Truk and Yap; capital Kolonia, on Ponape

Mid Glamorgan (two words, no hyphen) Welsh county

Middlesbrough, Cleveland *not* -borough

Middx. Middlesex, former English county, still used in postal addresses

Midlothian former Scottish county

Midsomer Norton, Avon

Midwest (one word), **Middle West** (two words) hazily defined area of the US generally taken to include Ohio, Indiana, Illinois, Iowa, Wisconsin, Missouri, Minnesota and Michigan

Mies van der Rohe, Ludwig (1886–1969) German-born US architect

mijnheer (Dut.)/**mynheer** sir; cap. when placed before a name as form of address

mile a unit of linear measurement equivalent to 5,280 ft, 1,760 yards, 1,609.34 metres; *see* Appendix for table of conversion to kilometres

mileage *not* milage

miles gloriosus (Lat.) *not* -sis; pronounced meel'-us glore-ee-oh'-sus; a braggart, particularly a braggart soldier

Milhaud, Darius (1892–1974) French composer

milieu environment

militate, mitigate The first means to act against; the second to soften or make more endurable

Milius, John (Frederick) (1944–) American film writer and director

Millais, Sir John Everett (1829–96) British painter

Millay, Edna St Vincent (1892–1950) American poet

millennium -ll-, -nn-; 1,000 years; *pl.* **millenniums** (pref.)/ **millennia** (alt.); note that adjs. millenary and millenarian have just one *n*

millepede (UK)/**millipede** (US)

Millet, Jean-François (1814–75) French painter

milli- prefix meaning one-thousandth

milliard (UK) seldom used term meaning 1,000 million, now replaced by billion

Milošević, Slobodan President of Serbia (1989–)

Milton Keynes, Buckinghamshire, pronounced keenz

Milwaukee, Wisconsin

Mindanao island in the Philippines

Mindszenty, József, Cardinal (1892–1975) Roman Catholic primate of Hungary, long opposed to Communist regime

Minneapolis largest city in Minnesota; twin city of St Paul, the state capital

Minnesota postal abbr. MN; traditional abbr. Minn.
Minorca/Menorca (Sp.) Balearic Islands, Spain
Minos in Greek mythology, a son of Zeus and Europa, and king of Crete
Minotaur in Greek mythology, a figure that is half man and half bull
Minsk capital of Belarus
minuscule *not* mini-
minutia a detail; *pl.* **minutiae**
mirabile dictu (Lat.) wonderful to relate
MIRAS (UK) pronounced my'-rus; mortgage interest relief at source
Miricioiu, Nelly (1952–) Romanian opera singer
MIRV multiple independently targeted re-entry vehicle, a type of ballistic missile
miscellaneous
mischievous *not* -ious
mise-en-scène stage or film scenery; or general setting of an event
Misérables, Les novel by Victor Hugo (1862)
mishandle
mishit
misogamist, **misogynist** The first, pronounced with a hard *g* sound, hates marriage; the second, pronounced with a *j* sound, hates women
misshape, **misshapen**
Mississauga suburb of Toronto
Mississippi river and state; postal abbr. is MS; traditional abbr. is Miss.
Missolonghi, Greece
misspell
misspend
misstate
misstep
mistakable
mistime
mistletoe

mistral cold, unpleasant wind in France

MIT Massachusetts Institute of Technology

mitigate, militate The first means to soften or make more endurable; the second to act against

Mitsukoshi Japanese department store chain

Mitterrand, François (Maurice Marie) (1916–) President of France 1981–

Miyazawa, Kiichi (1919–) Prime Minister of Japan 1991–93

mizen, mizen-mast (UK)/**mizzen, mizzenmast** (US)

Mlle, Mlles Mademoiselle, Mesdemoiselles

MLR (UK) minimum lending rate; now called base rate

Mme, Mmes Madame, Mesdames

MN Merchant Navy (UK); postal abbr. of Minnesota

Mnemosyne Greek goddess of memory

MO Medical Officer; postal abbr. of Missouri

Mo molybdenum

Mo. Missouri

Möbius strip (or **band**) a piece of paper or other material twisted in such a way as to form a continuous surface; named after its discoverer, German mathematician August Möbius (1790–1868)

Mobutu Sésé Seko (1930–) born Joseph Désiré Mobuto; President of Zaïre 1965–

Moby-Dick (hyphen) a novel by Herman Melville (1851)

moccasin

modem modulator/demodulator, a device that converts digital data into analogue electrical signals, which can then be sent down telephone lines

modicum *pl.* **modicums**

Modigliani, Amedeo (1884–1920) Italian artist

modus operandi (Lat.) the way of doing something

Mogadishu capital of Somalia

Mohammed (US, alt. UK) /**Muhammad** (UK, alt. US) (*c.* 570–632) the founder of Islam

Mohave North American Indian people; but see Mojave

Mohawk North American Indian people

Mohocks gang of young thugs in 18th-century London

Moi, Daniel arap (not cap.) (1924–) President of Kenya 1978–

Mojave/Mohave (alt.) **Desert**, California, pronounced moe-hah'-vee

mold (US)/**mould** (UK)

Moldova/Moldavia former republic of Soviet Union, now an independent state, capital Kishinev

Molière (1622–73) born Jean-Baptiste Poquelin; French playwright

molybdenum symbol Mo

Molyneaux, James (Henry) (1920–) Northern Ireland politician

Mombasa seaport in Kenya

Mona Lisa painting by Leonardo da Vinci, also called *La Gioconda*

monarchs *see* Appendix for list of kings and queens of England

Mönchen-Gladbach, Germany

Mondrian, Piet (1872–1944) born Pieter Cornelis Mondriaan; Dutch abstract painter

Monégasque from or of Monaco

Monet, Claude (1840–1926) French Impressionist painter

monetary units *see* Appendix for list of currencies of selected countries

mongolism congenital abnormality, properly called Down's syndrome

mongoose, *pl.* **mongooses**

moniker a name or nickname

Monmouth's Rebellion (1685) challenge to the monarchy of the Catholic James II of England led by the Protestant Duke of Monmouth, which ended with the latter's defeat at Sedgemoor

Monnet, Jean (1888–1979) French statesman

Monongahela river in West Virginia and Pennsylvania

mononucleosis (US), **glandular fever** (UK)

Monopolies Commission (UK) formally, the Monopolies and Mergers Commission

Monroe Doctrine policy stated by US President James Monroe in 1823 warning European powers not to interfere in the politics of the Americas

Monrovia capital of Liberia

Monserrat, Spain, but **Montserrat**, Leeward Islands

monsieur (Fr.) sir; cap. when used as a form of address; abbr. M.; *pl.* **messieurs**, abbr. MM.

Mont. Montana

Montagnard (Fr.) literally, 'mountain dweller'; name given to radical faction during French Revolution because of the elevated position of their seats in the National Convention

Montaigne, Michel (Eyquem) de (1533–92) French philosopher and essayist

Montecatini Italian spa

Monterey, California, but **Monterrey**, Nuevo León state, Mexico

Montesquieu, Charles Louis de Secondat, **Baron de la Brède et de** (1689–1755) French philosopher and jurist

Montessori system of teaching developed by Maria Montessori (1870–1952), Italian doctor and educator

Monteverdi, Claudio Giovanni Antonio (1567–1643) Italian composer

Montevideo capital of Uruguay

Montgomery (of Alamein), Bernard Law, Viscount (1887–1976) British field marshal

Montparnasse, Paris

Montpelier capital of Vermont

Montpellier, France

Mont-Saint-Michel, France (hyphens)

Montserrat, Leeward Islands, but **Monserrat**, Spain

More, Sir Thomas, also **St Thomas** (1478–1535) English statesman and author

Morgan le Fay sister of King Arthur

morganatic marriage one between noble and commoner in which the commoner and his/her descendants enjoy no privileges of inheritance

Morgenthau, Henry (1891–1967) American statesman, Secretary of the Treasury 1934–45

MORI poll Market & Opinion Research International
Morison, Samuel Eliot (1887–1976) *not* Morr-; American historian
Mormon Church officially, the Church of Jesus Christ of Latter-Day Saints
Morocco, Moroccan
Morrell, Lady Ottoline (1873–1938) English hostess
Morris, Gouverneur (1752–1816) American statesman, a signatory of the US Constitution
morris dancer (no caps.)
mortise lock
Morton, (Robert) Alastair (Newton) (1938–) South African-born British businessman
Morton Thiokol US chemicals company
Mosel (Ger.)/**Moselle** river and wine
Mosimann, Anton (1947–) Swiss-born chef
Moskva Russian for Moscow
Moslem (alt.)/**Muslim** (pref.)
Mosley, Sir Oswald (Ernald), Baronet (1896–1980) British politician, founded the British Union of Fascists (1932)
mosquito, *pl.* **mosquitoes**
Mossad Israeli secret service
Moss Side, Manchester
mot juste (Fr.) the right word
moto-cross motorcycle racing over rough terrain
MOT test (UK) annual roadworthiness test for cars
motto, *pl.* **mottoes**
mould (UK)/**mold** (US)
mountebank charlatan
Mourning Becomes Electra a play by Eugene O'Neill (1931)
moussaka
Moussorgsky/Mussorgsky, Modest Petrovich (1839–81) Russian composer
moustache (UK)/**mustache** (US) /**mustachio** (UK, US)
mousy *not* -ey
mouthy
movable/moveable (UK legal refs.)

Mozambique, but **Mozambicans**
mozzarella Italian cheese
MS manuscript; *pl.* **MSS**
MS Master of Science; Master of Surgery; *memoriae sacrum* (sacred to the memory of); postal abbr. of Mississippi; multiple sclerosis
MT postal abbr. of Montana
Mubarak, (Muhammad) Hosni (Said) (1928–) Egyptian President 1981–
mucus (noun), **mucous** (adj.)
Muenster/Munster Alsatian cheese
muesli
muezzin in Islam, an official who calls the faithful to prayer
mufti plain clothes worn by a person who usually wears a uniform
Mugabe, Robert (Gabriel) (1924–) Prime Minister of Zimbabwe 1980– , and President 1987–
Muhammad (UK, alt. US)/**Mohammed** (US, alt. UK) (*c.* 570–632) the founder of Islam
Muharraq Airport, Bahrain
Mühlhausen, Germany
mujahidin/mujahedin/mujahedeen guerrilla fighters in Islamic countries
Mukhabarat Iraqi secret police
mukluk a type of boot
mulatto, *pl.* **mulattos**
Mulhouse, France, pronounced moo-looz'
mullah a Muslim teacher of Islamic theology, a learned man
mulligatawny soup
Munch, Edvard (1863–1944) Norwegian artist
Mundt, Theodor (1808–61) German writer
Munro, H(ector) H(ugh) (1870–1916) British writer, principally of short stories, under the pen name Saki
Munster province of Ireland comprising six counties: Clare, Cork, Kerry, Limerick, Tipperary and Waterford; *see also* Muenster
Münster city in Germany; *see also* Muenster

Murchison Falls, Uganda; **Murchison River,** Australia

Murfreesboro, Battle of (1863) Union victory in US Civil War; sometimes called the Battle of Stones River

murmur *not* -mer

Murphy's Law: if anything can go wrong, it will

Murrumbidgee River, New South Wales, Australia

Murry, John Middleton (1889–1957) English critic and writer

Muscovite *not* Mos-; citizen of Moscow

Muses the nine daughters of Zeus and Mnemosyne who presided over the arts: Calliope (eloquence and epic poetry), Clio (History), Erato (elegiac poetry), Euterpe (music), Melpomene (tragedy), Polyhymnia (lyric poetry), Terpsichore (dancing), Thalia (comedy), and Urania (astronomy)

'Music hath charms to soothe a savage breast' *not* beast; from Congreve's play *The Mourning Bride* (1697)

Muslim (pref.)/**Moslem** (alt.)

Mussadeq/Mussadegh/Mussaddiq, Muhammad (1881–1967) Iranian Prime Minister 1951–3

Mussolini, Benito (Amilcare Andrea) (1883–1945) Italian Prime Minister 1922–43 and dictator

Mussorgsky/Moussorgsky, Modest Petrovich (1839–81) Russian composer

mustache (US)/**moustache** (UK) /**mustachio** (UK, US)

mutable, **mutability**, **mutableness**

mutatis mutandis (Lat.) with the necessary changes

muu-muu loose-fitting Hawaiian dress

Muzak (cap.) anodyne piped music

MW megawatt

mW milliwatt

Mwinyi, Ali Hassan (1925–) President of Tanzania 1985–

myalgic encephalomyelitis abbr. ME, a type of chronic flu

Myanmar Asian state, formerly called Burma

Mycenaean of the ancient Greek city of Mycenae or the Bronze Age civilization, of which Mycenae was an important site

Myddleton Square, London

My Lai, Vietnam, site of notorious massacre of villagers by US troops (1968)

mynheer/mijnheer (Dut.) mister, sir; cap. when placed before a name

myrrh

myxomatosis viral disease of rabbits

NAACP National Association for the Advancement of Colored People (US civil rights organization)

NAAFI (UK) Navy, Army, and Air Force Institutes

NACODS (UK) National Association of Colliery Overmen, Deputies and Shot-Firers

Nagorno-Karabakh Armenian-dominated enclave in former Soviet republic of Azerbaijan

Naipul, V(idiadhar) S(urajprasad) (1932–) Trinidad-born English writer

naïve, **naïvety** (UK, alt. US)/**naive**, **naivety** (US, alt. UK)

Nakasone, Yasuhiro (1918–) Prime Minister of Japan 1982–8

NALGO (UK) National and Local Government Officers' Association

namby-pamby

namable (US)/**nameable** (UK, alt. US)

Namen (Fl.)/**Namur** Belgian city

nano- prefix meaning one-billionth

Nantes, Edict of (1598) a bill of rights for French Protestants (Huguenots) issued by Henry IV. Its revocation by Louis XIV in 1685 led many thousands of Huguenots to flee the country

naphtha pronounced naff-tha, *not* nap-tha

Napoleon I (1769–1821) born Napoleon Bonaparte; Emperor of the French (1804–15)

narcissism excessive interest in oneself

narcissus bulbous flowering plant of the lily family; *pl.* **narcissi**/**narcissuses**

Narragansett Bay, Rhode Island

NASA (US) National Aeronautics and Space Administration

nasal *not* -el; of the nose

NASDAQ (US) National Association of Securities Dealers Automated Quotations

Nash/Nashe, Thomas (1567–1601) English dramatist

Nasser, Gamal Abdel (1918–70) Egyptian Prime Minister 1954–6 and President 1956–70

nasturtium

NAS-UWT National Association of Schoolmasters and Union of Women Teachers

Natchez, Mississippi

Nateley Scures, Hampshire, pronounced nate'-lee skew'-ers

National Coal Board (UK) former name of British Coal

National Institutes of Health, Bethesda, Maryland; note plural

National Westminister Bank, but **NatWest** (UK)

NATO North Atlantic Treaty Organization; members are Belgium, Canada, Denmark, France, Germany, Greece, Iceland, Italy, Luxembourg, The Netherlands, Norway, Portugal, Spain, Turkey, the UK and the US

NATSOPA (UK) National Society of Operative Printers, Graphical and Media Personnel; former name of trade union that merged with Sogat to become Sogat '82

Natty Bumppo note -pp-; main character in James Fenimore Cooper's *Leatherstocking Tales*

Natural History Museum, London, formally British Museum (Natural History)

naught, nought The first means nothing, as in 'His efforts came to naught'; the second is the figure zero (0); *see also* noughts and crosses

nauseate, nauseous Nauseate is a verb meaning to produce, or suffer, nausea. Nauseous is an adjective describing something that causes nausea. Therefore it is wrong to say, 'I feel nauseous'; you feel nauseated.

Navajo (pref.)/**Navaho** (alt.) North American Indian people

naval, navel The first pertains to ships; the second to belly buttons or any central point

navigable

Navistar US vehicle manufacturer, formerly called International Harvester

Nazarbayev, Nursultan President of Kazakhstan 1991–

Nazism *not* -ii-

n.b. (US)/**NB** (UK) *nota bene* (Lat.) note well

NBA (UK) Net Book Agreement

NBC (US) National Broadcasting Company, a television and radio network, not a station

NC postal and traditional abbr. of North Carolina

NCB *see* National Coal Board

NCCL (UK) National Council for Civil Liberties, now known as Liberty

ND postal abbr. of North Dakota; traditional abbr. is **N. Dak.**

N'djaména/Ndjamena formerly Fort Lamy; capital of Chad

'Ndrangheta, organized crime group in Calabria, Italy

NE postal abbr. of Nebraska; traditional abbr. is **Neb.**

Neagh, **Lough**, pronounced nay; largest lake in British Isles (153 sq miles/396 sq km), in Northern Ireland

neat's-foot oil

Nebuchadnezzar (*c.* 625–561 BC) King of Babylon (605–561 BC)

nebuchadnezzar an exceptionally large bottle of champagne, equivalent to 20 normal bottles

nebula, *pl.* **nebulae/nebulas**

necessary, necessity

NEDC (UK) National Economic Development Council, commonly called Neddy

nefarious

negligé (UK)/**negligee** (US)

negligible

Negretti & Zambra UK manufacturer of musical instruments

Nehemiah Jewish leader in fifth century BC after whom an Old Testament book is named

Nehru, Jawaharlal, Pandit (1889–1964) Indian Prime Minister 1947–64

neighbor (US)/**neighbour** (UK)

Neiman-Marcus pronounced nee'-man; US department store group

neologism a newly coined word

nephritis inflammation of the kidneys

ne plus ultra (Lat.) the acme, perfection

Neptune eighth planet from the Sun; Roman god of the sea, identified with the Greek god Poseidon

nerve-racking *not* wracking

Nervi, Pier Luigi (1891–1979) Italian architect

Nesbit, E(dith) (1858–1924) English writer

n'est-ce-pas? (Fr.) pronounced ness-pah'; is that not so?

Netherlands, The (cap.) The capital is Amsterdam, but the seat of government is The Hague

netsuke Japanese carved ornament

Nettles, Graig (1944–) *not* Craig; American baseball player

Netzahualcóyotl part of the Mexico City conurbation

Neuchâtel Swiss town and wine

Neufchâtel French town and cheese

Neuilly-sur-Seine suburb of Paris

neurasthenia chronic lethargy

Nev. Nevada

Neva river that flows through Leningrad

nevertheless (one word) *see also* none the less/nonetheless

Nevins, Allan (1890–1971) American historian

Newberry Library, Chicago

Newbery Airport, Buenos Aires. Officially, Aeroparque Jorge Newbery

Newcastle-under-Lyme (hyphens), Staffordshire

Newcastle upon Tyne (no hyphens), Tyne and Wear

New England unofficial American region comprising Connecticut, Maine, Massachusetts, New Hampshire, Rhode Island and Vermont

New Hebrides former name of Vanuatu

New Houghton, Derbyshire, pronounced new huff'-tun

Newton-le-Willows, Merseyside (hyphens)

New York City (caps.) comprises five boroughs, each coextensive with a state county (in brackets): the Bronx (Bronx

County), Brooklyn (Kings County), Manhattan (New York County), Queens (Queens County), and Staten Island (Richmond County)

NH postal and traditional abbr. of New Hampshire

Niagara Falls *not* Niagra

Niamey capital of Niger

Nibelungenlied German epic poem

niblick a golf club used for getting the ball out of bad lies

niceish

niche The preferred pronunciation is nitch, though neesh is also acceptable

nickel *not* -le

Nicklaus, Jack (William) (1940–) American golfer

Nicolson, Sir Harold George (1886–1968) *not* Nichol-; English diplomat, politician and writer

Nicosia/Levkosia (Grk), Cyprus

nicotine *not* -tene

Nielsen, Carl (1865–1931) Danish composer

Nietzsche, Friedrich Wilhelm (1844–1900) German philosopher. The adjective is **Nietzschean**

Nightingale, Florence (1820–1910) English nurse and hospital reformer

Nihon-Keizai Shimbun Japanese financial newspaper

Niigata, Honshu, Japan, note -ii-

Niihau note -ii-; a Hawaiian island

Nijinsky, Vaslav (1890–1950) Russian dancer and choreographer

Nijmegen, The Netherlands

nincompoop

Nisei literally, 'second generation'; term used in North America for native US or Canadian citizens born to immigrant Japanese parents and educated in the US or Canada; often loosely used to describe all Japanese expatriates, particularly in the context of World War II internment

Nissen hut named after its inventor, British engineer Peter Norman Nissen (1871–1930)

nitty-gritty

nitwit

Nitzchke, Oscar (1900–91) German architect

Nixon, Richard Milhous (*not* -house) (1913–) US President 1969–74

Nizhny Novgorod Russia; called Gorky during Communist era

NJ postal and traditional abbr. of New Jersey

Nkomo, Joshua (Mqabuko Nyongolo) (1917–) African Nationalist and Zimbabwean politician

Nkrumah, Dr Kwame (1909–72) Ghanaian Prime Minister 1957–60 and President 1960–6

NM postal abbr. of New Mexico; traditional abbr. is **N. Mex.**

no (US)/**Noh** (UK) highly stylized Japanese drama with song and dance

Nobel Prizes named after the Swedish inventor and industrialist Alfred Nobel (1833–96), whose will established and funded them. The prizes are for achievements in chemistry, economics, literature, peace, physics, and physiology or medicine. When giving the full titles, use caps., e.g. Nobel Prize for Literature

noblesse oblige (Fr.) nobility obligates; applied to duties that come with holding high rank

nobody (one word), but **no one**

noisome has nothing to do with noisiness; it describes a foul smell

nolo contendere (Lat.) 'I do not wish to contend'; tantamount to a plea of guilty, but leaves the defendant with the option of denying the same or similar charges in other proceedings

nom de guerre (Fr.) an assumed name. In most contexts it is a cliché

nom de plume a writer's pseudonym

nomenklatura secret list of names from which people in the USSR were chosen for advancement

nonagenarian person from 90 to 99 years old

non-Christian, but **unchristian**

non compos mentis (Lat.) not of sound mind

none Although none can always take a singular verb, there is no rule recognized by any authority on English grammar that it cannot equally well take a plural one

none the less (UK)/**nonetheless** (US) *see also* nevertheless

nonillion the figure 1 followed by 54 zeros (UK); 1 followed by 30 zeros (US). The number that Americans call nonillion is in Britain called quintillion. For obvious reasons, the terms should be used with considerable care

nonpareil peerless

nonplused (US)/**nonplussed** (UK)

non sequitur (Lat.) a conclusion that does not follow logically from the premiss, or a statement in which the ideas are jarringly unconnected, as in 'He was born in Liverpool and his shoes were brown'.

no one (two words, no hyphen), but **nobody** (one word)

Norge Norwegian name for Norway

normalcy is derided by many authorities. **Normality** is unobjectionable

Northants (no point) Northamptonshire

Northern Ireland part of the United Kingdom, comprising six counties: Antrim, Armagh, Down, Fermanagh, Londonderry and Tyrone

Nostradamus, Michel de Notredame (1503–66), French astrologer and prophet

nosy *not* nosey

nota bene (Lat.) abbr. n.b. (US)/NB (UK); note well

Notes from Underground novel by Dostoevsky (1864)

notwithstanding (one word)

Nouakchott capital of Mauritania

n'oubliez pas (Fr.) don't forget

noughts and crosses (UK)/**tick-tack-toe** (US) children's game; *see also* naught

nouveau riche (Fr.) mildly disparaging description of someone whose wealth is recently acquired; *pl.* ***nouveaux riches***

Novocaine (cap.)

Novokuznetsk, Russia

Novorossiisk, Russia

Novosibirsk, Russia

Novotný, Antonín (1904–75) Czech politician

NOW (US) National Organization for (*not* of) Women; women's rights organization

nowadays

NSPCC National Society for the Prevention of Cruelty to Children

Nuffield Radio-Astronomy Laboratories of the University of Manchester formal name of the observatory more commonly known as Jodrell Bank

Nuits-Saint-Georges French wine

Nuku'alofa/Nukualofa capital of Tonga

Nullarbor Plain, Australia

nullify

number Used with the definite article, number always takes a singular verb ('The number of people in the world is rising'); used with an indefinite article it always take a plural verb ('A number of people are unhappy')

numismatics the study or collection of coins or medals

numskull *not* numbskull

NUPE (UK) National Union of Public Employees

Nuremberg/Nürnberg German city

Nureyev, Rudolf (Hametovich) (1938–93) Soviet-born ballet dancer

Nuuk formerly Godthaab; capital of Greenland

NV postal abbr. of Nevada

NY postal and traditional abbr. of New York

Nyasaland former name of Malawi

Nyerere, Julius (Kambarage) (1922–) President of Tanganyika and then, after its union with Zanzibar, of Tanzania 1962–85

Nymphenburg Palace/Schloss Nymphenburg (Ger.), Munich

O, oh, oho The first normally appears only in literary or religious contexts; it is always capitalized and never followed by punctuation. The second is used in more general contexts to denote emotions ranging from a small sigh to an outcry; it is capitalized only at the start of sentences and normally followed by either a comma or exclamation mark. Oho, with or without an exclamation mark, denotes an expression of surprise

Oakenclough, Lancashire, pronounced oak'-en-klew

OAS Organization of American States; Organisation de l'Armée Secrète, underground group of French loyalists in Algeria in the 1950s

oast house barn for drying hops

Oates, Titus (1649–1705) anti-Catholic English cleric who reported a fictitious Jesuit plot to murder Charles II, as a result of which 35 innocent people were killed

OAU Organization of African Unity

Oaxaca pronounced wa-ha'-ka; city and state in southern Mexico

Obadiah Old Testament prophet

obbligato in music, an indispensable accompaniment

obeisance pronounced o-bay'-sunce; a show of deference

Oberammergau village in Bavaria, Germany, where a noted passion play is performed every 10 years

obiter dictum (Lat.) a remark made in passing; *pl.* ***obiter dicta***

objet d'art, *pl.* ***objets d'art***

objet trouvé (Fr.) a found object

oblique
obloquy pronounced ob-luh-kwee; verbal abuse; *pl.* **obloquies**
Obote, (Apollo) Milton (1925–) Prime Minister of Uganda 1962–6, and President 1966–71, 1980–85
O'Brien, Flann pen name of Brian O'Nolan (1911–66), Irish writer, who also wrote a column in the *Irish Times* under the pseudonym Myles na Gopaleen
obscurum per obscurius (Lat.) the obscure by the more obscure
obsidian glassy volcanic rock
obsolescence, **obsolescent**
obstetrics, **obstetrician**
obstreperous noisy, vociferous
obtuse angle one between 90 and 180 degrees
Occam's/Ockham's razor paring all presumptions to the minimum, a principle attributed to English philosopher William of Occam/Ockham (*c.* 1285–*c.* 1349)
occult
occur, **occurred**, **occurring**
ochlocracy government by mob rule
ochre (UK)/**ocher** (US)
Ocle Pychard, Hereford & Worcester, pronounced oak'-ull pitch'-urd
O'Connell, Daniel (1775–1847) Irish political activist
octocentenary 800th anniversary
octogenarian person from 80 to 89 years old
octopus, *pl.* **octopuses/octopodes** (US)
oculist
Oder–Neisse Line boundary between Germany and Poland
Odets, Clifford (1906–63) American playwright
Odiham, Hampshire, pronounced odium
odometer device for measuring distance travelled
odor, **odorless** (US)/**odour**, **odourless** (UK), but **odorize**, **odorous**, **odoriferous** (UK, US)
Odysseus (Grk)/**Ulysses** (Lat.) in Greek mythology, the King of Ithaca
OECD Organization for (*not* of) Economic Cooperation and Development. The members are Australia, Austria, Belgium,

Canada, Denmark, Finland, France, Germany, Greece, Iceland, Ireland, Italy, Japan, Luxembourg, The Netherlands, New Zealand, Norway, Portugal, Spain, Sweden, Switzerland, Turkey, the UK and the US

oedema (UK)/**edema** (US) swelling of body tissue as a result of abnormal retention of fluid

Oedipus in Greek mythology, character who solved the Sphinx's riddle, and killed his father and married his mother; subject of two plays by Sophocles

Oedipus complex term coined by Freud to describe a child's (usually a son's) feelings of love for the parent of the opposite sex mingled with dislike for the parent of the same sex

oenology/enology (alt. US) study of wines. A connoisseur is an oenophile

oesophagus, **oesophageal** (UK)/ **esophagus**, **esophageal** (US)

oestrogen, **oestrus** (UK)/**estrogen**, **estrus** (US)

oeuvre an artist's body of work

O'Faoláin, Seán (1900–91) Irish novelist and short story writer

Offaly county in Republic of Ireland

Offa's Dike/Dyke eighth-century earthwork between England and Wales

Offenbach, Jacques (1819–80) born Jakob Eberst; German-born French composer

offence (UK)/**offense** (US), but **offensive** (UK, US)

Official Report of Parliamentary Debates formal title of Hansard

off of is redundant; write 'Get off the table', *not* 'Get off of the table'.

Ogdon, John (Andrew Howard) (1937–89) British pianist

ogre

OH postal abbr. of Ohio

Oh, **Oho** *see* O, Oh, Oho

O'Hare International Airport, Chicago

O. Henry pen name of William Sydney Porter (1862–1910) American short story writer

Oireachtas pronounced ur'-akh-tus; the Irish legislature, comprising the President and the two assemblies, the Dáil Éireann and Seanad

Ojos del Salado Andean mountain on Chilean and Argentinian border, second highest peak in the western hemisphere (22,660 ft/6,910 m)

OK postal abbr. of Oklahoma

Okeechobee lake and inland waterway, Florida

Okefenokee Swamp, Florida and Georgia, pronounced oh-kee-fuh-no'-kee

Okeford Fitzpaine, Dorset, pronounced as spelled, but sometimes referred to by locals as fip-pen-ee ok-furd

Okhotsk, Sea of

Okla. Oklahoma

Olav V (1903–91) King of Norway 1957–91

Old Bailey, London, a street and the Central Criminal Court located there

Oldenburg, Claes (1929–) Swedish-born American sculptor

Old Lady of Threadneedle Street nickname for the Bank of England

Old Peculier (UK) *not* Peculiar; a beer brewed by Theakston

Olduvai Gorge, Tanzania

Olivetti formally, Ing. C. Olivetti & Co. SpA; Italian industrial group

Olivier, Laurence (Kerr), Baron (1907–89) English actor, producer and director

Omar Khayyám (*c.* 1050–*c.* 1125) Persian mathematician and poet

OMB (US) Office of Management and Budget

Ombudsman (cap.), **the** (UK) formally, the Parliamentary Commissioner for Administration

omelette (UK, alt. US) /**omelet** (US)

omit, **omitted**, **omitting**, **omissible**

omnipotent, **omniscient** The first means all-powerful; the second all-knowing

Onassis, Aristotle (Socrates) (1906–75) Greek shipping magnate

oneiric

oneself

onomatopoeia the formation of words based on the sounds they denote, as with buzz, bang and splash

onomatopoeical/onomatopoetical (alt. US)

on parle français (Fr.) French spoken here

on to (UK)/**onto** (US)

oolong tea

oozy

opaque

op. cit. *opere citato* (Lat.) in the work cited

OPEC Organization of Petroleum Exporting Countries. The members are Algeria, Ecuador, Gabon, Indonesia, Iran, Iraq, Kuwait, Libya, Nigeria, Qatar, Saudi Arabia, the United Arab Emirates and Venezuela

openness note -nn-

Opéra-Comique Paris theatre

opéra bouffe (Fr.) farcical opera

ophthalmology, **ophthalmic** note oph-, pronounced off-thal-, *not* opth-

Opium War war between Britain and China 1839–42, through which Britain gained control of Hong Kong

Oppenheimer, J(ulius) Robert (1904–67) American physicist, helped develop the first atomic bomb

Oporto/Pôrto, Portugal

opossum pronounced uh-poss'-um; type of marsupial found in the Americas; *see also* possum

oppressor

opus magnum, ***magnum opus*** (Lat.) The first is a great work; the second an author's principal work.

OR postal abbr. of Oregon

orange pekoe a tea

oratio recta, ***oratio obliqua*** (Lat.) The first means words as spoken, i.e., direct speech; the second means words as recorded, i.e., indirect speech

Orcadian of or from the Orkneys

ordinal numbers first, second, third, etc.; *see also* cardinal numbers

ordinance, **ordnance** The first is an authoritative decree; the second refers to military stores and materials

Ordiquhill, Grampian Region, Scotland; pronounced or'-duh-will

Ordnance Survey Department (UK) government map-making department, so called because it was originally a part of the Army Board of Ordnance

ordonnance the proper arrangement of parts in a literary, musical, artistic or architectural work

Ordzhonikidze, Russia, formerly, Dzaudzhikau

Oresteia trilogy by Aeschylus (*c.* 458 BC)

Orestes in Greek mythology, the son of Clytemnestra and Agamemnon

Öresund strait between Sweden and Denmark

Oriel College, Oxford

Orinoco South American river, rising in Venezuela

Orkney Islands, but a resident is an **Orcadian**

Orly Airport, Paris

Orlando, Vittorio Emanuele (1860–1952) Italian Prime Minister 1917–19

orology the study of mountains

Ortega y Gasset, José (1883–1955) Spanish philosopher

orthoepy correct pronunciation; the study of pronunciation. Curiously, there are two accepted pronunciations: or'-tho-ep-ee and or-tho'-ip-ee.

orthography correct or accepted spelling; the study of spelling

orthopaedics (UK)/**orthopedics** (US) area of medicine concerned with bones and muscles

Orwell, George pen name of British writer Eric Blair (1903–50)

Osborne, John (James) (1929–) English playwright

oscillate

oscilloscope

Osservatore Romano, L' Vatican newspaper

Ossett, West Yorkshire

Ostend/Oostende (Fl.) Belgian port

osteo- prefix meaning bone(s)

osteomyelitis infection in the bone or bone marrow
Österreich German name for Austria
Oswaldtwistle, Lancashire, pronounced oz'-wald-twiss-ull/oz'-ull-twiss-ull
Oświęcim (Pol.)/**Auschwitz** German concentration camp in Poland during World War II
otolaryngology the branch of medicine dealing with ear, nose and throat disorders
Ottawa, Ontario, capital of Canada
Otway, Thomas (1652–85) British playwright
Ouachita (pref.)/**Washita** (alt.) river and mountains in Arkansas and Oklahoma
Ouagadougou capital of Burkina Faso
oubliette dungeon with access only through a trap-door in the ceiling
Oudenarde, Battle of (1708)
Ouija board (cap. O)
'Ours is not to reason why, ours is but to do or die' is wrong. The lines from Tennyson's 'Charge of the Light Brigade' are 'Their's not to reason why,/Their's but to do and die.'
Ouse pronounced ooze; rivers in Northamptonshire (the Great Ouse), Yorkshire and Sussex
outspokenness note -nn-
ouzo Greek drink
Overbeck, Johann Friedrich (1769–1869) German painter
Overijssel province of The Netherlands
Overlord code name given to the Normandy invasion by Allied forces in 1944
overripe, **overrule**, **overrun**, etc. note -rr-
overweening *not* -weaning
Ovid, properly Publius Ovidius Naso (43 BC–AD 17) Roman poet
ovum, *pl.* **ova**
Oxford Movement a movement in the Church of England, begun at Oxford in 1833, seeking a return to certain Roman Catholic doctrines and practices
Oxford University colleges: All Souls, Balliol, Brasenose,

Christ Church, Corpus Christi, Exeter, Green, Hertford, Jesus, Keble, Lady Margaret Hall, Linacre, Lincoln, Magdalen, Merton, New College, Nuffield, Oriel, Pembroke, (The) Queen's, St Anne's, St Antony's, St Catherine's, St Cross, St Edmund Hall, St Hilda's, St Hugh's, St John's, St Peter's, Somerville, Trinity, University, Wadham, Wolfson, Worcester

Oxon. *Oxonia* (Lat.) Oxford or Oxfordshire; *Oxoniensis* (Lat.) of Oxford

Oxon: signature of the Bishop of Oxford

oxymoron the intentional mingling of contradictory ideas or expressions for rhetorical effect, as in 'getting nowhere fast'

Ozawa, Seiji (1935–) Japanese conductor

'Ozymandias' sonnet by Shelley (1818)

P

PA postal abbr. of Pennsylvania
pabulum food
PABX (UK) private automatic branch exchange
pachyderm thick-skinned animals such as elephants and rhinoceroses
paddywhack a tantrum
Paderewski, Ignace Jan (1860–1941) pronounced pad-der-reff'-skee; Polish concert pianist, composer and Prime Minister 1919–20
Padova (It.)/**Padua**
paean, **paeon**, **peon** Paean is a hymn or song of praise; paeon is a metrical foot in ancient Greek and Latin poetry; peon is a servant or peasant
paediatrics, **paediatrician** (UK)/**pediatrics**, **pediatrician** (US)
paedophile
paella Spanish dish of rice and chicken or seafood
Paganini, Niccolò (1782–1840) Italian violin virtuoso and composer
Pago Pago pronounced pango pango; capital of American Samoa
Pahlavi, Mohammed Reza (1919–80) Shah of Iran 1941–79
pail, **pale** The first is a small bucket; the second means lacking colour
Paine, Thomas (1737–1809) British-born American political philosopher and pamphleteer
Paisley, Rev. Ian (Richard Kyle) (1926–) Ulster Protestant clergyman and politician

Paiute Indians North American Indian peoples

pajamas (US)/**pyjamas** (UK)

Pakenham, Suffolk, pronounced pay'-ken-um

palaeology (UK)/**paleology** (US) study of antiquities

palaeontology (UK)/**paleontology** (US) study of fossils

Palaeocene (UK)/**Paleocene** (US) a geological epoch

palatable *not* -eable; pleasant to the taste

palate, **palette**, **pallet** Palate pertains to the mouth and taste. Palette is the board used by artists for holding and mixing paints. Pallet is a straw mattress, a machine part, a wooden platform on which freight is stood, and various specialized tools

palaver fuss

Palazzo Vecchio, Florence

palindrome a word or passage that reads the same forwards and backwards, as in 'A man, a plan, a canal: Panama'

palisade

Palladian architecture the style of architecture of Andrea Palladio (1508–80)

Pall Mall, London, pronounced pal mal or pel mel; *see also* pell-mell

pallor *not* -our; paleness

Palme, (Sven) Olof (1927–86) Swedish politician

Palmers Green, London (no apos.)

palomino type of horse; *pl.* **palominos**

palsy

panacea a universal remedy, something that cures all woes, not just a single ill

Pan Am former US airline

pandemonium

P&O should be printed closed up. It stands for Peninsular and Oriental Steamship Company

panegyric pronounced pann-a-jir'-ick; a formal speech of praise

Pangloss an excessively optimistic character in Voltaire's *Candide*, hence any optimistic person

panjandrum self-important person, pompous official

Pankhurst, Emmeline (1858–1928) English activist for

women's rights. Her daughters, **Dame Christabel Pankhurst** (1880–1958), **Sylvia Pankhurst** (1882–1960) and **Adela Pankhurst** (1885–1961), were similarly dedicated to women's causes.

pantyhose (US), **tights** (UK)

Pão de Açucar (Port.)/**Sugarloaf Mountain**, Rio de Janeiro

Paolozzi, Eduardo (1924–) Scottish sculptor

Papal Nuncio a prelate acting as an ambassador of the Pope

paparazzo roving photographer who stalks celebrities; *pl.* **paparazzi**

Pap test a test for uterine cancer and other disorders devised by Dr George Papanicolaou (1883–1962), a Greek-American doctor

papier mâché

papyrus writing material

Paracelsus Theophrastus Philippus Aureolus Bombastus von Hohenheim (1493–1541), Swiss physician and alchemist

paradisaical *not* -iacal; having the nature of a paradise

paraffin (UK), **kerosene** (US)

paraffin (US)/**paraffin wax** (UK)

paragon model of excellence

parakeet

parallel, paralleled, paralleling

paralyse (UK)/**paralyze** (US)

paranoia, paranoiac

paraphernalia note -pher-

paraquat herbicide

paraphrase

parasite

parasol

parbleu! (Fr.) exclamation of surprise

Parcheesi (cap.) (US), **ludo** (UK)

pardonnez-moi (Fr.) note hyphen; pardon me

par excellence (Fr.) pronounced par ek-sul-ahnss'; the best of its type

pariah person of low standing, a social outcast

Paribas short for Compagnie Financière de Paris et des Pays-Bas; French bank

pari passu (Lat.) with the same speed, at an equal rate

parka type of coat
Park Chung Hee (1917–79) President of South Korea 1963–79
Parkinson's disease
Parkinson's Law: 'Work expands to fill the time available for its completion', stated by C. Northcote Parkinson (1909–), British writer
parky (UK) chilly
parlay, parley The first means to make a gain on the back of another gain; the second, pronounced par-lee, is a conference.
Parliamentary Commissioner for Administration (UK) formal title of the government ombudsman
parlour (UK), **parlor** (US)
Parmenides of Elea (5th century BC) Greek philosopher
Parmesan cheese (cap. P)/***parmigiano*** (It., no cap.)
Parmigianino, Il Girolamo Francesco Maria Mazzola (1504–40), Italian painter
Parnassus, Mt, former name of Líakoura, a Greek mountain
Parnell, Charles Stewart (1846–91) Irish patriot
paroxysm
parquet flooring
Parr, Catherine (1512–48) sixth wife of Henry VIII
parricide the murder of a parent or close relative
Parry, Sir William Edward (1790–1855) British admiral and explorer
Parsifal opera by Wagner (1879)
Parthian shot a remark or blow made while retreating
parti pris (Fr.) a prejudice
Parti Québecois Canadian political party
Partridge, Eric (Honeywood) (1894–1979) New Zealand-born British lexicographer
parturition birth
parvenu (masc.)/**parvenue** (fem.) an upstart; a person who has risen above his original social class; *pl.* **parvenus** (masc.)/ **parvenues** (fem.)
Pasadena, California city near Los Angeles, home of the Rose Bowl, or Tournament of Roses, the most important annual college football match in the US

paso doble (Sp.) pronounced pass-o doe'-blay; type of dance
Pasolini, Pier Paolo (1922–75) Italian writer, actor and film director
passable, **passible** The first means capable of being passed ('The road was passable') or barely satisfactory ('The food was passable'); the second means capable of feeling or suffering
Passchendaele *not* -dale; Belgian village, scene of bloody battle in World War I
passe-partout a passkey; adhesive tape used in picture framing
Pasteur, Louis (1822–95) French chemist
pastille
pastis
pastrami
pâté de foie gras
Patek, Philippe Swiss watch manufacturer
Patel, Vallabhbhai (1875–1950) Indian politician
Patent Office, London *not* Patents
paterfamilias (one word) male head of house
Paterson, New Jersey note -t-, but pronounced as if spelled -tt-
pâtisserie
Pattenmakers Company (no apos.) *not* Pattern-
Pauli, Wolfgang (1900–58) Austrian-born physicist; Nobel Prize for Physics 1945
Pavarotti, Luciano (1935–) Italian tenor
pavilion *not* -ll-
pax vobiscum (Lat.) peace be with you
Pays-Bas French name for The Netherlands
Pb chemical symbol for lead
PBX (UK) private branch exchange
PC personal computer; police constable; Privy Council; Privy Counsellor
PCBs polychlorinated biphenyls, organic substance used in hydraulics and electrical systems; banned in most Western countries
peaceable
peak, **peek** The first is a point or summit; the second means to steal a look

Pearce, Sir Austin (William) (1921–) British businessman

Pears, Sir Peter (1910–) English tenor, pronounced 'Peers'

Pearse, Padraic (1879–1916) Irish writer and nationalist

Peary, Robert Edwin (1856–1920) pronounced peer'-ee; American admiral and explorer, first to reach North Pole (1909)

pease pudding

Peaston, Lothian, Scotland pronounced pay'-stun

peccadillo a minor fault; *pl.* peccadilloes

pederasty/paederasty (alt. UK) sexual relations between an adult male and a boy

pedlar (UK)/**peddler** (US) a traveller who sells wares

Peeblesshire note -ss-; former Scottish county

peek, peak The first means to steal a look; the second is a point or summit

peekaboo (no hyphens)

Peekskill, New York

Peel, Sir Robert (1788–1850) British Prime Minister 1834–5, 1841–6

peers The British peerage comprises, in descending order, the ranks duke, marquess, earl/countess, viscount and baron/baroness. Male peers below the rank of duke may be referred to as Lord (i.e., the Earl of Avon may be called Lord Avon), and all peeresses may be referred to as Lady. However, not every Lord is a peer. The eldest son of a duke, marquess or earl, for instance, may use one of his father's minor titles as a courtesy title and call himself the Marquess of X or Earl of Y, but he is not a peer and is not allowed to sit in the House of Lords. Younger sons of dukes and marquesses may put Lord in front of their names: Lord John X. Their wives are then called Lady John X. Daughters of dukes, marquesses and earls will similarly put Lady before their names: Lady Mary Y. Wives of other kinds of peers, and of knights and baronets, are referred to as Lady X or Lady Y; that is, their first names are not used. Sir John Bloggs's wife is simply Lady Bloggs, not Lady Mary Bloggs. Life peers are people of distinction who are elevated to the peerage but whose titles die with them.

Pei, I(eoh) M(ing) (1917–) Chinese-born American architect.

Peirce, Charles Sanders (1839–1914) American philosopher, pronounced 'Purse'

Pekingese dog

pekoe a tea

Pelagianism a heresy

pelargonium flowering plant popularly known as the geranium

Pelaw, Tyne & Wear, pronounced peel'-a

Pelé nickname of Edson Arantes do Nascimento (1940–) Brazilian soccer player

Peloponnese (UK)/**Peloponnesus** (US) /**Pelopónnisos** (Grk) southern peninsula of Greece

pelota another name for the game of jai alai

pell-mell in a state of confusion; *see also* Pall Mall

Pembroke, Dyfed, Wales; **Pembroke College,** Oxford; **Pembroke College,** Cambridge; all pronounced pem'-brook

pemmican dried meat

penance

PEN Club short for Poets, Playwrights, Editors, Essayists, and Novelists; an international association

pendant (noun)/**pendent** (adj.)

Penetanguishene, Ontario

penicillin

Peninsular and Oriental Steamship Company the British shipping company commonly known as P&O

Penney, J. C., US department store group

penniless *not* penny-

penn'orth a penny's worth

Penrhyndeudraeth, Gwynedd, Wales, pronounced pen-rin-die-drithe

Pensacola, Florida

Pentateuch the first five books of the Old Testament: Genesis, Exodus, Leviticus, Numbers and Deuteronomy

pentathlon, modern the five events are swimming, fencing, pistol shooting, cross-country running and cross-country horse-back riding

Pentecost the Christian Whit Sunday, the seventh Sunday after

Easter; the Jewish Shavuot, the sixth and seventh days of Sivan

peon, **paean**, **paeon** Peon is a servant or peasant; paean is a hymn or song of praise; paeon is a metrical foot in ancient Greek and Latin poetry

peony a flowering plant

PepsiCo (one word) **Inc.** US company that owns Pepsi-Cola

Pepys, Samuel (1633–1703) pronounced peeps; English Admiralty official, remembered for his diary

per ardua ad astra (Lat.) to the stars through adversities

per cent (UK)/**percent** (US), but **percentage** (UK, US)

per cent, **percentage point** If interest rates are 10 per cent and are raised to 11 per cent, they have gone up by one percentage point, but by 10 per cent in value (i.e., borrowers must now pay 10 per cent more than previously). In everyday contexts the distinction is not always vital, but in contexts in which the percentage rise is large and confusion is likely, the distinction is crucial

perceptible

Perceval, Spencer (1762–1812) British Prime Minister 1809–12

perestroika (Russ.) restructuring; the plan to modernize the Soviet economy and political system

perchance, **perforce** The first means possibly; the second without choice

Perelman, S(idney) J(oseph) (1904–79) American humorist

Perez de Cuellar, Javier (1920–) Peruvian diplomat, Secretary-General of the UN 1982–92

perfectible, **perfectibility**

perforce, **perchance** The first means without choice; the second possibly

perinatal pertaining to the period immediately before and after birth

peripatetic wandering

periphrasis using more words than necessary; circumlocution; *pl.* **periphrases**

perishable

periwinkle

Perlman, Itzhak (1945–) Israeli violinist

permissible
permitted, **permitting**
pernickety
Perón, (Maria) Eva (Duarte de) (1919–1952) nickname Evita; second wife of Juan Perón
Perón, Juan (Domingo) (1895–1974) President of Argentina 1946–55, 1973–4
Persephone in Greek mythology, queen of the underworld; identified with the Roman goddess Proserpina
Perseus in Greek mythology, son of Zeus who murdered Medusa
persevere, perseverance
persiflage idle banter
persimmon
personnel note -nn-
perspicacity, **perspicuity** The first means shrewdness; the second lucidity
pesos
pertinacious persistent
Pétain, Henri Philippe (1856–1951) French general and politician, head of the Vichy government 1940–44
Peter Principle the idea that people are promoted until they reach a level at which they are incompetent
Petri dish (cap. P)
Petrograd originally St Petersburg, then Leningrad, reverted to St Petersburg 1991
Petrovsk former name of Makhachkala, Russia
Pettenkofer, Max Joseph von (1818–1901) German chemist
Petticoat Lane famous Sunday morning market in East End of London. The street on which it is held is actually called Middlesex Street, and has been for well over 100 years
pettifog quibble over petty matters; legal trickery
petty bourgeois/***petit bourgeois*** (Fr.) a small businessman; member of the lower middle class
peu à peu (Fr.) little by little
Peugeot French car
peut-être (Fr.) perhaps

Pevsner, Sir Nikolaus (Bernhard Leon) (1902–83) German-born art historian best remembered for his encyclopaedic survey of English architecture, *The Buildings of England*
pfennig German coin worth 1/100th of a mark
PFLP Popular Front for the Liberation of Palestine
pH potential of hydrogen, a measure of acidity in a solution
Phalange political party in Lebanon
phalanx, *pl.* **phalanxes/phalanges**
pharaoh *not* -oah
pharmacopoeia a book containing descriptions of medicines and drugs
phenomenon *pl.* **phenomena**
Phidias (*c.* 498–*c.* 432 BC) Greek sculptor, responsible for all or part of the Parthenon
Philadelphia largest city in Pennsylvania
philanderer unfaithful person
Philip Morris US tobacco and diversified products company
Philippi ancient city in Macedonia
Philippians book of the New Testament
philippic a verbal denunciation
Philippines, Republic of the note -l-, -pp-; island state in the Pacific Ocean; capital Manila. Natives and citizens are Filipinos
Philippine Sea *not* -pines; part of the Pacific Ocean east of the Philippines
Philips formally, NV Philips Gloeilampenfabrieken; Dutch electrical company
philistine person who is indifferent or hostile to matters of culture
Phillips Collection, Washington, DC
Phillips Petroleum US oil group
Phillips Son & Neale London auction house
Philomel/Philomela poetic name for the nightingale
phlebitis inflammation of the veins
Phnom Penh pronounced puh-nom' penn; capital of Cambodia
phone *not* 'phone
phoney (UK)/**phony** (US)
Phyfe, Duncan (1786–1854) born Duncan Fife; Scottish-born American furniture maker

phylum a taxonomic division of animals and plants; *pl.* **phyla**

Physic, Regius Professor of, Cambridge University *not* Physics

physiognomy facial characteristics

physique bodily build

pi ratio of circumference to diameter of a circle, equivalent to 3.14159 . . .; the sixteenth letter of the Greek alphabet

pianissimo, pianississimo The first of these musical terms means very soft; the second means as softly as possible

Picard, Jean (1620–82) French astronomer

Picasso, Pablo (Ruiz y) (1881–1973) Spanish artist

picayune a trifling matter

Piccadilly

piccalilli a kind of pickle relish

Piccard, Auguste (1884–1962) Swiss physicist

piccolo a small flute pitched an octave higher than the ordinary instrument; *pl.* **piccolos**

pickaback use piggyback

picnic, **picnicked**, **picnicking**, **picnicker**

pico- prefix meaning one-trillionth

Pico della Mirandola, Count Giovanni (1463–94) Italian philosopher

pidgin, **creole** Pidgin is a language spontaneously devised by two or more peoples who have no common language. Pidgins are generally very rudimentary. If contact between the different peoples is prolonged and generations are born for whom the pidgin is their first tongue, the language will usually evolve into a more formalized system of speech called a creole. Most languages that are commonly called pidgins are in fact creoles

pièce de résistance (Fr.) most outstanding item, particularly applied to the finest dish in a meal

piecemeal

pied-à-terre (Fr.) (hyphens) a secondary residence; *pl.* ***pieds-à-terre***

Pied Piper of Hamelin

Pierce, Franklin (1804–69) US President 1853–7

Piero della Francesca (*c.* 1418–92) Italian artist
Pierre, South Dakota, pronounced peer; the state capital
Piers Plowman, The Vision of William Concerning epic poem by William Langland (*c.* 1360–99)
Pietermaritzburg, South Africa, capital of Natal
pigeonhole
piggyback *not* pickaback
Pikes Peak (no apos.) summit (14,100 ft/4,341 m) in Rocky Mountains, Colorado; named after Zebulon Montgomery Pike, its discoverer
pilaf/pilaff/pilau/pilaw Indian or Middle Eastern spiced rice dish
Pilipino language of the Philippines
Pilsener/Pilsner beer
Piłsudski, Józef (1867–1935) Polish statesman
pimento (UK)/**pimiento** (alt. US) *pl.* **pimentos** (UK)/**pimientos** (US)
PIN (UK), personal identification number, the individual code given to holders of cards for use in bank machines and the like
pineal gland
Pinero, Sir Arthur Wing (1855–1934) pronounced pin-nee'-ro; English comedic playwright
Ping-Pong (caps.)
Pinocchio note -cc-
Pinochet (Ugarte), Augusto (1915–) President of Chile 1973–90
pinscher, Doberman (US)/**Dobermann** (UK) breed of dog
pint a liquid measure equal to 20 ounces (UK)/16 ounces (US)
Pinturicchio nickname of Bernardino di Betto Vagio (1454–1513), Italian painter
Pinyin One of the two main international systems for romanizing Chinese names, Pinyin was devised in 1953 but has been in widespread international use only since about 1977; *see also* Chinese names
piquant pungent, alluring
pique resentment. 'Fit of pique' is a cliché
Piraeus port of Athens

Pirandello, Luigi (1867–1936) Italian author and playwright; Nobel Prize for Literature 1934

Piranesi, Giovanni Battista/Giambattista (1720–78) Italian artist and architect

piranha species of fish

Pirelli Italian tyre manufacturer

pirouette graceful turn on one foot

Pissarro, Camille (1830–1903) French painter

pistachio nut-bearing tree; *pl.* **pistachios**

pistil part of flower

pitiable, **pitiful**, **pitiless**, but **piteous**

Pitt, William, first Earl of Chatham (1708–78) called Pitt the Elder and 'the Great Commoner'; Prime Minister 1766–8; father of **William Pitt** (1759–1806), called Pitt the Younger, the youngest Prime Minister in British history, 1783–1801, 1804–6

Pitti Palace/Palazzo Pitti (It.), Florence

Pittsburgh, Pennsylvania, *not* -burg

pixels picture elements, the little squares from which computer graphics are composed

pixie *not* pixy; a sprite

Pizarro, Francisco (*c.* 1475–1541) Spanish *conquistador*, conquered Peru, founded Lima

pizzeria *not* -zza-; restaurant where pizzas are made

Plaid Cymru (Wel.) pronounced plide kum'-ree; Party of Wales, Welsh nationalist political party

Plaistow The district of London is pronounced plass'-to, the villages in Kent and West Sussex are pronounced place'-toe

Planck, Max (Karl Ernst Ludwig) (1858–1947) German physicist; Nobel Prize for Physics 1918

planetarium, *pl.* **planetariums/planetaria**

Plantagenets dynasty of English monarchs from Henry II to Richard III, 1154–1485

Plasticine (cap.)

plat du jour (Fr.) dish of the day

plateau, *pl.* **plateaux/plateaus**

platen the roller on a typewriter

plate tectonics *not* tech-; a theory of the structure of the Earth's crust and its movements

Plato (*c.* 427– *c.* 347 BC) Greek philosopher

Platt-Deutsch/Plattdeutsch German dialect, also called Low German

platypus, *pl.* **platypuses**

plausible, **plausibility**

Plautus, Titus Maccius, or Maccus (*c.* 250–184 BC) Roman writer of comedies

playwright *not* -write

PLC (UK) Public Limited Company, one whose shares are sold publicly and quoted on the stock market; equivalent to Inc. (US) or AG (Ger.). Many companies use 'plc' or 'Plc', but there is no logical reason for so doing

plead innocent is wrong. Under the British and American judicial systems, one pleads guilty or not guilty

Pleasley, Derbyshire, pronounced plez'-lee

plebeian common, vulgar, of the lower classes

plebiscite vote of the people

Pleiades in Greek mythology, the seven daughters of Atlas and Pleione; a cluster of stars in the constellation Taurus

Pleistocene a geological period

plenary full, complete. A plenary session of a council is one attended by all the members

plenitude *not* plenti-; an abundance

plentiful, but **plenteous**

plethora a glut

pleurisy inflammation of the membrane covering the lungs

Plexiglas (cap.) *not* -ss

Plimsoll line/mark point down to which a ship may be loaded

plimsolls rubber-soled canvas shoes

Pliny, Gaius Plinius Secundus known as **'the Elder'** (23–79) Roman writer on natural history

Pliny, Gaius Plinius Caecilius Secundus known as **'the Younger'** (62–113) Roman writer and orator, nephew of above

PLO Palestine Liberation Organization

plough (UK)/**plow** (US)

PLR Public Lending Right; system by which annual payments are made to British authors (but not, alas, non-British authors living in Britain) based on the number of times their books were borrowed from a sampling of libraries in the previous year

plumage

plumb

plummy rich in plums; an affected rich, full voice

Plutarch, properly Ploutarchos (*c.* 46–*c.* 120) Greek historian, biographer and philosopher

plutocrat person who has influence or power because of wealth

p.m./PM post meridiem (*not* -ien); after noon

PMS (US)/**PMT** (UK) premenstrual syndrome/tension

Pocahontas (*c.* 1595–1617) North American Indian princess, known for saving the life of John Smith, English settler in the New World

pocket borough a British parliamentary borough controlled by one person or group; common before parliamentary reforms of 1832

Podhoretz, Norman (1930–) American journalist and writer

Poe, Edgar Allan (1809–49) American poet and short story writer

pogrom methodical massacre of a minority group

Pöhl, Karl Otto (1929–) German banker

Poincaré, Jules Henri (1854–1912) French mathematician

Poincaré, Raymond Nicolas Landry (1860–1934) French statesman

poinsettia winter-flowering plant

pokey (US) slang for jail

poky small, cramped; slow (US)

Poliakoff, Stephen (1954–) British dramatist

poliomyelitis commonly shortened to polio, once also called (somewhat misleadingly) infantile paralysis

politburo/Politburo the chief committee of a Communist Party

Polizei (Ger.) police

Pollaiuolo, Antonio (1429–98) Italian painter, sculptor and goldsmith

Pollock, (Paul) Jackson (1912–56) American artist

Pollok House, Pollok Country Park, Pollokshaws Road, Glasgow

Pollyanna an optimistic person, particularly one who is foolishly so; after the heroine of a 1913 novel by Eleanor Porter

polonaise a slow Polish dance, or music for it

poltergeist

Poltoratsk former name of Ashkhabad, capital of Turkmenistan

polyandry state or practice of a woman having more than one husband at the same time

polygamy state or practice of having more than one mate at the same time

polyglot speaking several languages

polygyny state or practice of a man having more than one wife at the same time

polypropylene type of plastic

pomegranate a round fruit with many seeds

Pomeranian a toy breed of dog

pommy disparaging Australian term for a Briton

Pompeian of Pompeii, a Roman city destroyed by eruption of Mount Vesuvius in AD 79

Pompey, properly Gnaeus Pompeius Magnus (106–48 BC) Roman soldier and statesman

Pompidou Centre, Paris, formally, Le Centre National d'Art et de Culture Georges Pompidou; also called Centre Beaubourg

pompon *not* -pom; a ball or tuft of material

Ponce de León, Juan (1460–1521) Spanish explorer, discovered Florida

Pontefract, West Yorkshire

Ponte Vecchio a bridge over the Arno, Florence

Pont l'Évêque French town and type of cheese named after it

Pontypridd, Mid Glamorgan, Wales, pronounced pon-tay-preeth'

Pooh-Bah/pooh-bah person who holds many offices at once, from character in Gilbert and Sullivan's *The Mikado*

Popa, Vasko (1922–91) Yugoslav poet

poppadam/poppadom Indian thin, crisp, fried bread

populace, populous The first means the common people or a general population; the second heavily populated

porcupine

pore, pour The first means to examine carefully: one pores over a book; the second means to flow or rain heavily

port the left-hand side of a ship when looking forward; *see also* starboard

Port-au-Prince capital of Haiti

portentous *not* -ious

Port Eynon, West Glamorgan, pronounced port eye'-nun

Porthmadog, Gwynedd, Wales, pronounced porth'-mad-ogg, formerly Portmadoc

portico a porch supported by pillars; *pl.* **porticoes/porticos**

portmanteau word a word blending two others, e.g., smog = smoke + fog

Portmeirion, Gwynedd, Wales, Italianate village built by Sir (Bertram) Clough Williams-Ellis, and a brand of pottery that originated there

Port Moresby capital of Papua New Guinea

Porton Down common name for the Centre for Applied Microbiology and Research, the British government research station near Salisbury, Wiltshire, frequently associated with chemical warfare experiments

Porto-Novo capital of Benin

Portuguese

Poseidon Greek god of the sea; identified with the Roman god Neptune

poser, poseur The first is a puzzle; the second a person of affected manner

possum type of marsupial found in Australasia

postcode (UK)

poste restante

post-haste (UK)/**posthaste** (US) with speed

posthumous after death

postilion

post meridiem *not* -ien; abbr. p.m./PM; after noon
Post Office, The (UK) public corporation
post office (no caps.) the offices or buildings where postal business is done
postpartum after birth
postprandial after dinner
Postwick, Norfolk, pronounced pozz'-ick
potage soup
potassium
pot-pourri (UK)/**potpourri** (US) pronounced po-pur-ree'; a mixture of fragrant dried petals and spices; a medley; *pl.* **pot-pourris**
Potteries, the group of six towns in Staffordshire all associated with china and pottery production: Stoke-on-Trent, Burslem, Fenton, Hanley, Longton and Tunstall
Poughkeepsie pronounced puh-kip'-see; city in New York state
Poulenc, Francis (1899–1963) French composer
Poulton-le-Fylde, Lancashire (hyphens)
pound abbr. lb; unit of weight equal to 16 oz avoirdupois, 0.4536 kg, or 12 oz troy, 0.3732 kg
pour, pore The first means to flow or rain heavily; the second to examine carefully: one pores over a book
pourboire (Fr.) a gratuity
pour encourager les autres (Fr.) to encourage the others
Poussin, Nicolas (1594–1665) French painter
Powell, Sir Anthony (Dymoke) (1905–) pronounced po'-ull; English novelist
powwow a conference
Powys pronounced pow'(rhymes with cow)-iss; Welsh county containing the former counties of Montgomeryshire, Radnorshire and Breconshire
Powys, John Cowper (1872–1963) pronounced poe'-iss; English poet and novelist
PP parish priest
practical, practicable Anything that can be done and is worth doing is practical. Anything that can be done, whether or not it is worth doing, is practicable

praemonitus praemunitus (Lat.) forewarned is forearmed

Praetorian guard

Praha Czech spelling of Prague

practice (UK noun; US noun, vb)

practise (UK vb)

precautionary measure verbose way of saying 'precaution'

precipitant, **precipitate**, **precipitous** Precipitant and precipitate both indicate a headlong rush and are largely indistinguishable in meaning. However, precipitant tends to emphasize the abruptness of the rush, and precipitate the rashness of it. Precipitous means very steep; cliff faces are precipitous

précis pronounced pray'-see; a summary; *pl.* **précis**, pronounced pray'-seez

precondition, **preplanning**, **prerecorded**, etc. Pre- often adds nothing to the sense of the words to which it is affixed and can be removed. Recorded music is precisely the same as prerecorded music. Conditions for an agreement are the same as preconditions

precursor *not* -er; a forerunner

predilection preference

preferred (-rr-), but **preferable**, **preference** and **preferential**

prehensile able to grasp

premier, **première** The first is a government official of top rank, especially a prime minister; the second is a début

Preminger, Otto (1906–) Austrian-born American film director

premise an introductory statement

premise (US)/**premiss** (UK) a proposition from which a conclusion is drawn

premises always plural when referring to property; there is no such thing as a business premise

prepositions at end of sentences The lingering belief that sentences should not end with prepositions is entirely without foundation. Indeed, there are many sentences where the preposition could scarcely come anywhere but at the end: 'This bed hasn't been slept in'; 'What is the world coming to?'; 'I don't know what you are talking about.'

prerogative an exclusive right

Prescelly Mountains, Wales, pronounced press-ell'-ee

prescribe, **proscribe** The first means to order or instruct; the second to forbid or denounce. If you contract bronchitis, your doctor may prescribe antibiotics and proscribe smoking

Press Complaints Commission (UK) watchdog that replaced the Press Council in 1991

pressurize raise to a high pressure; maintain normal atmospheric pressure at high altitudes, as in an aircraft; but for the sense of to exert pressure, press is shorter

Prestatyn, Clwyd, Wales, pronounced press-tatt'-in

Presteigne, Powys, Wales, pronounced press-teen'

pretence (UK)/**pretense** (US)

pretension, **pretentious**

preternatural abnormal, beyond the bounds of nature

prevaricate, **procrastinate** The first means to be untruthful; the second to postpone doing

preventive (pref.)/**preventative** (alt.)

PRI *Partido Revolucionario Institucional* (Sp.)/Institutional Revolutionary Party, which has governed Mexico since 1929

pricey *not* -cy

Prideaux, Cornwall, pronounced prid'-ucks

'Pride goeth before a fall' is wrong. The quotation, from Proverbs, is 'Pride goeth before destruction, and an haughty spirit before a fall'

Priestley, J(ohn) B(oynton) (1894–1984) English novelist and playwright

prima donna leading female singer in an opera company, and, by extension, any arrogant or self-centred person; *pl.* **prima donnas**

prima facie at first sight

prime rate (UK) rate of interest charged by banks to their most creditworthy customers

primeval *not* -evil; very ancient, of earliest time; primitive

Primo de Rivera (y Orbaneja), Miguel (1870–1930) Spanish general and dictator 1923–30

primogeniture being the first-born child; the practice by which an entire inheritance passes to the first-born male child

primus inter pares (Lat.) first among equals

Princess Anne is now the Princess Royal, and, strictly, should not be referred to as Anne even after the first reference

Princes Risborough, Buckinghamshire

Princes Street, Edinburgh

Princes Town, Trinidad

Princetown, Devon

principal, **principle** Principal means of first importance (a school principal, a principal witness). A principle is something fundamental in terms of belief or understanding (a matter of principle, an agreement in principle)

Prinknash Abbey, Gloucestershire, pronounced prin'-idge

Pritchett, Sir V(ictor) S(awdon) (1900–) English writer and critic

privilege

Privy Council (UK) a group of about 350–400 senior figures, including all present and former members of the Cabinet, appointed for life, who ostensibly advise the monarch, though the position is now largely honorary. Members are Privy Councillors or Privy Counsellors

prix fixe (Fr.) pronounced pree feeks; fixed price; *pl.* ***prix fixes***

Prix Goncourt pre-eminent French literary award

p.r.n. *pro re nata* (Lat.) as necessary; used by doctors on prescriptions, meaning that a drug should be taken as required rather than at fixed intervals

proboscis an animal's trunk, long snout or feeding tube; *pl.* **proboscises**

proceed, but **procedure**

procrastinate, **prevaricate** The first means to postpone doing; the second to be untruthful

Procrustean producing or striving to produce absolute conformity, usually through severe or violent means; from Procrustes, a mythological Greek robber who made his victims fit a bed by stretching them or cutting off their limbs

Procter & Gamble *not* -tor; US household products group

proctor university or legal official
procurator fiscal public prosecutor in Scotland
proffer, proffered, proffering
profiterole cream-filled pastry
progenitor ancestor
program (US)/**programme** (UK), but use program for contexts involving computers
prognosis, *pl.* **prognoses**
Prohibition in the US (1920–33) was brought in by the 18th amendment to the Constitution and the Volstead Act, and repealed by the 21st amendment
Prokofiev, Sergei Sergeyevich (1891–1953) Russian composer
promissory note
prone, supine The first means face down; the second face up; *see also* prostrate
pronunciation *not* -nounc-
propaganda
propagate
propel, propelled, propeller, propelling
propellant (noun)/**propellent** (adj.) a mixture of propellant, but a propellent mixture
Propertius, Sextus (*c.* 48–*c.* 15 BC) Roman elegiac poet
prophecy (noun)/**prophesy** (vb) I prophesy war; that is my prophecy
propinquity nearness or similarity
proprietor, but **proprietary**
pro re nata (Lat.) abbr. p.r.n.; as necessary, used by doctors on prescriptions, meaning that a drug should be administered as required rather than at fixed intervals
prosciutto cured Italian ham
Proserpina/Proserpine Roman goddess of the underworld, wife of Pluto, analogous to the Greek goddess Persephone
prospector *not* -er
prosthesis, *pl.* **prostheses**
prostrate Most dictionaries define prostrate as lying face down, but some do not specify. In either case, it should be used only

with the sense of throwing oneself down in submission or for protection; a sleeping person is not prostrate. *See also* prone, supine

protagonist the principal character, not necessarily the hero. Although there can be only one protagonist to a novel, play or situation, there can be any number of antagonists

protégé (masc.)/**protégée** (fem.) one under the protection or tutelage of an experienced person; *pl.* **protégés** (masc.)/**protégées** (fem.)

pro tempore (Lat.) usually shortened to pro tem (no ital.); for the time being

protester *not* -or

protocol

prototype an original that serves as a model for later products of its type. Thus such expressions as 'first prototype', 'experimental prototype' and 'model prototype' are redundant

proved, proven Proved is the preferred past participle, but there are exceptions, notably in Scottish law, where there is a verdict of 'not proven', and in the oil-drilling expression 'proven reserves'

provenance place of origin

proverbial is wrongly used when there is no connection with a proverb

Prudhoe, Northumberland, pronounced prudd'-hoe

Prudhoe Bay, Alaska, pronounced prood'-hoe

Pryor, Richard (1940–) American comedian and actor

PSBR public sector borrowing requirement, the amount of money a government needs to borrow to meet its outgoings in a given fiscal year

pseudonym pen name

psittacosis sometimes called parrot fever; a disease of birds that can be passed to people

ptarmigan

pterodactyl

Ptolemy Macedonian-Egyptian royal dynasty, pronounced 'Toller-me'

Pty. Proprietary, the Australian, New Zealand and South African equivalent of PLC and Inc.

Public Lending Right (UK) abbr. PLR; system by which annual payments are made to British authors based on the number of times their books were borrowed from a sampling of libraries in the previous year

publicly *not* -cally

Public Record Office, London; *not* Records; abbr. PRO

public sector borrowing requirement abbr. PSBR; the amount of money a government needs to borrow to meet its outgoings in a given fiscal year

Puccini, Giacomo (Antonio Domenico Michele Secondo Maria) (1858–1924) Italian composer of operas

Pudd'nhead Wilson, The Tragedy of a novel by Mark Twain (1894)

puerile childish

puerperal pertaining to childbirth, as in puerperal fever

Puerto Rico Caribbean island state, formerly a US territory, now a self-governing commonwealth

Puget Sound, Washington state, pronounced pew'-jet

Pugin, Augustus Welby Northmore (1812–52) English architect

Pulitzer Prizes (US), annual journalism and literary awards, established by the will of Joseph Pulitzer (1847–1911)

pumice volcanic rock

pummel, pummeled, pumeling (US)/**pummel, pummelled, pummelling** (UK)

pumpernickel coarse wholemeal rye bread

Puncknowle, Dorset, pronounced punn'-ull

punctilious

Purcell, Henry (1659–95) pronounced purss'-ull; English composer

Purim pronounced poo-rim, *not* pyoo-rim; Jewish holiday

Purley, district of London, now part of Croydon; but Purleigh, Essex

purlieu, purlieus The first denotes bounds or limits; the second outlying areas or environs

purposely, purposefully The first means intentionally; the second with an objective in mind

purveyor
Pusan, South Korea
pusillanimous cowardly
putrid, but **putrefy**, **putrefaction**
Puttnam, David (1941–) British film producer
PVC polyvinyl chloride, a type of plastic
Pwllheli, Gwynedd, Wales, pronounced pool-thell'-ee
pygmy, *pl.* **pygmies**
pyjamas (UK)/**pajamas** (US)
Pyle, Ernie (Ernest Taylor) (1900–45) American journalist
Pym, Barbara (Mary Crampton) (1913–80) English novelist
Pym, John (1584–1643) English statesman
Pynchon, Thomas (1937–) American novelist
Pyongyang capital of North Korea
pyorrhoea (UK)/**pyorrhea** (US) infection of the gums, more formally called periodontal disease
Pyrenees, **Pyrenean**
Pyrrhic victory a victory won at too great a cost; *see also* Cadmean victory
Pythagoras (582–507 BC) Greek philosopher and mathematician
Pythagorean of or pertaining to Pythagoras

Qaddafi/Gaddafi, Muammar al- (1942–) Libyan head of state 1969–

Qantas Queensland and Northern Territory Aerial Service, Australian airline

Qatar Persian Gulf state

QC Queen's Counsel, a senior barrister. The initials should be separated from the name by a comma, e.g. John Bloggs, QC. Such people are said to have 'taken silk' because of the silk gowns they are entitled to wear

QED *quod erat demonstrandum* (Lat.), which was to be demonstrated

quadrennium a period of four years, and you will be more readily understood if you just say that rather than quadrennium

Quadring, Lincolnshire, pronounced kway'-dring

quadriplegia paralysis of all four limbs

quadruped *not* quadra-; four-legged animal

Quai d'Orsay the French Foreign Ministry, so called because it is on a street of that name in Paris

Quakers formally, the Society of Friends

quandary *not* quandry

quand même (Fr.) all the same

quango quasi-autonomous non-governmental organization

Qu'Appelle Canadian river

quark hypothetical subatomic particle

quart two pints: 40 fl oz (UK)/32 fl oz (US)

quasar quasi-stellar object

quaternary *not* quart-; of or pertaining to groups of four. When capitalized, it describes the geological period, part of the Cenozoic era, in which humans first appeared

quatercentenary *not* quart-; 400th anniversary

quatrefoil in architecture, a four-pointed tracery

quattrocento abbr. of *millequattrocento* (It.), 1400; the 15th century, especially in reference to Italian art and culture

quaver to tremble

queasy

Québecair Canadian airline

Québecois, Parti Canadian political party

Queen Elizabeth II (1926–) officially, Elizabeth the Second by the Grace of God, of the United Kingdom of Great Britain and Northern Ireland and of Her Other Realms and Territories, Queen, Head of the Commonwealth, Defender of the Faith, 1952–

Queen Mother (1900–) formally, Queen Elizabeth the Queen Mother (no punc.); *see also* Bowes Lyon

Queens (no apos.) borough of New York

Queensberry, Marquess of *not* -bury

Queen's Birthday day on which the British monarch's birthday is officially celebrated, the second Saturday of June (as opposed to the Queen's actual birthday, April 21)

Queensboro Bridge, New York

Queen's College, (The), Oxford; **Queens' College**, Cambridge

quelque chose (Fr.) something, a trifle

Quemerford, Wiltshire, pronounced kumm'-er-ford

¿qué pasa? (Sp.) what's up?

Quernmore, Lancashire, pronounced kwar'-mer

querulous fretful, peevish

query, **inquiry/enquiry** A query is a single question. An inquiry or enquiry may be a single question or an extensive investigation; *see also* inquiry/enquiry

que será, será (Sp.) whatever will be, will be. Also, *che sarà sarà* (It.)

Quesnay, François (1694–1774) French economist

qu'est-ce que c'est? (Fr.) what is this?

questionnaire note -nn-
Quetzalcoatl Aztec god
queuing *not* queueing
Quezon City capital of the Philippines 1948–76
quid pro quo tit for tat, a fair trade-off
quiescent
Quiller-Couch, Sir Arthur (1863–1944) Couch pronounced kootch; British scholar and author, whose novels were written under the pseudonym Q
qu'importe? (Fr.) what does it matter?
quincentenary 500th anniversary
Quincy, Illinois, pronounced kwin'-see
Quincy, Massachusetts, pronounced kwin'-zee
Quinquagesima the 50th day before Easter, the Sunday before Lent
quinquennial can mean either to last for five years or to occur every five years. Because of this ambiguity the word is almost always better replaced with a more specific phrase.
quinsy pronounced kwin'-zee; historic name for tonsillitis
quintessence, **quintessential**
quisling a person collaborating with a foreign enemy; a traitor; after **Vidkun Quisling** (1887–1945), pro-Nazi Norwegian Prime Minister appointed by Germany
Quito capital of Ecuador
qui vive, on the in a state of watchfulness
Qum holy city in Iran
quod erat demonstrandum (Lat.) abbr. QED; which was to be demonstrated
quod vide (Lat.) abbr. q.v.; which see, used for cross-references
Quonochontaug, Rhode Island
Quonset hut (US) prefabricated metal shelter, similar to a Nissen hut
quorum, *pl.* **quorums**
Quoyburray, Orkney, Scotland, pronounced kwy' (rhymes with eye)-burr-ee
Quy, Cambridgeshire, rhymes with eye
q.v. *quod vide* (Lat.) which see, used for cross-references

qwerty keyboard standard typewriter keyboard in English, so called because the first six letters of the first row of letters spell qwerty

Rabelais, François (*c.* 1494–*c.* 1553) French satirist

rabbet type of groove used to make a join in carpentry

rabbi, rabbinical

Rabin, Itzhak (1922–) Prime Minister of Israel 1974–7, 1992–

Racine, Jean (1639–99) French poet

raccoon (US)/**racoon** (UK)

Rachmaninov, Sergei Vasilyevich (1873–1943) Russian composer and pianist

rack, wrack Rack means to strain; wrack means to wreck. The expressions are nerve-racking, rack one's brains, wrack and ruin

racket (pref.)/**racquet** (alt.)

racy

radiator *not* -er

radius, *pl.* **radii/radiuses**

Raeburn, Sir Henry (1756–1823) Scottish artist

raffia fibre used for mats

Rafsanjani, Ali Akbar (Hashemi) (1934–) President of Iran 1989–

ragamuffin

ragout/***ragoût*** (Fr.)

Rainier III (1923–) formally, Rainier Louis Henri Maxence Bertrand de Grimaldi; Prince of Monaco 1949–

raise Cain, to

raison d'être (Fr.) reason for being

Rajasthan India, *not* -stan

raki spirit drunk in Eastern Europe and the Middle East

Ralegh, Sir Walter (1552–1618) -leigh often used but now considered incorrect; pronounced ral'-ee (UK)/rawl'-ee (US); English courtier, explorer and author

Raleigh, North Carolina, pronounced rawl'-ee

Raleigh bicycles pronounced ral'-ee (UK)/rawl'-ee (US)

RAM random access memory, a type of computer memory; Royal Academy of Music (London)

Ramadan ninth month of Muslim year, and a fast that takes place in that month

Ramblers' Association (UK) note apos.

Rameses (UK)/**Ramses** (US) name of twelve pharaohs of ancient Egypt

Ramphal, Sir Shridath (Surendranath) (1928–) Guyanese statesman; Secretary-General of the Commonwealth 1975–90

Ramsay, Allan (*c.* 1685–1758) Scottish poet, and father of **Allan Ramsay** (1713–84), Scottish artist

rancor (US)/**rancour** (UK), but **rancorous** (UK, US)

rand (no cap.) abbr. R (cap.); South African unit of currency

Ranelagh Gardens former pleasure gardens in Chelsea, now part of Chelsea Hospital Gardens

ranges of figures When dealing with large approximate sums, write '1 million to 2 million tons', *not* '1 to 2 million tons', '1–2 million tons', etc., unless you mean 'one ton to two million tons'

Ranks Hovis McDougall *not* Rank; British foods group

Ransom, John Crowe (1888–1974) American poet and critic

Ransome, Arthur (Mitchell) (1884–1967) British journalist and author, known particularly for children's books

Raphael Raffaello Santi/Raffaello Sanzio (1483–1520), Italian painter

Rappaccini's Daughter story by Nathaniel Hawthorne (1844)

Rappahannock River, Virginia

rappel (US), **abseil** (UK) to descend from a height by means of a rope

rappelled, rappelling

rapport harmonious relationship

rapprochement (Fr.) reconciliation

rara avis (Lat.) literally, a rare bird; an unusual and wonderful person or thing; *pl.* ***rarae aves***

rarefy, **rarefied**, **rarefaction**, but **rarity**

Rasmussen, Knud (Johan Victor) (1879–1933) Danish explorer

Rasselas, Prince of Abyssinia, The History of a novel by Samuel Johnson (1759)

Rastafarianism religious sect; *see also* Haile Selassie

ratatouille vegetable stew

Ratcheugh, Northumberland, pronounced ratch'-uff

rateable

Rathaus (Ger.) town hall

rational, **rationale** The first means of sound mind; the second is the basic reason for something

rattan a type of cane

ravage, **ravish** The first means to lay waste; the second to rape, carry off, or enrapture

Ravel, Maurice (1875–1937) French composer

Ravenna city in Emilia-Romagna, Italy

ravioli meat-filled squares of pasta

Rawalpindi city in Pakistan

raw sienna note -nn-; yellowish-brown pigment

Ray, Man (1890–1976) born Emanuel Rabinovitch; American artist, photographer and film-maker

Ray, Satyajit (1921–92) Indian film director

Rayleigh, Essex

raze means to reduce to ground level, so it is a tautology to say that a building is razed to the ground

razzmatazz

re- words A hyphen is needed to distinguish between a one-word form and a compound with a different meaning, such as recollect (remember) and re-collect (collect again), and recede (withdraw) and re-cede (give back again). In British usage a hyphen is also necessary when re- is followed by a word beginning with a separately pronounced *e*, as in re-educate and re-edit

Reagan, Ronald (Wilson) (1911–) US President 1981–9

realpolitik politics based on the achievable

rebus a poem or puzzle employing drawings in place of some words or syllables, such as an eye to represent the word I; *pl.* **rebuses**

recce (UK) pronounced wrecky; slang for reconnaissance

receptacle *not* -ticle

recherché far-fetched

Recife, Brazil

reciprocal, **reciprocate**, **reciprocity**

Reckitt & Colman UK household products group

reconnaissance

reconnoiter (US)/**reconnoitre** (UK)

reducible *not* -able

reductio ad absurdum (Lat.) to deflate an argument by proving it absurd

reebok antelope

Reekie, Auld (Scot.) Old Smoky, nickname for Edinburgh

refectory communal eating place

referendums

referral, **referred**, **referring**

reflector

refute means not simply to deny or dispute an allegation, but to prove it wrong

regalia is plural

Regan, Donald Thomas (1918–) American financier and author, Secretary of the Treasury 1981–5

Regent's Park, London

reggae a West Indian style of music

Reggio di Calabria and **Reggio nell' Emilia**, Italy

register office (UK) *not* registry

Registrar, Oxford

Registrary, Cambridge

regretfully, **regrettably** The first means with regret; the second unfortunately

rehabilitate

Reims (Fr., pref. UK, US)/**Rheims** (alt. UK) pronounced reemz in English, ranz in French; city in northeastern France.

The usual spelling of the adjective is Rhemish, but as this is bound to provoke confusion among readers it is perhaps better avoided

Reinhardt, Max (1873–1943) born Max Goldmann; Austrian theatrical producer

Relate formerly the Marriage Guidance Council

religieuse (Fr.) a nun; *pl.* ***religieuses***

religieux (Fr.) a monk; *pl.* ***religieux***

REM rapid eye movement

Remarque, Erich Maria (1898–1970) German-born American novelist

Rembrandt (Harmensz/Harmenszoon van Rijn) (1606–69) Dutch painter

Remembrance Sunday (UK) *not* -berance; the Sunday nearest 11 November, formerly Armistice Day, the day on which World War I ended and on which the dead of the two world wars are commemorated

reminiscence

remissible

remittance, **remitted**

remittent

remunerate *not* renum-

Renaissance, the in European art, roughly the period 1300–1500

rendezvous, *sing.* and *pl.*

renegade

renege *not* renegue/renig

reneged, **reneging**

Renoir, Pierre Auguste (1841–1919) French painter and father of **Jean Renoir** (1894–1979), French film director

renown *not* reknown

repartee

repast a meal

repel, **repellent**

repetition, **repetitive**

replete not merely full, but overfull, stuffed

replica an exact copy. A scale model is not a replica. Only something built to the same size and using the same materials is a replica

repository

reprehensible

reproducible

Repubblica, La (cap. R) note -bb-; Italian newspaper

rescuable

Resnais, Alain (1922–) French film director

Resolution Trust Corporation (US) federal agency concerned with bankrupt savings and loan associations

respirator *not* -er

restaurateur *not* -rant-; a restaurant proprietor or manager

resuscitate, **resuscitator**

retraceable

retroussé (masc.)/**retroussée** (fem.) turned up, particularly applied to noses

retsina Greek white wine flavoured with resin

Reuters (no apos.) formally, Reuters PLC; news agency

reveille pronounced reh-val'-lee (UK)/rev'-uh-lee (US)

revelation

Revelation, Book of *not* -tions

reversible

revert back is always redundant; use just revert

revertible

Reykjavik capital of Iceland

Reynolds News (no apos.)

Rhadamanthus in Greek mythology, a son of Zeus and Europa, and a judge of the dead

Rhein German spelling of Rhine

rhinestone artificial diamond

rhinoceros,*pl.* **rhinoceroses**

Rhodesia renamed Zimbabwe 1980

rhododendron

Rhondda, Mid Glamorgan, Wales

Rhône river, France

rhumb-line (UK)/**rhumb line** (US)

rhythm, **rhythmic**

RI postal and traditional abbr. of Rhode Island; Royal Institute of Painters in Water Colours (UK), Royal Institution (UK)
RIBA Royal Institute of British Architects
Ribbentrop, Joachim von (1893–1946) German politician
ribonucleic acid abbr. RNA
Ricardo, David (1772–1823) English political economist and politician
Richelieu, Armand Jean du Plessis, Cardinal, Duc de Richelieu (1585–1642) French Prime Minister 1624–42
Richler, Mordecai (1931–) Canadian writer
rickets bone disease chiefly affecting children
rickettsia micro-organism that can transmit various diseases to humans
rickety
ricochet, **ricocheted**, **ricocheting**
ridable (US)/**rideable** (UK, alt. US)
Riesling pronounced rees'-ling; a German white wine
Rievaulx Abbey, North Yorkshire, pronounced ree'-vo
riffraff
Rigoletto an opera by Verdi (1851)
rigor (US)/**rigour** (UK), but **rigorous** (UK, US)
rigor mortis
Rijksmuseum, Amsterdam
Riksdag Swedish parliament
Riley, the life of
Rilke, Rainer Maria (1875–1926) Austrian poet
Rimbaud, (Jean Nicolas) Arthur (1854–91) French poet
'Rime of the Ancient Mariner', 'The' poem by Samuel Taylor Coleridge (1798)
Rimsky-Korsakov, Nikolai/Nicholas Andreyevich/Andreievich (1844–1908) Russian composer
Ringling Brothers and Barnum & Bailey Circus America's premier circus
Rio de Janeiro, Brazil
Rio Grande *not* Rio Grande River
Rio Tinto-Zinc note position of hyphen; British mining company

Rip Van Winkle story by Washington Irving (1819)

risible pertaining to laughter, causing laughter

risotto Italian dish of rice cooked in stock with meat or other ingredients

rissole deep fried minced meat or fish ball or patty

RITA Russian Information Telegraph Agency, Soviet News agency; formerly called TASS

Rive Gauche (Fr.) the Left Bank (of the Seine)

Riyadh/Ar Riyad (Arab.) capital of Saudi Arabia

Rizzio, David (1540–66) court musician to, and favourite of, Mary Queen of Scots

RMT Rail, Maritime and Transport workers' union

RNA ribonucleic acid

RNLI Royal National Life-boat Institution

Roanoke, Virginia

Robespierre, Maximilien François Marie Isidore de (1758–94) French Revolutionary

Robins, A. H. US pharmaceuticals company

Rochefoucauld, François, Duc de La (1613–80) properly La Rochefoucauld, François, Duc de; French writer known for his maxims

Rockefeller, John D(avison) (1839–1937) American businessman, co-founder of Standard Oil, and philanthropist; grandfather of **Nelson A(ldrich) Rockefeller** (1908–79), American politician, US Vice-President 1974–7

rock 'n' roll

rococo

Rodgers, Richard (1902–79) American composer

Rodin, **(François) Auguste (René)** (1840–1917) French sculptor

Roedean School, Brighton

Roederer, Louis, champagne

Roeg, Nicolas (Jack) (1928–) pronounced roag; British film director

Rogers, Ginger (1911–) born Virginia Katherine McMath; actress and dancer

Rogers, Richard (George) (1933–) British architect

Roget's Thesaurus of English Words and Phrases compiled by Peter Mark Roget (1779–1869) and first published in 1852

Rohmer, Éric (1920–) born Jean-Marie Maurice Henri Joseph Scherer; French film director

Rohmer, Sax pen name of Arthur Sarsfield Ward (1883–1959), British writer

Rolls-Royce (hyphen)

roly-poly

ROM read-only memory, a type of computer memory

roman-à-clef (Fr.) a novel about real people but using fictitious names; *pl.* ***romans-à-clef***

roman-fleuve (Fr.) a long novel, or series of novels, chronicling several generations of a family, a saga; *pl.* ***romans-fleuves***

Romania *not* Ru-

Roman numerals *see* Appendix

Romanov dynasty that ruled Russia 1613–1917

Romansch/Romansh language spoken in parts of Switzerland

Romberg, Sigmund (1887–1951) Hungarian-born American composer of operettas

Rommel, Erwin (Johannes Eugen) (1891–1944) German field marshal, commander of the Afrika Korps, known as the Desert Fox

Romney, George (1734–1802) English painter

Romsey, Hampshire, pronounced 'Rumzi'

Roosevelt, Franklin Delano (1882–1945) US President 1933–45

Roosevelt, Theodore (1858–1919) US President 1901–08

ropy *not* ropey

Roquefort a French cheese, from the village of Roquefort-sur-Soulzon

Rorschach test psychological test involving ink blots; devised by **Hermann Rorschach** (1884–1922), a Swiss psychiatrist and neurologist

Roseau capital of Dominica

Rosebery, Archibald Philip Primrose, Earl of (1847–1929) *not* -berry; British Prime Minister 1894–5

Rosenberg, Julius (1918–53) and **Ethel** (1915–53) Americans controversially executed as Russian spies

Rosenborg Castle, Copenhagen

Rosenkavalier, Der an opera by Richard Strauss (1911)

Rosetta stone stone fragment that helped archaeologists to decipher Egyptian hieroglyphs

Rosh Hashanah/Hoshanah Jewish New Year, usually late September or early October

Rosmersholm a play by Henrik Ibsen (1886)

RoSPA (UK) Royal Society for the Prevention of Accidents

Rossetti, Dante Gabriel (1828–82) English poet and painter, one of the founders of the Pre-Raphaelite Brotherhood, and brother of **Christina (Georgina) Rossetti** (1830–94), a poet

Rossini, Gioacchino Antonio (1792–1868) Italian composer

Rostand, Edmond (1868–1918) *not* -mund; French playwright and poet

Rostenkowski, Dan (1928–) American politician

Rostropovich, Mstislav (Leopoldovich) (1927–) Russian-born American cellist and conductor

rosy *not* rosey

Rotavator (cap.)

Rothko, Mark (1903–70) Russian-born American artist

Rothmans International (no apos.) British tobacco company

Rothschild family of European financiers. Among the more distinguished members are: **Nathaniel Mayer Victor, Baron Rothschild** (1910–90), English scientist and public servant; **Edmund Leopold de Rothschild** (1916–), British banker; **Baron Élie Robert de Rothschild** (1917–), French banker; **Baron Robert de Rothschild** (1911–), Belgian diplomat

Rottweiler breed of dog

Rouault, Georges Henri (1871–1958) pronounced róo-oh'; French expressionist painter

Roubiliac, Louis François (1695–1762) French sculptor

rouble (UK)/**ruble** (US) Russian unit of currency

Rousseau, Henri ('Douanier') (1844–1910) French painter

Rousseau, Jean Jacques (1712–78) Swiss-born French political theorist

Routledge & Kegan Paul British publisher

Rowland, Roland W. (1917–) *not* Rowlands; nickname 'Tiny'; born R. W. Fuhrhop; British businessman

Rowlandson, Thomas (1756–1827) English caricaturist

Royal and Ancient Golf Club, St Andrews, Fife, Scotland

Royal Dutch-Shell Group (hyphen) Anglo-Dutch oil company

Royal Welch Fusiliers, **Royal Welch Regiment** *not* Welsh

RSVP *répondez s'il vous plaît* (Fr.) please reply. The term is not used in France

RTE Radio Telefís Éireann, Irish broadcasting corporation

Rubáiyát of Omar Khayyám, The, Persian verses

rubella, **rubeola** both are names for measles

Rubens, Peter Paul (1577–1640) Flemish painter

Rubinstein, Artur (1886–1982) Polish-born American pianist

Rüdesheimer pronounced roo'-dess-hy-mer; German wine

Ruhr industrial region of Germany

Rukeyser, Louis (Richard) (1933–) American economic commentator

'Rule, Britannia' note comma (and consider that its absence reverses the meaning); British patriotic song

rumba a lively dance of Cuban origin

rumbustious

rumor (US)/**rumour** (UK)

Rumpelstiltskin

Runnymede meadow in Surrey, near Windsor, where King John signed the Magna Carta in 1215

Runcie, Dr Robert (Alexander Kennedy) (1921–) Archbishop of Canterbury 1980–91

rupee unit of Indian currency

Ruritania fictional country in *The Prisoner of Zenda*, and by extension a romantic, unreal country

Rush and Tompkins *not* Tomkins; British construction group

Ruskin, John (1819–1900) English author and art critic

Russian alphabet *see* Cyrillic alphabet

Ruth, George Herman (1895–1948) nickname 'Babe'; American baseball player renowned for hitting home runs

Ruy Lopez type of opening move in chess

Ruysdael/Ruïsdael, Jacob van (1628–82) pronounced royz'-dale; Dutch artist
Ruzyne Airport, Prague
Rwanda central African republic; capital Kigali
Ryukyu Islands, Japan
Ryun, Jim (1948–) American distance runner

S

Saab-Scania Swedish car and aviation company
Saarbrücken, Germany
Saarinen, Eero (1910–61), Finnish-born American architect, and son of **Gottlieb Eliel Saarinen** (1873–1950), also a noted architect
Sabena World Airlines formerly Sabena Belgian Airlines
sabotage, saboteur
saccharin, **saccharine** The first is an artificial sweetener; the second means sugary
Sackville-West, V(ictoria Mary) (1892–1962) nickname 'Vita', English writer
sacrilege, sacrilegious
Saddam Hussein (al-Takriti) (1937) President of Iraq 1979–
Sadler's Wells London theatre
Saenger Performing Arts Center, New Orleans, Louisiana
safflower
Saffron Walden, Essex
Sagittarius a sign of the Zodiac
sago, *pl.* **sagos**
Sahara means desert, so Sahara Desert is a tautology
Saigon former name of Ho Chi Minh City, Vietnam
St Albans, Hertfordshire, but **St Alban's Head**, Dorset
St Andrews, Fife, Scotland site of St Andrews University and golf's most revered institution, The Royal and Ancient Golf Club
St Andrew's Day (apos.) 30 November
St Anne's College, Oxford

St Antony's College, Oxford
St Barthélemy, French West Indies
St Bartholomew's Hospital, London, commonly called Bart's, the oldest hospital in England
St Benet's Hall, Oxford
St Catharines, Ontario
St Catharine's College, Cambridge
St Catherine's College, Oxford
St Christopher and Nevis, Federation of formal name of Caribbean state commonly known as St Kitts-Nevis
St Clement Danes London church
St Croix, US Virgin Islands, pronounced kroy; formerly Santa Cruz
St Edmund Hall, Oxford
St Edmund's House, Cambridge
Saint-Exupéry, Antoine (Marie Roger) de (1900–44) French aviator and author
St Helens, Merseyside
St Helens, Mount, active volcano in Washington state, which erupted on 18 May 1980
St Helier, Jersey
St James's, Court of the place to which diplomats to Britain are posted
St James's Park, **St James's Palace**, **St James's Square**, London
St John Ambulance Brigade *not* John's
St John's Wood, London
St-Just-in-Roseland, Cornwall
St Katharine's Dock, London *not* Kather-
St Kitts-Nevis formally, the Federation of St Christopher and Nevis
St Leonards-on-Sea, East Sussex
St Louis, Missouri
St Maarten/St Martin Caribbean island divided into Dutch and French sides, respectively
St Martin-in-the-Fields *not* Martin's; London church
St Michael's Mount, Cornwall

St Neots, Cambridgeshire
St Paul, Minnesota
St Paul's Cathedral, London
St Peter's, Rome
St Petersburg, Russia
St Swithin's/Swithun's Day 15 July. According to legend, rain on that day will be followed by 40 days of the same
St Vitus's dance
sake *not* saki; Japanese rice wine
Sakharov, Andrei (Dimitrievich) (1921–89) Russian physicist and dissident; Nobel Peace Prize 1975
Saki pen name of H(ector) H(ugh) Munro (1870–1916), English short story writer
salable (US)/**saleable** (UK)
Salammbô a novel by Flaubert (1862)
Salazar, António (de Oliveira) (1889–1970) dictatorial Prime Minister of Portugal 1932–68
saleable (UK)/**salable** (US)
Salinas de Gortari, Carlos (1944–) President of Mexico 1988–
Salinger, J(erome) D(avid) (1919–) American novelist
Salinger, Pierre (Emil George) (1925–) American journalist and writer
Sallie Mae (US) nickname for Student Loan Marketing Board
Sallust, properly Gaius Sallustius Crispus (86–34 BC) Roman historian and politician
salmonella bacteria that causes food poisoning and various diseases; named after its discoverer, American Dr D. J. Salmon (1850–1914)
Salomon Brothers Inc. US investment bank
Salop (no point) abbr. of Shropshire
SALT strategic arms limitation talks. The expression 'SALT talks', though sometimes criticized as redundant, is often unavoidable
saltpeter (US)/**saltpetre** (UK)
saluki breed of dog
salutary *not* -tory; beneficial

Salvadoran *not* -ean; of El Salvador

Sam Browne belt wide belt with a strap worn diagonally across the chest

samizdat underground publication of banned texts in the USSR

Samlesbury, Lancashire, pronounced samz'-bur-ee

Samson *not* Samp-; legendary man of great strength

samurai (*sing.* and *pl*)

Sana'a, Yemen

sanatorium, *pl.* **sanatoriums/sanatoria**

sanctimonious

Sand, George pen name of Amandine Aurore Lucile Dupin, Baronne Dudevant (1804–76) French writer

sandal type of shoe

sandalwood

Sandburg, Carl (1878–1967) American poet and writer

Sandinistas/Sandinists revolutionary party in Nicaragua that took power in 1979; named after **General Augusto César Sandino** (1895–1934), a Nicaraguan revolutionary

Sandwich Islands former name of Hawaii

sang-froid pronounced sang-frwah'; unflappability

Sangre de Cristo Mountains, Colorado and New Mexico

sangria Spanish drink

sanitary *not* -tory

San Joaquin Valley pronounced san wah-keen'; farming region of central California

San Luis Obispo, California *not* Louis

San Salvador capital of El Salvador

sansculotte/*sans-culotte* (Fr.) literally, 'without breeches'; an extreme revolutionary or republican. French revolutionaries were so called because they wore pantaloons rather than breeches

sanserif/sans-serif a typeface without serifs

Santa Ana, California *not* Anna

Santa Isabel former name of Malabo, capital of Equatorial Guinea

Santayana, George (1863–1952) born Jorge Augustin Nicolás

Ruiz de Santayana; Spanish-born American poet, novelist and philosopher

Santo Domingo formerly Ciudad Trujillo; capital of the Dominican Republic

São Paulo, largest city in Brazil

sapphire note -pp-; precious stone

Sappho (*c.* 620 BC–*c.* 565 BC) Greek poetess

Sarajevo capital of Bosnia; until recently, chiefly remembered as place where Archduke Francis Ferdinand of Austria, a nephew of the Emperor, was assassinated in 1914, precipitating World War I

Sara Lee Corporation US foods group

sarcoma a malignant tumour in connective tissue, bone or muscle; *pl.* **sarcomas/sarcomata**

sarcophagus stone coffin; *pl.* **sarcophagi**

Sargasso Sea area of Atlantic Ocean where masses of floating seaweed are found

Sargent, John Singer (1856–1925) American painter, based in London

sarsaparilla pronounced sass'-puh-rilla; plant of the lily family, and American soft drink, no longer produced, flavoured with it

Sartre, Jean-Paul (1905–80) French philosopher, dramatist and novelist

Sarum ancient name of Salisbury, Wiltshire

Sarum: signature of the Bishop of Salisbury

SAS Scandinavian Airlines System; Special Air Service (UK)

Saskatchewan Canadian province and river

Saskatoon, Saskatchewan, Canada

sasquatch North American abominable snowman

sassafras North American tree, source of flavouring

Sassoon, Siegfried (Lorraine) (1886–1967) British poet

satellite

Satie, Erik Alfred Leslie (1866–1925) French composer

Sauchiehall Street, Glasgow, pronounced sock'-ee-hall

saucisse (Fr.) pork sausage

saucy *not* -ey

sauerbraten (Ger.) dish made of marinated beef

sauerkraut pickled chopped cabbage

Sault Sainte Marie pronounced soo saint ma-ree'; towns in Michigan and Ontario, and a canal linking Lake Huron and Lake Superior

Sausalito, California

Sauterne, **Sauternes** The first is a sweet white French wine; the second the village in Gironde from which it comes

sauve qui peut (Fr.) literally, 'save who can'; to flee wildly; every man for himself

savanna (US, alt. UK)/**savannah** (UK, alt. US) tropical and subtropical grassland

Savannah, Georgia

Savernake, Wiltshire, pronounced sav'-er-nack

Savile Row, London

savoir-faire (Fr.) social grace

savoir-vivre (Fr.) good breeding

Savonarola, Girolamo (1452–98) Italian religious and political reformer

saxophone musical instrument invented by Adolphe Sax (1814–94), a Belgian

SC Signal Corps (US); South Carolina; Special Constable (UK); Staff Corps (UK); Supreme Court

Sca Fell, but **Scafell Pike**, Cumbria. Both are mountains in the Lake District. Scafell Pike is the highest in England at 3,206 feet

Scala, La opera house in Milan. Formally, Teatro alla Scala

scalene triangle one with no equal sides

scallywag (Britain), **scalawag** (US) a rascal. Note one-l-in US spelling

scaloppine Italian dish

Scandinavia not Scanda-

Scapigliatura, La 19th century Italian literary movement. Literally, 'the dishevelled ones'

Scarborough, North Yorkshire. But it is the Earl of Scarbrough

scarce, scarcely

scared (frightened), **scarred** (disfigured)

scarf *pl.* **scarves** or **scarfs**

Scarlatti, Alessandro (1659–1725) and **Domenico** (1683–1757), father and son composers from Italy

scary *not -ey*

sceptic, scepticism (UK)/**skeptic, skepticism** (US)

schadenfreude (Ger.) pronounced shah-den-froy-duh; deriving pleasure from the misfortunes of others

Schaefer Stadium, Foxboro, Massachusetts, home of the New England Patriots football team

Schaffhausen/Schaffhouse (Fr.), Switzerland

Schaffner, Franklin (1920–89) American film director

Scheherazade fictional sultan's wife, narrator of *The Arabian Nights;* title of composition by Rimsky-Korsakov

Schenectady, New York, pronounced skuh-nek'-tuh-dee

Scheveningen suburb of The Hague, The Netherlands

Schiaparelli, Elsa (1890–1973) Italian-born French fashion designer

Schiller, (Johann Christoph) Friedrich von (1759–1805) German poet, playwright and historian

schilling Austrian unit of currency

Schiphol Airport, Amsterdam

Schleiermacher, Friedrich Daniel Ernst (1768–1834) German philosopher

schlemiel (Yidd.) a fool

Schlesinger, Arthur M(eier) (1888–1965) American historian, and father of **Arthur M(eier) Schlesinger Jr** (1917–), American historian

Schleswig-Holstein province of Germany

Schlieffen, Alfred, Count von (1833–1913) Prussian field marshal and military strategist

Schliemann, Heinrich (1822–90) German archaeologist

schmaltz maudlin sentimentality

Schnabel, Artur (1882–1951) Austrian-born American pianist

schnapps a strong alcoholic drink

Schnauzer breed of dog

schnitzel veal cutlet

Schnitzler, Arthur (1862–1931) Australian novelist and playwright

Schoenberg/Schönberg, Arnold (1874–1951) Austrian composer

Schomburg Center for Research in Black Culture, New York

Schönbrunn Palace, Vienna

Schopenhauer, Arthur (1788–1860) German philosopher

Schubert, Franz (Peter) (1797–1828) Austrian composer

Schulberg, Budd (1914–) American screenwriter

Schulz, Charles M(onroe) (1922–) American comic-strip cartoonist

Schuman, Robert (1886–1963) Luxemburg-born French statesman who devised the Schuman Plan, which led to the setting-up of the European Coal and Steel Community

Schumann, Clara Josephine Wieck (1819–96) German pianist and composer, and wife of **Robert (Alexander) Schumann** (1810–56), German composer

schuss downhill run in skiing

Schütz, Heinrich (1585–1672) German composer

Schuylkill pronounced skoo'-kill; river in Pennsylvania

schwa an unstressed and indistinct vowel sound, denoted by the symbol ə

Schwabing district of Munich

Schwarzenegger, Arnold (1947–) Austrian-born film actor

Schwarzkopf, (Olga Maria) Elisabeth (1915–) Polish-born German soprano

Schwarzwald (Ger.) the Black Forest

Schwechat Airport, Vienna

Schweitzer, Albert (1875–1965) German theologian, medical missionary, philosopher and musician; established Lambaréné mission, French Equatorial Africa; Nobel Peace Prize 1952

Schweiz, die German name for Switzerland

Schygulla, Hanna (1943–) German film actress

Science Museum, London, formally National Museum of Science and Industry

Scilly, Isles of pronounced silly; group of islands off tip of Cornwall; adj. Scillonian

scintilla a tiny amount

Scofield, Paul (1922–) British actor

Scorsese, Martin (1942–) American film director

Scotch, Scottish, Scots Except for Scotch whisky and well-established expressions such as Scotch broth and Scotch mist, Scottish and Scots are preferred. In particular, a person from Scotland is Scottish, *not* Scotch. The army unit is the Scots Guards

Scotch tape US brand of sticking tape; *see also* Sellotape

scot-free to escape without penalty

Scottish terrier breed of dog

scouse native and dialect of Liverpool

scrutiny means close examination, so the common expression 'close scrutiny' is a tautology. The word is almost always better used without qualification

scurrilous grossly obscene or abusive

Scylla and Charybdis In Greek mythology Scylla (pronounced silla) was a six-headed monster who lived beside a treacherous whirlpool called Charybdis (pronounced kuh-rib-dis) off the coast of Sicily, so Scylla and Charybdis signify a highly unattractive dilemma

SD postal abbr. of South Dakota

SDI (US) Strategic Defence Initiative, commonly called 'star wars'; plan propounded by President Reagan in 1983 to erect a 'shield' of weapons in space over the US to keep out incoming missiles

SDRs special drawing rights; rights of members of the International Monetary Fund to draw on monies set up by the Fund to solve temporary balance of payment problems

Seaborg, Glenn (Theodore) (1912–) American nuclear chemist and physicist; Nobel Prize for Chemistry 1951

Seanad Éireann pronounced shin-add' air-ann'; upper house of Irish parliament

SEAQ Stock Exchange Automatic Quotations system, used on London Stock Exchange

Sears, Roebuck & Co. US stores group, usually called Sears. The Sears Tower in Chicago, Illinois, the company's headquarters, is the tallest building in the world at 110 stories and 1,454 ft/443 m

SEATO South-East Asia Treaty Organization
Sebastopol (alt., hist.)/**Sevastopol** Crimean city and Black Sea port
SEC (US) Securities and Exchange Commission, the regulatory body for US stock markets; but the Securities Exchange Act
secateurs pruning clippers
secede
Securities and Exchange Commission *see* SEC
Securities and Investments Board (UK) abbr. SIB; regulatory body for investment businesses
sedentary
Sedgemoor, Battle of (1685) at which forces of James II defeated Duke of Monmouth
Segovia, Andrés (1894–1987) Spanish guitarist
se habla español (Sp.) Spanish spoken here
seigneur lord of a manor, feudal lord
seize
Sejm Parliament of Poland
Selassie, Haile *see* Haile Selassie
Selfridges (no apos.) London department store
Sellafield nuclear plant in Cumbria, formerly called Windscale
Sellotape (cap.) UK brand of sticking tape; *see also* Scotch tape
Selznick, David O(liver) (1902–65) American film producer
semblance
Sendero Luminoso (Sp.) Shining Path, Peruvian revolutionary group
Seneca, Lucius Annaeus (*c.* 4 BC–AD 65) Roman philosopher, statesman and playwright
Senegal West African republic; capital Dakar
Senhor*, *Senhora*, *Senhorita (Port.) first syllable pronounced sun; Mr, Mrs, Miss
Senna, Ayrton (1960–) Brazilian formula-one racing car driver
'Sennacherib, The Destruction of' poem by Byron (1815)
Sennett, Mack (1884–1960) born Michael Sinnott; Canadian-born American film producer and director
Señor*, *Señora*, *Señorita (Sp.) first syllable pronounced sen; Mr, Mrs, Miss

Seoul pronounced sole; capital of South Korea. An alternative name among the Koreans is Kyongsong

Sephardi a Jew of Spanish or Portuguese origin; *pl.* **Sephardim**; *see also* Ashkenazi

seppuku hara-kiri

septicaemia (UK)/**septicemia** (US) blood poisoning

septuagenarian *not* septa-; person 70–79 years old

Septuagesima third Sunday before Lent, 70th day before Easter

seraglio a harem

Serengeti National Park, Serengeti Plain, Tanzania

sergeant

seriatim *not* -tum; in a series, one after another

sesquipedalian a long word

Session, Court of supreme court of Scotland

settee

Seurat, Georges Pierre (1859–91) French painter

seven deadly sins, the avarice, envy, gluttony, lust, pride, sloth and wrath

Seven Wonders of the World the Hanging Gardens of Babylon, the Great Pyramids of Egypt, the Colossus of Rhodes, the Mausoleum at Halicarnassus, the temple of Artemis at Ephesus, the statue of Zeus at Olympia, and the Pharos at Alexandria

Sevilla (Sp.)/**Seville**, Spain

Sèvres porcelain

sewage, sewerage The first is waste; the second the system that carries the waste away

Sexagesima second Sunday before Lent, 60th day before Easter

Seychelles island republic in Indian Ocean; capital Victoria; adj. Seychellois

Seymour, Jane (*c.* 1509–37) third wife of Henry VIII

Seymour, Lynn (1939–   ) Canadian-born British ballerina

S4C *Sianel Pedwar Cymru* (Wel.), Channel Four Wales, Welsh-language television channel

's-Gravenhage pronounced skrah-ven-hah'-guh; formal name for The Hague

Shadow Cabinet (caps.)

shaikh use sheikh

Shakerley, Greater Manchester, pronounced shack'-er-lee

Shakespearean (US)/**Shakespearian** (UK, alt. US)

shaky (*not* -ey), **shakiness**

shallot a plant related to the onion

'Shalott', 'The Lady of' poem by Tennyson (1833)

Shamir, Yitzhak (1915–) born Yitzhak Jazernicki; Prime Minister of Israel 1983–4, 1988–92

Shandong (Pinyin)/**Shantung** Chinese province; capital Jinan

Shangri-La a paradise, from the novel *Lost Horizon* (1933) by James Hilton

Shankill Road, Belfast *not* -hill

shanks's mare or **pony** to travel on foot

Shansi *see* Shanxi

shan't shall not

Shantung *see* Shandong

Shanxi (Pinyin)/**Shansi** Chinese province; capital Taiyuan

SHAPE Supreme Headquarters, Allied Powers, Europe

Sharpeville Massacre fatal shooting of 67 black South African demonstrators by police at black township of Sharpeville, near Johannesburg, on 21 March 1960

Shaw, George Bernard (1856-1950) Irish dramatist and essayist

Shays' Rebellion *not* Shay's; uprising by American farmers in 1786–7 led by Daniel Shays of Massachusetts

Shea Stadium, New York, home of the New York Mets baseball team

Shedd Aquarium, Chicago

sheikh *not* shaikh

shekel Israeli unit of currency

Shelley, Mary Wollstonecraft (1797–1851) English writer, and second wife of **Percy Bysshe Shelley** (1792–1822), English poet

shenanigans antics

Shepard, Alan (Bartlett) (1923–) US astronaut, the first American in space (1961)

Shepard, Sam (1943–) born Samuel Shepard Rogers; American actor and playwright

Shepherd, Cybill (1949–) American actress
Shepherd Market, London *not* -herd's
Shepherd's Bush, London
Shepton Beauchamp, Somerset; Beauchamp is pronounced bee-chum
Sheraton, Thomas (1751–1806) English furniture designer
Sherborne, Dorset, pronounced shur'-burn. Pupils of the public school there are called Shirburnians
Sherbourne, Warwickshire
Sherburn, Durham
Sheremetyevo Airport, Moscow
sheriff
Sherpa (cap.) a Himalayan people living in Tibet and Nepal
's Hertogenbosch city in The Netherlands, commonly called Den Bosch
Shevardnadze, Eduard (Amvrosiyevich) (1928–) former Soviet politician, now President of Georgia
shibboleth a word or phrase that distinguishes one group from another, a password
Shiite/Shi'ite member of the Shiah branch of Islam
Shikoku Japanese island
shiksa (Yidd.) a disparaging term for a non-Jewish girl
shillelagh pronounced shi-lay'-lee; Irish cudgel
Sholokov, Mikhail (Aleksandrovich) (1905–84) Russian novelist; Nobel Prize for Literature 1965
Shooters Hill, London
Short Brothers PLC Belfast aircraft manufacturer, commonly known as Shorts (no apos.)
Shostakovich, Dmitri Dmitriyevich (1906–75) Russian composer
Shrewsbury, Shropshire, pronounced shroze'-bury/shrews'-bury
shriek
shrivel, **shrivelled**, **shrivelling** (UK)/**shriveled**, **shriveling** (US)
shrove past tense of shrive, to give confession
Shrovetide the three days before Ash Wednesday

Shrove Tuesday the day before Ash Wednesday

Shultz, George (Pratt) (1920–) American statesman

Shute, Nevil pen name of Nevil Shute Norway (1899–1960) British novelist

shy, shyer/shier, shyest/shiest

SIB (UK) Securities and Investments Board, regulatory body for investment businesses

Sibelius, Johan Julius Christian (1865-1957) Finnish composer

sibilant hissing

sic (Lat.) thus; used, usually in square brackets, to show that a word or passage is being quoted correctly despite any errors or infelicities it may contain

Sichuan (Pinyin)/**Szechwan** Chinese province; capital Chengdu

sic transit gloria mundi (Lat.) so passes the glory of the world

Siddons, Sarah (1755–1831) leading English actress of her day

Sidgwick & Jackson British publisher

Sidney, Sir Philip (1554–86) English courtier, soldier and poet

SIDS Sudden Infant Death Syndrome

siege

Siegfried Line defensive fortification built by Germany along its western border before World War II

Siena, Italy

Sierra Leone republic in West Africa; capital Freetown

signatory

Sign of Four, The *not* the Four; a Sherlock Holmes story

signor, signora, signorina (It.) Mr, Mrs, Miss

Sikkim former Himalayan kingdom annexed by India in 1975

Sikorsky helicopters

silhouette

silicon chip *not* -cone

sillabub (alt. UK)/**syllabub** a dessert

Sillitoe, Alan (1928–) English novelist

silvan (pref.)/**sylvan** (alt.)

s'il vous plaît (Fr.) please

simile, metaphor Both are figures of speech in which two things are compared. A simile likens one thing to another, dissimilar one: 'He ran like the wind', 'She took to racing as a duck takes to water'. A metaphor acts as if the two compared things are identical and substitutes one for the other, thus comparing the beginning of time to the beginning of a day produces the metaphor 'the dawn of time'

simpatico (It.)/***simpático*** (Sp.) friendly, congenial

simulacrum a likeness or copy; a deceptive substitute

sinecure a profitable or advantageous position requiring little or no work

sine qua non (Lat.) a necessary condition

sinfonietta a small orchestra

singe, **singed**, **singeing**

Singin' in the Rain *not* Singing; classic MGM musical (1952)

Sinhalese main population group of Sri Lanka

Sinn Fein (Gaelic) pronounced shin fane; literally, 'we ourselves'; Irish nationalist movement and political party

Sioux North American Indian group

siphon/syphon (alt. UK)

sirocco a hot wind from the Sahara becoming moist as it reaches southern Europe

Sisyphus in Greek mythology, a king of Corinth who was condemned for eternity to push a heavy stone up a hill, only to have it roll down again. Hence Sisyphean describes some endless task

Sithole, Rev. Ndabaningi (1920–) Zimbabwean clergyman and politician

sitz bath type of hip bath

Sixth Avenue, New York; former, but still widely used, name for the Avenue of the Americas

sizeable (UK)/**sizable** (US)

SJ Society of Jesus, Jesuits

Skagerrak note -rr-; channel of the North Sea lying between Norway and Denmark

skedaddle

skein pronounced skane; flock of geese in flight or bundle of thread or yarn

skeptic, **skepticism** (US)/**sceptic**, **scepticism** (UK)

ski, **skied/ski'd**, **skiing**

skiddoo (archaic slang) to depart hastily
skilful (UK)/**skillful** (US)
skilless note -ll-; this clumsy word, meaning to be without skills, is better avoided
skirmish
skulduggery (pref.)/**skullduggery** (alt.)
Skvorecky, Josef (1924–) Czech novelist, resident in Canada
SLD (UK) Social and Liberal Democrats, political party
sleight of hand *not* slight; conjuring trick
sloe a bluish-black wild plum
sloe-eyed having eyes the colour of sloes
sloe gin gin flavoured with sloes
slough Pronounced to rhyme with cow, it means a swamp or bog; pronounced to rhyme with rough, it means to shed skin. Slough, Berkshire, also rhymes with cow
smart alec/aleck
Smetana, Bedřich (1824–84) Czech composer
smidgen/smidgin a small amount
Smith, Sydney (1771–1845) English journalist, cleric and wit
Smiths Industries (no apos.) British aerospace and defence group
Smithsonian Institution, Washington, DC; an institution for the promotion of knowledge, comprising many museums and academic and artistic organizations in Washington and elsewhere in the US, originally funded by **James Smithson** (*c.* 1765–1829), an English chemist who had never been to the US
smoky
smolder (US)/**smoulder** (UK)
Smollett, Tobias (George) (1721–71) Scottish novelist
Smuts, Jan Christiaan (1870–1950) Prime Minister of South Africa 1919–24, 1939–48
Smyrna former name of Izmir, Turkish city on Aegean
snippet
SNP Scottish National Party
Soane's Museum, Sir John, London, note apos.
sobriquet pronounced so-bri-kay'; a nickname

Society of Friends formal name of the Quakers
Socrates (469-399 BC) Greek philosopher
Sofia/Sofiya (Bulg.) capital of Bulgaria
Sogat '82 (UK) trade union formed from the merger of Sogat (the Society of Graphical and Allied Trades) and NATSOPA (the National Society of Operative Printers, Graphical and Media Personnel)
Soho district of London and Birmingham
SoHo, Manhattan district; short for South of Houston Street
soi-disant (Fr.) self-styled
soigné (Fr. masc.)/***soignée*** (Fr. fem.) well groomed
sojourn
soliloquy speech given for the benefit of oneself
Solomon R. Guggenheim Museum New York City
soluble, **solvable** The first is something that can be dissolved; the second something that can be solved
Solzhenitsyn, Alexander (Isayevich) (1918–) Russian novelist
somersault
Somoza (Debayle), Anastasio (1925–80) President of Nicaragua 1967–72, 1974–9
sonar sound navigation and ranging
Sondheim, Stephen (1930–) American composer and lyricist
son et lumière (Fr.) night-time sound and light show
Sophocles (495–406 BC) Greek playwright
sophomoric juvenile. In the US a sophomore is a second-year student in high school, college or university
Sorbonne, Paris; formally, Académie Universitaire de Paris
sortie a quick attack, especially by the besieged on their besiegers; one mission by a single military aircraft
Sotheby's formally, Sotheby's Holdings Inc., formerly Sotheby Parke Bernet & Co.; auctioneers
souchong a Chinese tea
soufflé light, puffy dish made with egg whites
souffle (no accent) pronounced soo'-full; a murmuring sound
souk market in Arab countries
soupçon a very small amount
sou'wester rain hat with a broad brim at the back; a southwest wind

Soviet Union comprised 15 Union Republics: Armenia, Azerbaijan, Byelorussia, Estonia, Georgia, Kazakhstan, Kirghizstan, Latvia, Lithuania, Moldavia, Russia, Tadzhikistan, Turkmenistan, Ukraine and Uzbekistan; formally ceased to exist in 1991

soya beans (UK)/**soybeans** (US)

Spanish Guinea former name of Equatorial Guinea

special, **especial** The first means for a particular purpose; the second to a high degree. A special meal may be especially delicious

special drawing rights abbr. SDRs; rights of members of the International Monetary Fund to draw on monies set up by the Fund to solve temporary balance of payment problems

speciality (UK)/**specialty** (US) pronounced spess-ee-al'-i-tee (UK)/spesh'-ul-tee (US); an area of specialization

specie coin, as opposed to paper money

species, genus The first is a subgroup of the second. The convention is to capitalize the genus, but not the species. People are of the genus *Homo* and the species *sapiens*: *Homo sapiens*; *pls.* **species, genera**

Spencer, (Edward John), Earl (1934–92)

Spengler, Oswald (1880–1936) German philosopher

Spenser, Edmund (1552–99) English poet

Spetsai, Greece

spicy *not* -ey

Spielberg, Steven (1946–) American film director and producer

spigot

spiky *not* -ey

spina bifida spinal defect

spinnaker a type of sail

spinney small woodland

Spinoza, Baruch de (1632–77) Dutch philosopher

Spitsbergen Norwegian island in the Arctic Ocean

spittoon note -tt-

splendor (US)/**splendour** (UK)

split infinitive The belief that it is a serious breach of grammar to split an infinitive (that is, to put an adverb between 'to' and a verb, as in 'to boldly go') is without foundation. There is nothing wrong with splitting an infinitive, and it is practically impossible to find a recognized authority who condemns it

Spokane, Washington state, pronounced spo'-kann

spoliation *not* spoil-; to ruin or plunder

spontaneous, **spontaneity**

sporran the pouch worn on the front of a Scotsman's kilt

springbok an antelope

Square Mile nickname for the City of London

squeegee device for cleaning windows

Sri Lanka formerly Ceylon; island state off the toe of India; capital Colombo

staccato

stadtholder Dutch governor

Stakhanovite a Soviet worker held up to the nation as a paragon; now sometimes applied to workers elsewhere

stalactite, **stalagmite** A stalactite hangs down from the roof or ceiling of a cave, and a stalagmite rises from the floor

Stalin, Joseph (1879–1953) Russian leader

stanch, **staunch** The first means to stop the flow; the second means loyal

stanchion *not* -eon; a post or pillar

Standard Chartered Bank (UK) *not* Standard and Chartered

Stanislavsky system of acting developed by **Konstantin Stanislavsky** (1863–1938), Russian actor, director and teacher

Stansted Airport, Essex

staphylococcus, *pl.* **staphylococci** type of bacteria

starboard the right-hand side of a ship when looking forward; *see also* port

Stasi *Staatssicherheitsdienst* (Ger.), Ministry for State Security in East Germany before unification

Staten Island, New York

stationary, **stationery** The first means standing still; the second is writing paper and envelopes

status pronounced stay'-tus

Steele, Sir Richard (1672–1729) English essayist and dramatist

Steffens, (Joseph) Lincoln (1866–1936) campaigning American journalist
Stendhal not -dahl; pen name of Marie Henri Beyle (1783–1842), French writer
Sterne, Laurence (1713–68) English clergyman and author
Stesichorus (*c.* 640–555 BC) Greek poet
stethoscope
Stevens, Wallace (1879–1955) American poet
Stevenson, Adlai (Ewing) (1900–65) American politician, helped to found the UN and was US delegate to it 1961–5
Stevenson, Robert Louis (Balfour) (1850–94) Scottish writer
sticky *not* -ey
Stieglitz, Alfred (1864–1946) American photographer
Stiffkey, Norfolk, parish of the infamous rector, pronounced 'Stookie'
stiletto, *pl.* **stilettos/stilettoes** (alt. US)
Stirling, Sir James (1926–92) British architect
Stockhausen, Karlheinz (1928–) German composer
Stockton, Earl of title of Harold Macmillan
Stoke-on-Trent, Staffordshire. It is a city, not a town
STOL short takeoff and landing
stolport airport with short runways designed for STOL aircraft
stony
Stopes, Marie (1880–1958) English birth-control pioneer and palaeobotanist
storey (UK)/**story** (US) the horizontal division, or floor, of a building; *pl.* **storeys** (UK)/**stories** (US)
Storey, David (Malcolm) (1933–) English novelist and playwright
Storting Norwegian parliament
Stow-on-the-Wold, Gloucestershire
Strachey, (Giles) Lytton (1880–1932) English biographer
Stradivarius a violin or other string instrument made by **Antonio Stradivari/Stradivarius** (*c.* 1645–1737)
strait a tight space or restricted opening, hence **straitjacket, straitened circumstances, strait-laced**
Stranraer, Dumfries and Galloway, Scotland

Strasbourg/Strassburg (Ger.) city in France

Strategic Defence Initiative abbr. SDI; commonly called 'star wars'; plan propounded by President Reagan in 1983 to erect a 'shield' of weapons in space over the US to keep out incoming missiles

Stratford-upon-Avon, Warwickshire, but Stratford-on-Avon District Council

stratum, *pl.* **strata**

Strauss, Johann, the Younger (1825–99) Austrian violinist, conductor and composer, known for his many waltzes, polkas, marches and operettas. Confusingly, his father, **Johann Strauss the Elder** (1804–49), brothers **Eduard Strauss** (1835–1916) and **Josef Strauss** (1827–70), and son **Johann Strauss III** (1866–1939) were all also composers. None of them should be confused with the next entry

Strauss, Richard (1864–1949) German composer of operas and other musical works

Stravinsky, Igor (Fedorovich) (1882–1971) Russian-born American composer

Streep, Meryl (1951–) American actress

Streisand, Barbra (1942–) *not* -bara; American singer and actress

strike action The word 'action' is almost always redundant here; it is enough to say workers are planning to strike

Strindberg, (Johan) August (1849–1912) Swedish playwright and writer

Stroessner, Alfredo (1912–) pronounced shtross'-ner; President of Paraguay 1954–89

Stroganoff (cap.) strips of meat cooked in a sour-cream sauce

'struth British expletive

strychnine pronounced strick'-neen (UK)/strick'-nine (US); poison

Stuka German dive bomber in World War II

stupefy *not* -ify

stupor *not* -our

Sturm und Drang (Ger.) storm and stress

Stuttgart capital of Baden-Württemberg, Germany

Stuyvesant, Peter (1592–1672) Dutch governor of New Netherlands (1646–64), which later became New York

stylus, *pl.* **styluses/styli**

stymie thwart, immobilize

Styx the river flowing round Hades

sub judice (Lat.) pronounced sub joo-diss-ee/soob yoo-di-keh, awaiting judicial consideration. In the UK details of cases that are *sub judice* (i.e. awaiting trial) cannot be publicly discussed or published

subpoena a writ ordering a person to appear in court

sub rosa (Lat.) under the rose, in secret

sub silentio (Lat.) in silence

subterranean

succès d'estime (Fr.) an undertaking that makes little or no profit but wins critical acclaim

succès fou (Fr.) a huge success, a smash hit

succinct

succubus a female evil spirit that has sexual relations with a sleeping man; *see also* incubus

Sucre official capital of Bolivia, although the seat of government is La Paz

Sudetenland German-speaking area of Czechoslovakia annexed by Hitler as part of the Munich Pact (1938), and returned to Czechoslovakia 1945

Suetonius (Gaius Suetonius Tranquillus) (*c.* 70–*c.* 160), Roman historian and biographer

suggestible

sui generis (Lat.) in a class of its own

suing *not* sueing

sukiyaki Japanese dish

Suleiman I (*c.* 1490–1566) called 'the Magnificent'; Sultan of the Ottoman Empire 1520–66

sulfur (US)/**sulphur** (UK)

Sullavan, Margaret, (1911–60) Hollywood actress; not Sulli-

Sully Prudhomme pen name of René François Armand Prudhomme (1839–1907), French poet; Nobel Prize for Literature 1901

sulphur (UK)/**sulfur** (US)

Sulzberger, Arthur Ochs (1926–) American newspaper publisher

Sunni member of Islamic mainstream

Sununu, John H. (1939–) American politician

Sun Yat-sen (1866–1925) Chinese statesman and revolutionary, guiding force behind revolution of 1911

Suomen Tasavalta (Fin.)/**Republic of Finland**

superfluous, superfluity

supersede *not* -cede

Sûreté French criminal investigation department, Paris

Surinam formerly Dutch Guiana; South American republic; capital Paramaribo

surreptitious

surrounded To be surrounded a thing must be entirely closed in. To say that it is 'surrounded on three sides' is a poor use of the word

Surtees, Robert Smith (1803–64) English writer

surveillance

survivor *not* -er

susceptible

Susquehanna a river flowing through New York state, Pennsylvania and Maryland

Sussex former county of England, now divided into East Sussex and West Sussex. Therefore it is wrong to say Arundel, Sussex; it is Arundel, West Sussex. *See also* Yorkshire

sustenance

susurrate whisper

suttee Hindu practice of a widow throwing herself on her husband's funeral pyre

Suva capital of Fiji

Suwannee River river running through Georgia and Florida, immortalized in songs as the Swanee

Sverige (Swed.)/**Sweden**

swap (*pref.*)/**swop** (alt.)

Swedenborg, Emanuel (1688–72) born Emanuel Swedborg; Swedish scientist and religious philosopher

Swinburne, Algernon Charles (1837–1909) English poet
swinge rhymes with hinge; a hard blow
Swissair (one word)
Swithin's/Swithun's Day, St 15 July. According to legend, rain on that day will be followed by 40 days of the same
Switzerland/die Schweiz (Ger.)/**Suisse** (Fr.)/**Svizzera** (It.)
sycamore tree
Sydney, New South Wales, largest city in Australia
syllabub/sillabub (alt. UK) a dessert
symbiosis a relationship that benefits both parties
Synge, J(ohn) M(illington) (1871–1909) pronounced sing; Irish playwright
synonym
syphilis *not* -ll-
syphon (alt.)/**siphon** (pref.)
Szczecin formerly Stettin; Polish river-port
Szechwan/Sichuan (Pinyin) Chinese province

T

tableau *pl.* **tableaux**, pronounced tab-loze
table d'hôte set meal at a fixed price
tablespoonfuls
tabula rasa (Lat.) a blank slate, the mind at birth
tachycardia abnormally fast heartbeat
Tacitus, Publius or **Gaius Cornelius** (c. 55–120) Roman historian
taffeta fabric
tagliatelle type of pasta
Taine, Hippolyte (Adolphe) (1828–93) French historian and critic
Taipei pronounced tye-pay'; capital of Taiwan
Taittinger champagne
Taiwan, formerly Formosa; officially, the Republic of China; capital Taipei
Taiyo Kobe Bank, Japan
Tajikistan/Tadzhikistan Central Asian republic, formerly part of Soviet Union, capital Dushanbe
Taj Mahal mausoleum at Agra, India
Takashimaya Company Limited largest Japanese retail group
Takeshita, Noburu (1924–) Japanese Prime Minister 1987–9
Taklimakan desert in China
Tale of a Tub, A; satire by Johnathan Swift (1704)
Tales of Hoffmann, The, opera by Jacques Offenbach (1881)
talisman *pl.* **talismans**
Tallahassee capital of Florida
Tallahatchie river in Mississippi

Talleyrand(-Périgord), Charles Maurice de, Prince of Benevento (1754–1838) French statesman

Tallinn capital of Estonia

Tallis, Thomas (c. 1505–85) English musician

tally-ho hunting cry

Talmud sacred Hebrew writings, the main body of laws for Judaism, in two parts: the Mishna, containing the laws themselves, and the Gemara, containing later commentaries and elaborations

Tamaulipas Mexico

tambourine percussion instrument of stretched material and jingling discs

tameable

Tamerlane (1336–1405) Mongol conqueror, but the play by Christopher Marlowe is *Tamburlaine the Great*

Tameside, Greater Manchester

Tammany Hall originally a Democratic Party club, now a committee, in New York City

tam-o'-shanter Scottish cap, named after the hero in the Burns poem 'Tam o'Shanter'

T'ang/Tang Dynasty ruled China 618–907

Tanguy, Yves (1900–55) French-born American painter

Tanjug Yugoslav news agency

Tannoy (UK) make of public-address system

Tantalus in Greek mythology, a son of Zeus condemned in Hades to sit up to his chin in a pool of water that recedes when he bends to drink it, and under branches of grapes that rise as he tries to grasp them

Tanzania African country formed by the merger of Tanganyika and Zanzibar (1964); capital Dodoma

Taoiseach pronounced tee'-sock; Prime Minister of Ireland

taradiddle/tarradiddle nonsense

tarantella Neopolitan dance

tarantula spider

target, targeted, targeting

tariff

tarpaulin

tartar a sauce; dental plaque

Tartar intractable, violent person; sometimes spelt **Tatar** member of a Turkic-speaking people in central Asia

Tartuffe play by Molière (1664)

Tashkent capital of Uzbekistan

TASS *Telegrafnoye Agenstvo Sovyetskovo Soyuza*; Soviet news agency; now called RITA, for Russian Information Telegraph Agency

Tate Gallery, London and Liverpool

tattoo

Taufa'ahau Tupou IV (1918–) King of Tonga 1965–

tautological/tautologous

taxiing, taxied

taxonomy the science of classification of organisms

Tbilisi formerly Tiflis; capital of Georgia

Tchaikovsky, Peter Ilich (1840–93) Russian composer

Teamsters (US) formally, the International Brotherhood of Teamsters, trade union of road hauliers

Teatro alla Scala formal name of Milan opera house commonly called La Scala

Tebbit, Norman (1931–) British Conservative politician

Teachta Dála Southern Irish MP

Technicolor (cap.) *not* -our

tectonics *not* tech-; study of structure and movement of the Earth's crust; *see also* plate tectonics

tee-hee/te-hee (alt. UK) laughter

Teesside, Cleveland; note -ss-;

Tees-side Airport

teetotaler (US)/**teetotaller**(UK)

Tegucigalpa capital of Honduras

Tehran (pref.)/**Teheran** (alt.) capital of Iran

Tehuntepec, **Isthmus of** narrowest part of Mexico

Teignmouth, Devon, pronounced tin'-muth

Teilhard de Chardin, Pierre (1881–1955) French scientist, priest and philosopher

Telemachus in Greek mythology, the son of Odysseus and Penelope

Telstar communications satellite
temblor *not* trem-; an earthquake
temporary respite All respites are temporary
tempus fugit (Lat.) time flies
tendentious biased
Tenerife, Canary Islands
Tenn. Tennessee
Tenniel, Sir John (1820–1914) English cartoonist and illustrator
Tennyson, Alfred, Baron (1809–92) known as Alfred, Lord Tennyson; English poet; Poet Laureate 1850–92
Tenochtitlán Aztec capital on site of modern Mexico City
tepee *not* tee-; North American Indian tent
tequila Mexican drink
tera- prefix meaning 1 trillion
Terence, properly Publius Terentius Afer (c. 190–159 BC) Roman comedy writer
terminus, *pl.* **termini/terminuses**
terracotta
terra firma dry land
terra incognita (Lat.) unknown territory
terrazzo stone flooring material
terrine an earthenware bowl, and the food prepared in it
Tess of the D'Urbervilles novel by Thomas Hardy (1891)
tetchy touchy, ill-tempered
tête-à-tête
Tevere Italian name for the Tiber
Tex. Texas
TGV *Train à Grande Vitesse*, high-speed French train
TGWU (UK) Transport and General Workers' Union
Thackeray, William Makepeace (1811–63) English novelist
thalassic pertaining to the seas
thalassocracy dominance of the seas
Thanksgiving Day formal title of the US holiday celebrated on the fourth Thursday in November, usually referred to simply as Thanksgiving; Canadian holiday celebrated on the second Monday in October
Thant, U (1909–74) Burmese diplomat; Secretary-General of

the United Nations 1962–71. U is a Burmese honorific, roughly equivalent to Mr, not a first name

Thatcher, Margaret (Hilda) (1925–) British Prime Minister 1979–90

theater (US)/**theatre** (UK)

'Their's not to reason why,/Their's but to do and die' lines from the Tennyson poem 'The Charge of the Light Brigade'

Theophrastus (*c.* 372–286 BC) Greek philosopher

therapeutic

Thermopylae, Greece, a pass between the mountains and the sea, used throughout history as an invasion route

Thermos (cap.) vacuum flask for keeping liquids at or near original temperature

thesaurus, *pl.* **thesauri/thesauruses**

thesis, *pl.* **theses**

THF Trusthouse Forte, British hotels group

thingamy/thingummy/thingamajig/thingamabob

thinness, **thinnest**

Third World (caps.)

Thirty-nine Articles the points of doctrine which must be agreed to when taking orders in the Church of England

Thirty Years/Years' War (1618–48) war between Catholic and Protestant factions fought principally in Germany

Thomas Aquinas, St (1225–74) properly, Aquinas, St Thomas; Italian theologian, canonized 1323

Thomas, Dylan (1914–53) Welsh poet

Thompson, Daley (Francis Morgan) (1958–) British decathlete

thorax, *pl.* **thoraces/thoraxes**

Thoreau, Henry David (1817–62) American naturalist, poet and writer

Thornburgh, Dick (1932–) pronounced thorn-burg, *not* burra; American jurist

Thorndike, Dame (Agnes) Sybil (1882–1976) English actress

thorny *not* -ey

Thorvaldsen, Albert Bertel (1770–1844) Danish sculptor of statues on an epic scale

though, although The two are interchangeable except as an adverb placed after the verb, where only though is correct, and with the expressions 'as though' and 'even though', where idiom precludes although

Threadneedle Street, City of London. The Old Lady of Threadneedle Street is the Bank of England

3i (UK) pronounced three-eye; Investors in Industry

Three Mile Island nuclear power station, Harrisburg, Pennsylvania

threshold

thrived/throve

Through the Looking-Glass and What Alice Found There note hyphen; full title of children's book by Lewis Carroll (1871)

Thucydides (*c.* 460–*c.* 400 BC) Greek historian of the Peloponnesian War

Thunderer, The nickname for *The Times* (UK), now seldom used

Tiahuanaco Indian ruins in Bolivia

Tiananmen Square, Peking

Tibullus, Albius (*c.* 54–19 BC) Roman elegiac poet

tic douloureux formally, trigeminal neuralgia; disorder of the facial nerves

tickety-boo

tick-tack-toe (US), **noughts and crosses** (UK) a children's game

tiddly-winks a game

Tiepolo, Giovanni Battista (1696–1770) Italian artist

Tierra del Fuego South American archipelago

Tiffany, Charles Lewis (1812–1902) American jeweller, who founded the famous New York jewellery store, and father of **Louis Comfort Tiffany** (1848–1933), American designer, known for design and production of Tiffany glass and Tiffany lamps

tilde pronounced till'-duh; the mark (˜) used in Spanish to denote the sound 'ny', as in *señor*

Tilden, (William Tatem) Bill (1893–1953) American tennis player, three times world champion, and writer

timber, timbre The first is wood; the second refers to sound
Timbuktu/Tombouctou (Fr.) small city in Mali; names used to signify any very remote place
time, at this moment in a carelessly wordy way of saying 'now'
tin lizzie a Model T Ford, not any old car
tinnitus persistent ringing in the ears
Tin Pan Alley district of New York where music publishers were once congregated
tinsel
Tintagel, Cornwall
tintinnabulation ringing sound of bells
Tintoretto Jacopo Robusti (1518–94), Italian artist
Tipperary town and county in Republic of Ireland
Tippett, Sir Michael (Kemp) (1905-) English composer
tipsy *not* -ey; slightly intoxicated
tiramisu Italian dessert
tire (US)/**tyre** (UK) casing around wheel of a vehicle
tiro (UK, alt. US)/**tyro** (US, alt. UK) a novice; *pl.* **tiros/tyros**
Tirol (Ger.)/**Tirolo** (It.)/**Tyrol** region of Austria and Italy
'Tis Pity She's a Whore *not* 'Tis A; play by John Ford (1633)
Titanic White Star passenger liner that sank on 14 April 1912 with the loss of 1,513 lives
titfer (UK) Cockney rhyming slang for hat: tit for tat = hat
Titian/Tiziano Vecellio (It.) (*c.* 1490–1576) Italian painter
titillate
titivate
Tito, Marshal (1892–1980) born Josip Broz; Prime Minister of Yugoslavia 1945–53, President 1953–80
TLS *Times Literary Supplement*
tmesis interposing a word between the syllables of another, as in abso-bloody-lutely
TML Transmanche Link, consortium that built the Channel tunnel
TN postal abbr. of Tennessee
TNT trinitrotoluene, an explosive
to all intents and purposes is a tautology; use 'to all intents'

toboggan
toby jug (no caps.)
Tocqueville, Alexis (Charles Henri Maurice Clérel) de (1805–59) French politician and historian
together with is not the same, grammatically, as 'and'. 'With' is a preposition, *not* a conjunction, and so does not govern the verb. Thus 'The man, together with a woman arrested earlier,' requires a singular verb: 'was being questioned', *not* 'were being questioned'
Tojo, Hideki (1884–1948), Japanese Prime Minister 1941–4, executed as a war criminal
Tolkien, J(ohn) R(onald) R(euel) (1892–1973) English philologist and author of fantasies
Tolpuddle martyrs six farm labourers from Dorset village of Tolpuddle sentenced in 1834 to seven years' transportation to Australia for trade union activities; pardoned 1836
Tolstoy/Tolstoi, Count Leo/Lev (Nikolayevich) (1828–1910) Russian novelist
tomato, *pl.* **tomatoes**
tomorrow
ton, tonne There are two kinds of ton: a long ton (used in the UK), weighing 2,240 lb/1,016 kg, and a short ton (used in the US, Canada), weighing 2,000 lb/907 kg. A tonne is a metric ton, which weighs 2,204 lb/1,000 kg
Tonbridge, Kent, but **Tunbridge Wells**, Kent
tonnages of ships Deadweight tonnage is the amount of cargo a ship can carry. Displacement tonnage is the weight of the ship itself. Gross tonnage measures the theoretical capacity of a ship, based on its dimensions. When discussing ship tonnages, it is only fair to the reader to give some brief idea of what they signify
Tontons Macoute civilian militia, supporters of Duvalier regimes in Haiti
Tony Broadway equivalent of the Oscar; *pl.* **Tonys**
TOPIC Teletext Output of Price Information by Computer; London Stock Exchange viewdata service
topsy-turvy
Torino Italian for Turin

tormentor *not* -er

tornadoes

Torquay, Devon

Torquemada, Tomás de (1420–98) Spanish monk who organized the Inquisition

Tortelier, Paul (1914–90) French cellist

tortuous, torturous The first means winding and circuitous; the second pertains to torture

Torvill, Jayne (1957–) British figure skater, generally in partnership with **Christopher Dean** (1958–)

torsos

tournedos choice cut of beef

Toscanini, Arturo (1867–1957) Italian conductor

Toulouse-Lautrec(-Monfa), Henri (Marie Raymond) de (1864–1901) French painter

toupee (no accent)

Tournai, Belgium

Tournay, France

tourniquet pronounced toor-ni-kay' (UK)/toor-ni-kut (US); a device for stopping the flow of blood

tout à l'heure (Fr.) soon, presently, a moment ago

tout de suite (Fr.) pronounced toot sweet; immediately

tout le monde (Fr.) everybody

tovarich/tovarish/*tovarishch* (Russ.) comrade

toward (US)/**towards** (UK)

toweling (US)/**towelling** (UK)

toxaemia (UK)/**toxemia** (US) blood poisoning

traceable

tractor

Tracy, Spencer (Bonadventure) (1900–67) prolific American actor

tradable

trade mark (UK)/**trademark** (US)

traffic, **trafficker**, **trafficking**

Tralee, County Kerry, Ireland

tranquility, **tranquilizer** (US)/ **tranquillity**, **tranquillizer** (UK)

transalpine, **transatlantic**, **transpacific**, etc.
transgressor *not* -er
transient impermanent
transistor *not* -er
transitive verb one that requires a direct object. 'Give', for example, is a transitive verb. In 'He gave me the book', 'book' is the direct object and 'me' the indirect object; *see also* intransitive
translucent a material through which light passes but images cannot be clearly seen, as with frosted glass
Transmanche Link abbr. TML; consortium of companies that built the Channel Tunnel
transmitter *not* -or
tranship/ment
transsexual note -ss-; a person who has changed sex or is physically of one sex but psychologically of the other
Trans World Airlines (no hyphens) abbr. TWA
Trappist monk note -pp-
trattoria Italian restaurant; *pl.* **trattorie**
traveled, **traveler** (US)/**travelled**, **traveller** (UK)
Traviata, La opera by Giuseppe Verdi (1853)
treble, **triple** There is no fixed distinction between the two. Treble is established in the UK in certain expressions ('treble chance'), but is seldom encountered in the US
treiskaidekaphobia fear of the number 13
trek, **trekked**
trenchant pithy
Treuhandanstalt German government agency responsible for privatizing or closing former East German state companies
trillion, **billion** In the US and now almost always in the UK billion signifies one thousand million (1,000,000,000), but in France and Germany (and formerly in the UK) it signifies one million million (1,000,000,000,000). In the US and generally but not invariably in Britain trillion signifies one million million, but in France and Germany it is one million million million (1,000,000,000,000,000,000)
Trintignant, Jean-Louis (**Xavier**) (1930–) French actor

triple *see* treble, triple

triptych a painting on three panels hinged together

trireme ancient Greek ship with three banks of oars

Tristan da Cunha British island colony in the south Atlantic

Tristram Shandy, Gentleman, The Life and Opinions of novel by Laurence Sterne (1760–67)

trivia is plural

troglodyte a cave-dweller

troika a group of three; a vehicle pulled by three horses abreast

Troilus and Cressida play by Shakespeare (*c.* 1601). The poem by Geoffrey Chaucer is 'Troylus and Cryseyde'

Trollope, Anthony (1815–82) English novelist, and son of **Frances Trollope** (1780–1863), English novelist and travel writer

trompe-l'oeil (Fr.) pronounced tromp-loy; painting designed to make the viewer believe he is looking at a three-dimensional object

Trooping the Colour (UK) *not* of the, Colours; an annual event on the second Saturday in June celebrating the monarch's official (*not* actual) birthday

Trotsky/Trotski, Leon (1879–1940) born Lev Davidovich Bronstein; Russian revolutionary

troubadour

trousseau, *pl.* **trousseaus/trousseaux**

Trovatore, Il opera by Giuseppe Verdi (1853)

Trudeau, Pierre Elliott (1919–) note -ll-, -tt-; Canadian politician, Prime Minister 1968–79, 1980–84

true facts A tautology. All facts are true; things that are not true are not facts

Truffaut, François (1932–84) French film director

Trujillo (Molinas), Rafael (Leonidas) (1891–1961) dictatorial President of the Dominican Republic 1930–61

Truman, Harry S (1884–1972) There is usually no point after the S, as he had no middle name; the middle S stands for nothing. American politician, President 1945–53

Trusthouse Forte *not* Trust House; abbr. THF; British hotels group

tsar (UK)/**czar** (US)

TSB (UK) Trustee Savings Bank

tsetse fly

Tshombe, Moïse (Kapenda) (1919–69) Prime Minister of the Congo (now Zaïre), 1964–5

tsunami a tidal wave

TUC (UK) Trades Union Congress

Tuckahoe, New York state

Tucson, Arizona, pronounced too'-sahn

Tudjman, Franjo President of Croatia (1990–)

Tugendhat, Sir Christopher (Samuel) (1937–) British civil servant

Tuileries, Paris

Tu'ipelehake, Prince Fatahefi (1922–) Prime Minister of Tonga 1970–

Tullamore, County Offaly, Ireland

tumor (US)/**tumour** (UK)

tumult, **turmoil** Both describe situations of confusion and agitation. Tumult applies only to people, but turmoil applies to both people and things. Tumultuous, however, can describe things as well as people

tunnel, **tunneled**, **tunneling**, (US) /**tunnel**, **tunnelled**, **tunnelling** (UK)

turbid, **turgid** The first means impenetrable, muddy; the second inflated or bombastic

Turkmenistan former republic of Soviet Union, now an independent state, capital Ashkhabad

Turner, J(oseph) M(allord) W(illiam) (1775–1851) English artist

turquoise a semiprecious stone, and the colour associated with it

Tuskegee, Alabama, home of **Tuskegee Institute**, renowned college for blacks

Tussaud's, Madame, pronounced too'-sawdz/ too'-soadz; London waxworks museum established by **Marie Grosholtz Tussaud** (1761–1850), Swiss wax modeller

Tutankhamun (*c.* 1359–*c.* 1340 BC) Egyptian pharaoh

tutti-frutti

TWA Trans World Airlines

Twain, Mark pen name of Samuel Langhorne Clemens (1835–1910), American author

2000 is correct for the year, *not* 2,000

TX postal abbr. of Texas

Tyndale/Tindale, William (*c.* 1484–1536) English biblical scholar

Tyne and Wear (no hyphens) former English metropolitan county

Tynwald *not* the; Isle of Man parliament and supreme court

tyrannosaur any two-footed, carnivorous dinosaur of the genus *Tyrannosaurus*

Tyrannosaurus rex the largest tyrannosaur, and the largest carnivorous land animal of all time

tyrannous

tyre (UK)/**tire** (US) the casing of the wheel of a vehicle

tyro (UK, alt. US)/**tiro** (US, alt. UK)

Tyrol/Tirol (Ger.)/**Tirolo** (It.) region of Austria and Italy

Tyrrhenian Sea stretch of the Mediterranean between Italy, Corsica, Sardinia and Sicily

U

U a Burmese honorific, roughly equivalent to Mr

UAE United Arab Emirates

UAL United Airlines

UAR United Arab Republic, title used by Egypt and Syria together 1958–61, and by Egypt alone 1961–71

Übermensch (Ger.) superman

ubiquitous, ubiquity

U-boat *Unterseeboot*, German submarine

Uccello, Paolo (1397–1475) born Paolo di Dono; Italian painter

Uccellina National Park, Tuscany, Italy

UCLA University of California at Los Angeles

UDI unilateral declaration of independence, usually associated with Rhodesia's action on 11 November 1965

UDR Ulster Defence Regiment, largely part-time reserve force in Northern Ireland

Ueberroth, Peter (Victor) (1937–) American businessman, former commissioner of Major League baseball

UEFA Union of European Football Associations

Ueno Park, station, district, Tokyo

Uffizi Gallery/Galleria degli Ùffizi (It.) Florence

UHF ultra high frequency

UHT ultra heat tested, process for 'long-life' milk products

UKAEA United Kingdom Atomic Energy Authority

ukase an edict

Ukraine former republic of Soviet Union, now an independent state, capital Kiev

ukulele

Ulaanbaatar/Ulan Bator capital of Mongolia
Ullmann, Liv (1939–) Norwegian actress
Ullswater, Cumbria
ulna the larger bone in the forearm; *pl.* **ulnae/ulnas** (alt. US)
Ulster province of Ireland, *not* coextensive with Northern Ireland; three counties are in the Republic
ultimatums
ululate to howl or hoot
Ulysses (Lat.)/**Odysseus** (Grk) also a novel by James Joyce
umbilicus *not* -cas; the umbilical cord
unadulterated pure, not debased
un-American, **un-British**, etc.
unanimous, **unanimity**
una voce (Lat.) with one voice, unanimously
unbiased
unbribable *not* -eable
unchristian, but **non-Christian**
UNCTAD United Nations Conference on (*not* for) Trade and Development, agency set up in 1964 with the purpose of smoothing trade differences between nations and promoting economic development
unctuous oily
underdog (one word)
Underground (cap.) London underground railway
Under Milk Wood (three words) Dylan Thomas play for voices (1954)
underwater (one word)
under way (two words)
un-English, **un-British**, etc.
UNESCO United Nations Educational, Scientific and Cultural Organization
unexceptional, **unexceptionable** The first means not remarkable; the second not open to objections
Ungaretti, Giuseppe (1888–1970) Italian poet
unget-at-able note 'unget' is one word
unguent soothing cream or lotion
unhonored (US)/**unhonoured** (UK)

unicameral a legislature having just one chamber
UNICEF United Nations Children's Fund (formerly, United Nations International Children's Emergency Fund)
UNIDO United Nations Industrial Development Organization
uninterested, disinterested The first means not caring; the second neutral
Union of Soviet Socialist Republics/Soyuz Sovyetskikh Sotsialisticheskikh Respublik (Russ.) abbr. USSR; *see also* Soviet Union; ceased to exist in 1991
unique means the only one of its kind. A thing cannot be 'more unique' or 'one of the most unique', etc.
unison all together
Unisys US computer company
United Airlines *not* Air Lines; abbr. UAL
United Arab Emirates formerly the Trucial States; composed of Abu Dhabi, Ajman, Dubai, Fujaira, Ras al Khaima, Sharja and Umm al Qaiwain
United Arab Republic abbr. UAR; title used by Egypt and Syria together 1958–61, and by Egypt alone 1961–71
United Kingdom abbr. UK; formally, the United Kingdom of Great Britain and Northern Ireland; comprising England, Scotland, Wales and Northern Ireland
University College London (no comma)
unlabeled (US)/**unlabelled** (UK)
unlicensed
unmanageable
unmistakable
unmovable
unnamable (US)/**unnameable** (UK, alt. US) note -nn-
unnatural note -nn-
unnecessary note -nn-
unnerved note -nn-
unnumbered note -nn-
unparalleled
unpractical/impractical The words are synonyms
unraveled (US)/**unravelled** (UK)
unridable/unrideable (alt. US)

unrivaled (US)/**unrivalled** (UK)

UNRRA United Nations Relief and Rehabilitation Administration

unselfconscious

unshakable (US)/**unshakeable** (UK, alt. US)

untimely death Generally fatuous; few deaths are timely

unwieldy

up-and-coming (hyphens)

Upanishads ancient Hindu metaphysical treatises

UPI United Press International

Upper Volta former name of Burkina Faso

Uppsala, Sweden, pronounced op-sahl'-la

upsilon *not* -ll-; twentieth letter of Greek alphabet

upsy-daisy

uraemia (UK)/**uremia** (US) toxic blood condition associated with kidney failure

Urdang, Laurence (1927–) American lexicographer

urethra urinary duct; *pl.* **urethrae/urethras**

Uriah Heep character in Dickens's *David Copperfield*

Urquhart pronounced erk'-ert; Scottish name

Ursa Major (Lat.) Great Bear, a constellation

Ursa Minor (Lat.) Little Bear, a constellation

ursine like or of a bear

Ursuline order of nuns named after St Ursula

Uruguay *not* Ura-; South American republic; capital Montevideo

USAF United States Air Force

usage, use The words are largely interchangeable. In general, usage appears in contexts involving languages ('modern English usage') and use in most other cases

USAir (one word) a US airline

USDAW (UK) Union of Shop, Distributive and Allied Workers

usquebaugh/*uisge beatha* (Gaelic) whisky

USSR *see* Union of Soviet Socialist Republics

usufruct the right to use another's property so long as no damage is done, as with footpaths across farmland

usurious adj. of usury

usury the practice of lending money at a grossly inflated rate of interest

USX formerly United States Steel Corporation

UT postal abbr. of Utah

U Thant (1909–74) Burmese diplomat; Secretary-General of the United Nations 1962–71. U is a Burmese honorific, roughly equivalent to Mr, so in alphabetical listings the name should actually appear under T

Uther Pendragon legendary father of King Arthur

utilize to make use of something that wasn't intended for the job ('He utilized a coat hanger to repair the car'); to make the most practical possible use of something ('The farmers utilized every square inch of the hillside'). In other senses 'use' is generally better

Utrillo, Maurice (1883–1955) French artist

Utsunomiya, Honshu, Japan

Uttar Pradesh Indian state; capital Lucknow

utterance

Utzon, Jørn (1918–) Danish architect

uvula the piece of flesh hanging at the back of the mouth above the throat

uxoricide the murder of a wife by her husband, and the man who commits such a crime

Uzbekistan former Soviet republic; capital Tashkent

V

VA postal abbr. of Virginia
vacillate note -c-, -ll-
vacuum
vade-mecum a handbook carried on the person for constant use
vagabond
vagary, *pl.* **vagaries**
vagrant, **vagrancy**
Vaishnava Hindu devotee of Vishnu
valance a short drapery
Val-d'Isère ski resort in French Alps
valediction a farewell speech; adj. **valedictory**
Valenciennes lace
Valera, Éamon de (1882–1975) properly, de Valera, Éamon; US-born Prime Minister of Ireland 1919–21, 1932–48, 1957–9, and President 1959–73
valetudinarian a person, particularly an invalid, obsessed with his or her health
Valhalla in Norse mythology, a great hall of slain warriors, presided over by Odin
valiant *not* -ent
Valium (cap.) brand of tranquillizer
Valkyrie in Norse mythology, one of the 12 handmaidens of Odin
Valladolid province and its capital in Castile, Spain
Vallance, Iain (1943–) British business executive
Valle d'Aosta region of Italy; capital Aosta
Valletta capital of Malta

valor(US)/**valour** (UK), but **valorous** (UK, US)

vamoose to flee or leave hurriedly

Vanbrugh, Sir John (1664–1726) English architect and playwright

Van Buren, Martin (1782–1862) US President 1837–41

Van de Graff, Robert Jemison (1901–67) American physicist and inventor

van der Post, Sir Laurens (Jan) (1906–) South African writer and explorer

Van Dyck, Sir Anthony (1599–1641) Flemish painter; use Vandyke (one word) for a painting by him, and as adj., i.e. Vandyke beard, Vandyke collar

Vänern, Lake largest lake in Sweden

van Eyck, Jan (*c.* 1380–1440) Flemish painter, and brother of **Hubert van Eyck** (*c.* 1366–1426), who may also have been a painter

van Gogh, Vincent (Willem) (1853–90) Dutch painter

Vanuatu formerly the New Hebrides; island republic in the south Pacific; capital Port Vila

vaquero (Sp.) cowboy

Vargas, Getulio Dornelles (1883–1954) President of Brazil 1930–45, 1951–4

varicella medical name for chickenpox

varicose veins

variegated diversified in appearance, particularly in colour

Varig Brazilian airline

Varity Corporation, formerly Massey-Ferguson

Varna formerly Stalin; Bulgarian city

Vasari, Giorgio (1511–74) Italian art historian

VAT (UK) value added tax

Vaughan Williams, Ralph (1872–1958) English composer

Vauquelin, Louis Nicolas (1763–1829) French chemist

VCR (US) video cassette recorder, called a video recorder in the UK

VDU visual display unit, a computer screen

Veblen, Thorstein (Bunde) (1857–1929) American economist

Vecchio, Palazzo, Florence; the famous bridge across the Arno is the **Ponte Vecchio**

VE day (UK)/**V-E Day** (US) 8 May 1945, date of Allied victory in Europe in World War I

veins, but **venous** (adj.)

Velázquez/Velásquez, Diego Rodriguez de Silva y (1599–1660) Spanish painter

veld (pref.)/**veldt** (alt.) grassland

vellum the finest type of parchment

venal, **venial** The first means corruptible; the second pardonable

vendetta feud

vendible

veneer

venerable

venery archaic word for hunting, and for sexual intercourse

Venezuela *not* -uala; South American republic; capital Caracas

vengeance

Veni, vidi, vici (Lat.) I came, I saw, I conquered

venomous

venous *not* vein-; pertaining to veins

ventilator *not* -er

ventre à terre (Fr.) full out, at top speed

Venus' fly-trap (US)/**Venus's fly-trap** (UK)

Venus's comb note -s's; same possessive form for other such constructions: Venus's girdle, Venus's looking glass, etc.

veranda (pref.)/**verandah** (alt.) in US called a porch

verbal agreement, because it can mean either a written or spoken agreement, can be ambiguous. Where the manner of agreeing is important, it is generally better to describe it as an oral or a written agreement

verbatim precisely the same words

verboten (Ger.) pronounced fer-boat-en; forbidden

verdant green

Verdi, Giuseppe (Fortunino Francesco) (1813–1901) Italian opera composer

verdigris green rust on copper or brass

Vereeniging, Transvaal, South Africa

Vergil use **Virgil**

verisimilitude air of truth, quality of being realistic

Verlaine, Paul (Marie) (1844–96) pronounced vair-len; French poet

Vermeer, Jan (1632–96) also known as Jan van der Meer van Delft; Dutch painter

vermicelli type of pasta

vermilion *not* -ll-;, bright red

Vermillion towns in Kansas and South Dakota

vermouth

vernal pertaining to the spring. The vernal equinox is about 21 March

Verne, Jules (1828–1905) French novelist

Veronese, Paolo (1528–88) born Paolo Cagliari; Italian painter

Verrazano-Narrows Bridge, New York City

Verrocchio, Andrea del (1436–88) born Andrea di Michele di Francesco de' Cione; Italian painter and sculptor

Versailles palace near Paris

vertebra, *pl.* **vertebrae**

Verwoerd, Hendrik Frensch (1901–66) Dutch-born South African Prime Minister 1958–66

Vespucci, Amerigo (1454–1512) Italian navigator and explorer after whom America was named

vestibule entrance room or hall

Veterans Administration (US) former name of the Department of Veterans Affairs

Veterans Day (no apos.) 11 November; US holiday honouring all armed forces veterans

veto, *pl.* **vetoes**

vetoed, **vetoing**

Veuve Clicquot champagne

vexatious *not* -cious

VHF very high frequency

viable with reference to plants and animals generally, it means capable of living; with reference to ideas or plans, it means practicable

via dolorosa (Lat.) way of sadness, used to describe the road taken by Jesus to the Crucifixion

vicereine female viceroy; the wife of a viceroy

vichyssoise a creamy potato and leek soup
vicious
vicissitude a change of circumstance
Vicksburg, Mississippi
Vico, Giovanni Battista (Giambattista) (1668–1744) Italian philosopher and historian
victualer (US)/**victualler** (UK) pronounced vittler; a provider of food or drink
vie, **vying**
Vienna, Congress of (1814–15) congress at which victorious European powers carved up disputed territories at the end of the Napoleonic Wars
Vientiane capital of Laos
Vietnam South-east Asian nation, divided into North Vietnam and South Vietnam 1954–76; capital, Hanoi
Vieux Carré French quarter of New Orleans, Louisiana
vieux jeu (Fr.) old-fashioned
vigilance, **vigilant**
vigilante person who takes the law into his or her own hands
vignette a decoration or sketch; an image with no definite border; a literary sketch
Vigny, Alfred Victor, Comte de (1797–1863) French poet, playwright and novelist
vigor (US)/**vigour** (UK), but **vigorous** (UK, US)
vilify *not* -ll-; defame
Villa-Lobos, Heitor (1887–1959) *not* Hector; Brazilian composer
Ville Lumière (Fr.) City of Light, nickname of Paris
Villette novel by Charlotte Brontë (1853)
vinaigrette *not* vinegar-; salad dressing
vin ordinaire an inexpensive wine
Viollet-le-Duc, Eugène Emmanuel (1814–79) French architect
virago a fierce woman; *pl.* **viragos**
Virgil anglicized name of Publius Vergilius Maro (70–19 BC), Roman poet
Virgin Islands comprise the British Virgin Islands (capital Road Town), and the Virgin Islands of the United States (capital Charlotte Amalie)

virtuoso, *pl.* **virtuosi/virtuosos**
vis-à-vis (Fr.) face to face, with regard to
viscera internal organs; *sing.* **viscus**
Visconti, Count Luchino (1906–76) Italian stage and film director
viscous sticky
Vishnu Hindu god
visitable
vis major (Lat.) greater force; *pl.* ***vires majores***
visor shield for eyes
VISTA (US) Volunteers in Service to America
vita brevis, ars longa (Lat.) life is short, art is long
vitiate contaminate, ruin
Viti Levu main island of Fiji and location of Suva, the Fijian capital
vitreous, **vitriform** The first means something made, or having the quality, of glass; the second describes something having the appearance of glass
vitrify to make vitreous
vituperate, **vituperative**
vivacious, **vivacity**
vivat regina! (Lat.) long live the queen
vivat rex! (Lat.) long live the king
viva voce an oral examination
vivify to bring to life
viz. *videlicet* (Lat.), namely, that is to say
Vizcaíno, Sebastián (*c.* 1550–1615) Spanish explorer
VJ day (UK)/**V-J Day** (US) 15 August 1945 (UK), date fighting officially stopped, marking Allied victory over Japan in World War II; 2 September 1945 (US), day surrender signed by Japan
Vlaanderen (Fl.)/**Flanders** note -aa-
Vladivostok, Russia
Vlaminck, Maurice de (1876–1958) French artist and writer
Vlissingen, The Netherlands
vocal cords *not* chords
vociferous outspoken

Volapük artificial language devised in 1879 by Johann Schleyer, a German linguist

volatile

vol-au-vent puff-pastry case filled with savoury foodstuffs and sauce

volcano, *pl.* **volcanoes**

volcanology (US), **vulcanology** (UK) science of volcanoes

Volcker, Paul (1927–) American banking executive and government official

Volgograd formerly Stalingrad and, before that, Tsaritsyn, Russia

Volkswagen *not* -on; abbr. VW; formally, Volkswagenwerk AG

Volstead Act (US) act passed in 1919 to enforce Prohibition

Völsunga Saga Scandinavian epic

Voltaire pen name of François-Marie Arouet (1694–1778), French writer; adj. is **Voltairean**

volte-face a complete change or reversal, especially an unexpected one

voluptuous

von Braun, Wernher (1912–77) German-born American rocket designer

von Karajan, Herbert (1908–89) properly, Karajan, Herbert von; Austrian conductor, principal conductor of Berlin Philharmonic 1955–89

Vonnegut, Kurt, Jr (1922–) American novelist

von Stroheim, Erich (1885–1957) born Hans Erich Maria Stroheim von Nordenwall, German-born Hollywood actor and director

voodoo, *pl.* **voodoos**

voortrekker (Afrikaans) a pioneer

Vorster, Balthazar Johannes (1915–83) South African politician

vortex, *pl.* **vortexes/vortices**

vox populi (Lat.) voice of the people

Voyageurs National Park Minnesota

voyeur one who enjoys watching others engaging in sex

VT postal abbr. of Vermont
VTOL vertical take-off and landing
Vuillard, (Jean) Édouard (1868–1940) French artist
vulcanology (UK)/**volcanology** (US) science of volcanoes
vulpine of a fox
vying

WA postal abbr. of Washington state
WAAC (UK) Women's Army Auxiliary Corps
WAAF (UK) Women's Auxiliary Air Force
WAC (US) Women's Army Corps
wacky (pref.)/**whacky** (alt.) crazy
WAF (US) Women in the Air Force
Wagadugu (alt.)/**Ouagadougou** (pref.) capital of Burkina Faso
Wagner, (Wilhelm) Richard (1813-83) German composer
wagon
Waikiki beach and district of Honolulu, Hawaii
wainscot, **wainscoting** panelling
waistcoat (UK), **vest** (US)
waiver, **waver** The first is a relinquishment of a claim; the second means to hesitate
Wajda, Andrzej (1926–) pronounced vie'-duh; Polish film director
Wakayama, Honshu, Japan
Walden Pond small lake in Massachusetts associated with Henry David Thoreau
Waldenses puritanical Christian sect originating in the 12th century
Waldheim, Kurt (1918–) Austrian politician, Secretary-General of the United Nations 1972–82 and President of Austria 1986–92
Wałesa, Lech (1943–) pronounced lek vah-wend'-suh; Polish trade union leader; Nobel Peace Prize 1983; President of Poland 1990–

walkie-talkie

wallaby species of small kangaroo

Wallace, Alfred Russel (*not* -ll) (1823–1913) English naturalist

Wallace, Sir Richard (1818–90) English art collector and philanthropist

Wallace, Sir William (*c.* 1274–1305) Scottish patriot

Wallenberg, Raoul (1912–47?) Swedish diplomat who helped to save thousands of Hungarian Jews from being sent to concentration camps during World War II

Wallis and Futuna Islands a French overseas territory in the south Pacific

Wallis, Sir Barnes Neville (1887–1979) British aeronautical engineer and inventor

Walloon a French-speaking Belgian

Walpurgis night night of 30 April, when witches were once thought to gather

Walton, Izaak (1593–1683) *not* Isaac; English biographer and naturalist

Wampanoag a North American Indian group of the Algonquian people

wampum small beads once used by North American Indians as money

Wanamaker, Sam (1919–) American author and director

Wankel engine type of internal combustion engine, designed by German engineer Felix Wankel (1902–)

Wardour Street, London

warp and woof a foundation or base

Warrnambool, New South Wales, Australia

Warsaw Pact an economic union of, and a defensive treaty between, the Communist countries of Europe, signed in 1955 by Albania (withdrew 1968), Bulgaria, Czechoslovakia, East Germany (withdrew on merger with West Germany 1990), Hungary, Poland, Romania and the USSR

WASP white Anglo-Saxon Protestant

Wassermann test blood test for syphilis, named after German bacteriologist August von Wassermann (1866–1925)

wastage *not* waste-

wasteland (one word), but the T. S. Eliot poem is 'The Waste Land'

wastrel good-for-nothing person

'Water, water, everywhere, /'Nor any drop to drink' are the lines from the Coleridge poem 'The Rime of the Ancient Mariner'

Waterman, Dennis (1948–) British actor

Waterston, Sam (1940–) not -son; American actor

Watling Street a Roman road between Shropshire and Dover, passing through London

Watt, James (1736–1819) Scottish inventor

Watteau, Jean-Antoine (1684–1721) French painter

Watusi an African people

Waukegan, Illinois

Waugh, Evelyn (1903–66) first name pronounced eev'-a-lin; English novelist

waver, waiver The first means to hesitate; the second is the relinquishment of a claim

Waverley Station, Edinburgh

wavy *not* wavey

WCTU Women's Christian Temperance Union

weasel

Weatherill, (Bruce) Bernard (1920–) British politician

Webb, (Martha) Beatrice (1858–1943) economist, social reformer and historian working jointly with her husband, **Sidney James Webb**, Baron Passfield (1859–1947)

Weber, Carl Maria (Friedrich Ernst) von (1786–1826) German composer and pianist

Webern, Anton von (1883–1945) Austrian composer

Webber, Andrew Lloyd (no hyphen) properly Lloyd Webber, Andrew

Weddell Sea, Antarctica

Wedgwood china *not* Wedge-

weevil type of beetle

Wehrmacht German armed forces 1935–45

Weill, Kurt (1900–50) pronounced vile; German-born American composer

Weimar Republic German republic 1919–33
Weimaraner breed of dog
Weir, Peter (1944–) Australian film director
weird
Weizmann, Chaim (1874–1952) pronounced vites'-mun; Russian-born Israeli scientist and statesman, President of Israel 1948–52
Welch, Raquel (1944–) *not* Rac-; American actress
Welch Regiment and **Royal Welch Fusiliers**, but the *Welsh Guards*
Welles, (George) Orson (1915–85) American film actor and director
Wellesley College, Wellesley, Massachusetts
wellington boots (no caps.)
weltschmerz (Ger.) sadness over the state of the world
Welwyn Garden City, Hertfordshire, pronounced well'in
Wemyss village and castle, Fife; **Wemyss Bay**, Strathclyde, pronounced wimz/weemz
Wendy house (cap. W) (UK) play-house for children
Wensleydale, North Yorkshire
werewolf, *pl.* **werewolves**
Wertmuller, Lina (1928–) born Arcangela Felice Assunte Wertmuller von Elgg, Italian film director
West, Mae (1892–1980) American actress
West, Nathanael note -ael; pen name of Nathan Wallenstein Weinstein (1903–40) American novelist
Westchester, New York, but **West Chester**, Delaware and Pennsylvania
Westdeutsche Landesbank Girozentrale, West German Bank.
Westmeath, County, Ireland
Westmorland, *not* -more-; former county of England
Westpac Banking Corporation, Australian Bank
West Point-Pepperell US textiles company
West Virginia abbr. WV; a state, entirely separate from neighbouring Virginia; capital Charleston (not to be confused with the more famous city of that name in South Carolina)
Westward Ho!, Devon (exclamation mark)

wether a castrated sheep
whacky (alt.)/**wacky** (pref.)
whammy (US) a curse
wharf, *pl.* **wharves/wharfs**
Wharfedale, North Yorkshire
Wharton, Edith (Newbold Jones) (1862–1937) American novelist
wheedle coax
wheeze
whelk edible mollusc
whet one's appetite
Which? (UK) note question mark is part of title; magazine published by Consumers' Association
whim, whimsy (pref.)/**whimsey** (alt.)
whinny the sound a horse makes
whippet breed of dog
whippoorwill North American bird, so named because of its call
whirligig
whiskey (US., Irel.)/**whisky** (UK)
Whistler, James Abbott McNeill (1834–1903) American painter
Whit Sunday the seventh Sunday after Easter
Whitaker's Almanack
White Friars Carmelites
White Paper, **Green Paper** (UK) A Green Paper is a consultative document, outlining Government proposals for discussion. A White Paper outlines the Government's planned legislation
whitish *not* white-
Whittam Smith, Andreas (1937–) (no hyphen) British journalist and newspaper executive
Whittier, John Greenleaf (1807–92) American poet
whittle to pare wood; to reduce gradually
whiz, whizzed, whizzing
whiz-kid *not* **whizz-**
whodunit note -n-; a mystery story

whortleberry
Who's Who
Whyte & Mackay Scotch whisky
WI postal abbr. of Wisconsin
Wichita, Kansas
widdershins (alt. UK)/**withershins**; pronounced widdershins; anticlockwise
widget a gadget or other small undefined item
wield
Wien German for Vienna
Wiener, Norbert (1894–1964) American mathematician, developed science of cybernetics
Wiener schnitzel fried breaded veal cutlet
Wiesbaden, Germany, *not* Weis-, pronounced Veez
Wilde, Oscar (Fingall O'Flahertie Wills) (1854-1900) Irish poet and playwright
wildebeest gnu; *pl.* **wildebeeste/wildebeests**
wilful (UK)/**willful** (US)
Wilkes-Barre Pennsylvania, pronounced wilks-barrah/wilks-barry
Wilkes Land, Antarctica (two words, no apos.)
Wilkie, Sir David (1785–1841) Scottish painter
Williams-Ellis, Sir (Bertram) Clough (1883–1978) British architect who designed and built village of Portmeirion in Gwynedd, Wales
Willkie, Wendell L(ewis) (1892–1944) American businessman, who had never before held public office, chosen by Republican Party as its presidential candidate in 1940; defeated by Franklin Delano Roosevelt
will-o'-the-wisp
Wills, Garry (1934–) US historian; *not* Gary
willy-nilly
Wilshire Boulevard, Los Angeles; *not* Wilt-
Wilson, (James) Harold, Baron (1916–) British politician, Prime Minister 1964–70, 1974–6
Wimbledon tennis club; officially, the All-England Lawn Tennis and Croquet Club

Wimpey/Wimpy The first is a UK construction company; the second a fast-food chain
Windhoek capital of Namibia
Winger, Debra (1952–) *not* Deborah; American film actress
Winnipeg capital of Manitoba, Canada
wintry not -ery
Wisbech, Cambridgeshire, pronounced wiz'-beach
wishy-washy
wistaria climbing flowering shrub, **not** wisteria
witch hazel (US)/**wych-hazel** (UK)
withal *not* -all; in addition, moreover
Withers, Googie (1917–) British actress
withershins/widdershins (alt. UK) pronounced widdershins; anticlockwise
withhold note -hh-
Wittgenstein, Ludwig (Josef Johann) (1889–1951) Austrian-born British philosopher
Witwatersrand South African region in which Johannesburg is located
wizened shrivelled
Wodehouse, Sir P(elham) G(renville) (1881–1975) pronounced wood-house; English-born American comic writer
Wobegon, Lake fictional town in novels by Garrison Keillor
woebegone
Wolf, Hugo (1860–1903) Austrian composer
Wolfe, Thomas (Clayton) (1900–38) American novelist
Wolfit, Sir Donald (1902–68) English actor-manager
Wollongong, New South Wales, Australia
Wollstonecraft, Mary (1759–97) English author, and mother of Mary Wollstonecraft Shelley
Wolsey, Thomas, Cardinal (c. 1475–1530) English clergyman and statesman, Lord Chancellor 1515–29
wondrous *not* -erous
wonky erratic, unreliable, not straight
Woods Hole Oceanographic Institution, Woods Hole, Massachusetts
woofer type of loudspeaker

woolen (US) **woollen** (UK), but **woolly** (UK, US)

Woolf, (Adeline) Virginia (1882–1941) English novelist; founder of the Hogarth Press with her husband, **Leonard (Sidney) Woolf** (1880–1969)

Woollcott, Alexander (Humphreys) (1887–1943) American journalist and critic

woollen (UK) /**woolen** (US), but **woolly** (UK, US)

Woolley, Monty (1888–1963) American film actor

Woolloomooloo, Sydney, Australia

Woolsack (UK) large cushion on which the Lord Chancellor sits in the House of Lords

Woonsocket, Rhode Island

Woosnam, Ian (1958–) British golfer

Worcestershire pronounced woos-ter-shur; former English county, now part of the county of Hereford & Worcester

workaholic

World Bank officially, the International Bank for Reconstruction and Development, but this title rarely used, even on first reference

worshiped, **worshiper** (US)/ **worshipped**, **worshipper** (UK, alt. US)

worsted fabric *not* -stead

WRAC (UK) Women's Royal Army Corps

wrack, **rack** Wrack means to wreck; rack to strain. The expressions are wrack and ruin, nerve-racking, rack one's brain

WRAF (UK) Women's Royal Air Force

Wrangell-St Elias National Park, Alaska

wreak havoc

wreath (noun)

wreathe (vb)

Wright, Frank Lloyd (1869–1959) American architect

Wright, Wilbur (1867–1912) and **Orville** (1871–1948) brothers and aviation pioneers. Their historic flight was at Kitty Hawk, North Carolina, on 17 December 1903

WRNS (UK) Women's Royal Naval Service. A member is a Wren

Wrocław, Poland, formerly Breslau (Ger.)

WRVS (UK) Women's Royal Voluntary Service

wunderkind *not* wonder- pronounced voon-der-kint; a prodigy

WV postal abbr. of West Virginia

WY postal abbr. of Wyoming

Wycherley, William (1640–1716) English playwright

Wyclif/Wycliffe, John (*c.* 1320–84) pronounced wick-liff; English religious reformer

Wykehamist student of Winchester College, English public school; named after William of Wykeham, its founder (pronounced wick'-um)

Wymondham, Norfolk, pronounced win'-dum

Wythenshawe, Greater Manchester

Xavier, St Francis (1506–52) Spanish missionary, one of the founders of the Jesuit order

Xenophon (*c.* 430–*c.* 350 BC) Greek historian and soldier

xerography (no cap.) photocopying process

Xerox (cap.) brand of photocopier and the copies it produces

Xerxes (519–465 BC) Persian king, defeated by Greeks at Salamis

Xianggang (Pinyin)/**Hong Kong**

Xinhua pronounced shin-hwa; Chinese news agency

Xizang (Pinyin)/**Tibet**

X-ray

xylophone

Y

yacht

yakuza (Jap.) Japanese organized crime groups that specialize in blackmailing companies

Yangon formerly Rangoon, capital of Myanmar (formerly Burma)

yarmulke/yarmulka (alt. UK) skullcap worn by Jews

yashmak veil worn by Muslim women

Yastrzemski, Carl (Michael) (1939–) American baseball player

yclept named, known as

ye, as in Ye Olde Antique Shoppe, is *not* pronounced 'yee'. The *y* is a transcription of the Old English character thorn, which was pronounced as *th*.

Yeats, W(illiam) B(utler) (1865–1939) Irish poet

Yeltsin, Boris President of Russia 1991–

Yerevan capital of Armenia

Yeşilköy Airport, Istanbul pronounced yesh-il-keah-ee

Yevtushenko, Yevgeny (Aleksandrovich) (1933–) Russian poet

yobbo, *pl.* **yobbos**

yoghurt (UK)/ **yogurt** (US)

yoicks (UK) fox-hunter's call

Yoknapatawpha County fictional county in William Faulkner novels

Yokohama, Japan

Yokosuka, Japan

Yom Kippur Jewish holy day, also called Day of Atonement

Yorkshire is not one county, but five: North Yorkshire, West Yorkshire, South Yorkshire, Humberside and Cleveland. It is not enough to say Bradford, Yorkshire; it is Bradford, West Yorkshire

Yourcenar, Marguerite pen name of Marguerite de Crayencour (1903–87) Belgian-born French-American writer

Yugoslavia; formerly included the now sovereign republics of Bosnia-Hercegovina, Croatia, Macedonia and Slovenia; now comprises the republics of Montenegro and Serbia, and the autonomous provinces of Kosovo and Vojvodina within Serbia

YTS (UK) Youth Training Scheme

Z

Zaandam, **Zaanstad**, The Netherlands
zabaglione Italian dessert
Zacatecas city and state in central Mexico
Zaïre formerly, Democratic Republic of Congo (*not* the Congo); central African republic; capital Kinshasa
Zambezi African river
Zambia formerly Northern Rhodesia; African republic; capital Lusaka
Zanuck, Darryl F(rancis) (1902–79) American film producer and studio executive; and father of **Richard Darryl Zanuck** (1934–), a film producer
Zarathustra/Zoroaster (Grk) (*fl.* sixth century BC) Persian prophet, founder of the religion Zoroastrianism
Zeebrugge Belgian port, and site of disaster in which the UK ferry *Herald of Free Enterprise* sank with the loss of 188 lives on 6 March 1987
Zeitgeist (Ger.) spirit of the age
Zeffirelli, Franco (1923–) Italian film, theatre and opera director
Zeil, Mount, Northern Territory, Australia
Zell am See (no hyphens) Austrian resort
Zeneca bioscience company demerged from ICI in 1993
Zeppelin German military airship in World War I
Zermatt, Switzerland
zeros
Zeus the greatest of the Greek gods

Zhao Ziyang (1919–) Prime Minister of China 1980–7, General Secretary of Chinese Communist Party 1987–9

Zhonghua Renmin Gongheguo (Mandarin)/**People's Republic of China**

Zhou Enlai (Pinyin)/**Chou En-lai** (1898–1976) pronounced jo-en-lie; Prime Minister of China, 1949–76

Zia (ul-Haq), Muhammad (1924–88) President of Pakistan 1977–88

Ziegfeld, Florenz (1867–1932) American musical theatre producer

ziggurat ancient pyramidal temple in Iraq

Zimbabwe formerly Rhodesia; African republic; capital Harare

Zinnemann, Fred (1907–) Austrian-born American film director

Zip Code US postal code

złoty Poland's basic unit of currency; *pl.* **złotys**

zoetrope 19th-century optical toy

Zoroaster (Grk)/**Zarathustra** (*fl.* sixth century BC) Persian prophet, founder of the religion Zoroastrianism

Zorrilla y Moral, José (1817–93) Spanish poet

Zsigmond, Vilmos (1930–) Hungarian-born American cinematographer

zucchini (It., US), **courgette** (Fr., UK)

Zukor, Adolph (1873–1976) Hungarian-born American film producer and studio executive

zum Beispiel (Ger.) abbr. *z.B.*; for example

zut alors (Fr.) a cry of astonishment

Zvereva, Natalia (1960–) Soviet tennis player

Zweig, Ferdynand (1896–1988) note -dyn-; Polish-born British social scientist

Zweig, Stefan (1881–1942) Austrian writer

zwieback a kind of rusk

Zwingli, Ulrich/Huldreich (1484–1531) Swiss religious zealot

APPENDIX

Words ending in *–able and –ible*

–able	*–ible*
abominable	accessible
amenable	admissible
appreciable	collapsible
available	collectible (US, alt. UK)
collectable (UK, alt. US)	compatible
conformable	comprehensible
confusable	contemptible
culpable	credible
delectable	deductible
dependable	defensible
describable	digestible
estimable	discernible
execrable	divertible
expandable	exhaustible
dispensable	forcible
impassable	impassible
impressionable	incorrigible
innumerable	irresistible
inscrutable	perceptible
inseparable	perfectible
knowledgeable	reprehensible
manageable	resistible
marriageable	revertible
peaceable	suppressible
perishable	
recognizable	

refusable
reputable
salable (US, alt. UK)
saleable (UK, alt. US)
separable
sizable (US, alt. UK)
sizeable (UK, alt. US)
unconscionable

Major airports

Abbr	*City*	*Airport Name*
AMS	Amsterdam	Schíphol
ATH	Athens	Hellinikon
ATL	Atlanta	Hartsfield Atlanta International
BCN	Barcelona	El Prat
SFX	Berlin	Schönefeld
THF		Tempelhof
TXL		Tegel
BOS	Boston	Logan International
EZE	Buenos Aires	Ministro Pistarini
ORD	Chicago	O'Hare International
CPH	Copenhagen	Kastrup
HAM	Hamburg	Fuhlsbuttel
HEL	Helsinki	Helsinki–Vantaa
LHR	London	Heathrow
LGW		Gatwick
LAX	Los Angeles	Los Angeles International
VNY		Van Nuys (pronounced Van Nize)
MAD	Madrid	Barajas
YUL	Montreal	Dorval
YMX		Mirabel
SVO	Moscow	Sheremetyevo
VKO		Vnukovo
DME		Domodedovo
MUC	Munich	Riem
EWR	Newark	[New Jersey] International

JFK	New York	John F. Kennedy International
LGA		La Guardia
FBU	Oslo	Fornebu
GEN		Gardermoen
ORY	Paris	Orly
CDG		Charles de Gaulle
FCO	Rome	Leonardo da Vinci (Fiumicino)
CIA		Ciampino
GRU	São Paulo	Guarulhos International
VCP		Viracopos
CGH		Congonhas
SEL	Seoul	Kimpo International
SIN	Singapore	Changi
ARN	Stockholm	Arlanda
BMA		Bromma
SYD	Sydney	Kingsford Smith
TPE	Taipei	Chiang Kai-shek International
TLV	Tel Aviv	Ben Gurion
HND	Tokyo	Haneda
NRT		Narita
YYZ	Toronto	Lester B. Pearson International
IAD	Washington, DC	Dulles International
WAS		National

Temperature conversion table

Celsius★	← *F/C* →	*Fahrenheit*★	*Celsius*★	← *F/C* →	*Fahrenheit*★
−18	0	32	0	32	90
−15	5	41	2	35	96
−12	10	50	4	40	104
−9	15	59	7	45	113
−7	20	68	10	50	122
−4	25	77	38	100	212
−1	30	86			

★ *figures rounded off to the nearest whole number*

Distance conversion table

km →	miles/*km*	← miles	*km* →	miles/*km*	← miles
1.6	1	0.6	48.3	30	18.6
3.2	2	1.2	64.4	40	24.9
4.8	3	1.9	80.5	50	31.1
6.4	4	2.5	96.6	60	37.3
8.0	5	3.1	112.7	70	43.5
9.7	6	3.7	128.7	80	49.7
11.3	7	4.3	144.8	90	55.9
12.9	8	5.0	160.9	100	62.1
14.5	9	5.6	402.3	250	155.3
16.1	10	6.2	804.7	500	310.7
32.2	20	12.4			

★ *figures rounded off to one decimal place*

Metric prefixes

Prefix	*Meaning*	*Prefix*	*Meaning*
deci-	one-tenth	deka-	10
centi-	one-hundredth	hecto-	100
milli-	one-thousandth	kilo-	1000
micro-	one-millionth	mega-	1 million
nano-	one-billionth	giga-	1 billion
pico-	one-trillionth	tera-	1 trillion

European vehicle identification codes

Code	*Country*	*Code*	*Country*
A	Austria	IRL	Ireland
AL	Albania	IS	Iceland
AND	Andorra	L	Luxembourg
B	Belgium	MC	Monaco
BG	Bulgaria	N	Norway
CH	Switzerland	NL	Netherlands
D	Germany	P	Portugal
DK	Denmark	PL	Poland
E	Spain	RO	Romania
F	France	RSM	San Marino
FL	Liechtenstein	S	Sweden
GB	Great Britain	SCV	Vatican City
H	Hungary	SF	Finland
I	Italy	TR	Turkey

Monarchs of England

Saxons and Danes

802–39	Egbert
839–58	Ethelwulf
858–60	Ethelbald
860–65	Ethelbert
865–71	Ethelred
871–99	Alfred
899–924	Edward (the Elder)
924–39	Athelstan
939–46	Edmund
946–55	Edred
955–9	Edwy
959–75	Edgar
975–8	Edward (the Martyr)
978–1016	Æthelred (the Unready)
1016	Edmund (Ironside)
1016–35	Canute/Cnut
1035–7	Harold (*regent*)
1037–40	Harold I
1040–42	Harthacanute
1042–66	Edward (the Confessor)
1066	Harold II

Normans

1066–87	William I (the Conqueror)
1087–1100	William II (Rufus)
1100–1135	Henry I

House of Blois

1135–54	Stephen

House of Plantagenet

1154–89	Henry II
1189–99	Richard I (Coeur de Lion)
1199–1216	John
1216–72	Henry III
1272–1307	Edward I
1307–27	Edward II
1327–77	Edward III
1377–99	Richard II

House of Lancaster

1399–1413	Henry IV
1413–22	Henry V
1422–61	Henry VI

Appendix

House of York

1461–70	Edward IV

House of Lancaster

1470–71	Henry VI

House of York

1471–83	Edward IV
1483	Edward V
1483–5	Richard III

House of Tudor

1485–1509	Henry VII
1509–47	Henry VIII
1547–53	Edward VI
1553–8	Mary I
1558–1603	Elizabeth I

House of Stuart

1603–25	James I
1625–49	Charles I
1660–85	Charles II
1685–8	James II
1689–94	William III and Mary II
1694–1702	William III alone
1702–14	Anne

House of Hanover

1714–27	George I
1727–60	George II
1760–1820	George III
1820–30	George IV
1830–37	William IV
1837–1901	Victoria

House of Saxe-Coburg

1901–10	Edward VII

House of Windsor

1910–36	George V
1936	Edward VIII
1936–52	George VI
1952–	Elizabeth II

Select list of main units of currency

Country	Currency	Country	Currency
Afghanistan	afghani	Ghana	cedi
Albania	lek	Greece	drachma
Algeria	dinar	Guatemala	quetzal
Argentina	peso	Guinea	franc
Australia	dollar	Haiti	gourde
Austria	schilling	Honduras	lempira
Belgium	franc	Hong Kong	dollar
Bolivia	bolivianopeso	Hungary	forint
Brazil	cruzeiro	Iceland	króna
Bulgaria	lev	India	rupee
Canada	dollar	Indonesia	rupiah
Chile	peso	Iran	rial
China	renminbi yuan	Iraq	dinar
		Ireland	punt
Colombia	peso	Israel	shekel
Costa Rica	colón	Italy	lira
Czech Republic	koruna	Jamaica	dollar
		Japan	yen
Denmark	krone	Kenya	shilling
Egypt	pound	Korea, North	won
El Salvador	colón	Korea, South	won
Ethiopia	birr	Kuwait	dinar
Finland	markka	Laos	kip
France	franc	Lebanon	pound
Germany	mark	Libya	dinar

Luxembourg	franc	South Africa	rand
Malawi	kwacha	Spain	peseta
Malaysia	ringgit	Sweden	krona
Malta	lira	Switzerland	franc
Mexico	peso	Syria	pound
Morocco	dirham	Taiwan	dollar
Netherlands	guilder	Tanzania	shilling
New Zealand	dollar	Thailand	baht
Nicaragua	córdoba	Tunisia	dinar
Nigeria	naira	Turkey	lira
Norway	krone	Uganda	shilling
Panama	balboa	UK	pound
Paraguay	guaraní	Uruguay	peso
Peru	inti	USA	dollar
Philippines	peso	USSR	rouble
Poland	złoty	Venezuela	bolívar
Portugal	escudo	Vietnam	dong
Puerto Rico	US dollar	Yugoslavia	dinar
Romania	leu	Zaïre	zaïre
Saudia Arabia	riyal	Zambia	kwacha
Singapore	dollar	Zimbabwe	dollar
Slovakia	koruna		

Numerals

Arabic	Roman	Arabic	Roman
1	I	50	L
2	II	60	LX
3	III	90	XC
4	IV	100	C
5	V	500	D
6	VI	1,000	M
7	VII	5,000	V̄
8	VIII	10,000	X̄
9	IX	50,000	L̄
10	X		

READ MORE IN PENGUIN

READ MORE IN PENGUIN

LANGUAGE/LINGUISTICS

Sociolinguistics Peter Trudgill

Women speak 'better' English than men. The Eskimo language has several words for snow. 1001 factors influence the way we speak. Professor Trudgill draws on languages from Afrikaans to Yiddish to illuminate this fascinating topic and provide a painless introduction to sociolinguistics.

The English Language David Crystal

A guided tour of the language by the presenter of BBC Radio 4's *English Now*: the common structures that unify the language; the major variations from Ireland to the Caribbean; the 'dialects' of chemists and clergy, lawyers and truckers.

Bad Language Lars-Gunnar Andersson and Peter Trudgill

As this witty and incisive book makes clear, the prophets of gloom who claim that our language is getting worse are guided by emotion far more than by hard facts. The real truth, as Andersson and Trudgill illuminate in fascinating detail, is that change has always been inherent in language.

Our Language Simeon Potter

'The author is brilliantly successful in his effort to instruct by delighting ... he contrives not only to give a history of English but also to talk at his ease on rhyming slang, names, spelling reform, American English and much else ... fascinating' – *Higher Education Journal*

Grammar Frank Palmer

In modern linguistics grammar means far more than cases, tenses and declensions – it means precise and scientific description of the structure of language. This concise guide takes the reader simply and clearly through the concepts of traditional grammar, morphology, sentence structure and transformational-generative grammar.

Language and Learning James Britton

'The theoretical complexities of language acquisition and use are patiently presented and most skilfully and entertainingly illustrated with examples from children's speech and writing' – *Educational Review*

READ MORE IN PENGUIN

A SELECTION OF FICTION AND NON-FICTION

Money for Nothing P. G. Wodehouse

Lester Carmody of Rudge Hall is not altogether a good egg. Rather the reverse, in fact. For his intention is to inherit a large sum from the family silver by arranging its theft… 'His whimsical, hilarious stories aimed to do nothing more than amuse' – *Sunday Express*

Lucky Jim Kingsley Amis

'Dixon makes little dents in the smug fabric of hypocritical, humbugging, classbound British society … Amis caught the mood of post-war restiveness in a book which, though socially significant, was, and still is, extremely funny' – Anthony Burgess

The Day Gone By Richard Adams

'He is the best adventure-story-writer alive … Answers to the literary and personal puzzles of the Mr Adams phenomenon lie buried like truffles in his admirable autobiography' – A. N. Wilson in the *Daily Telegraph*

Romancing Vietnam Justin Wintle

'Justin Wintle's journal is a memorable, often amusing, always interesting diary of a tour of duty in a land where sharp-end history pokes round every corner' – *Yorkshire Post*. 'Compelling reading' – *Sunday Telegraph*

Travelling the World Paul Theroux

Now, for the first time, Paul Theroux has authorized a book of his favourite travel writing, containing photographs taken by those who have followed in his footsteps. The exquisite pictures here brilliantly complement and illuminate the provocative, wry, witty commentaries of one of the world's greatest travellers.

READ MORE IN PENGUIN

A SELECTION OF FICTION AND NON-FICTION

Brightside G. H. Morris

Stuffed with magic, coal grit and wayward, Rabelaisian humour, this wonderful trilogy chronicles the lives of three generations of the Brightsides – a family with an appetite for the extraordinary. 'We've just mined a seam of home-produced – and Northern – magic realism' – *Observer*

Chasing the Monsoon Alexander Frater

In 1987 Alexander Frater decided to pursue the astonishing phenomenon of the Indian summer monsoon and this fascinating account of his journey reveals the exotic, often startling discoveries of an ambitious and irresistibly romantic adventure.

Love in the Time of Cholera Gabriel García Márquez

'For fifty years a breath-taking beauty, now old and just widowed, has recoiled in pride and guilt from her secret lover. His desolate obsession has led him into an enigmatic existence in spite of his renown in business. One Pentecost, love found a new tongue with which to speak. Unique Márquez magic of the sadness and funniness of humanity' – *The Times*

The Invisible Woman Claire Tomalin

'Made visible is Nelly Ternan, and in the process, Tomalin gives us the world of a nineteenth-century actress and most importantly, the real world of Charles Dickens, whose passion for her ... changed his life, his career and his work' – Melvyn Bragg in the *Independent*

Shots from the Hip Charles Shaar Murray

His classic encapsulation of the moment when rock stars turned junkies as the sixties died; his dissection of rock 'n' roll violence as citizens assaulted the Sex Pistols; his superstar encounters, from the decline of Paul McCartney to Mick Jagger's request that the author should leave – Charles Shaar Murray's *Shots from the Hip* is also rock history in the making.

READ MORE IN PENGUIN

A SELECTION OF OMNIBUSES

Italian Folktales Italo Calvino

Greeted with overwhelming enthusiasm and praise, Calvino's anthology is already a classic. These tales have been gathered from every region of Italy and retold in Calvino's own inspired and sensuous language. 'A magic book' – *Time*

The Penguin Book of Ghost Stories Edited by J. A. Cuddon

An anthology to set the spine tingling, from the frightening and bloodcurdling to the witty and subtle, to those that leave a strange and sinister feeling of unease and fear, including stories by Zola, Kleist, Sir Walter Scott, M. R. James, and A. S. Byatt.

The Collected Dorothy Parker

Dorothy Parker, more than any of her contemporaries, captured in her writing the spirit of the Jazz Age. Here, in a single volume, is the definitive Dorothy Parker: poetry, prose, articles and reviews. 'A good, fat book … greatly to be welcomed' – Richard Ingrams

Graham Greene: Collected Short Stories

The thirty-seven stories in this immensely entertaining volume reveal Graham Greene in a range of moods: sometimes cynical, flippant and witty, sometimes searching and philosophical. Each one confirms V. S. Pritchett's statement that Greene is 'a master of storytelling'.

The Stories of William Trevor

'Trevor's short stories are a joy' – *Spectator*. 'Trevor packs into each separate five or six thousand words more richness, more laughter, more ache, more multifarious human-ness than many good writers manage to get into a whole novel' – *Punch*

READ MORE IN PENGUIN

REFERENCE

The Penguin Dictionary of Literary Terms and Literary Theory
J. A. Cuddon

'Scholarly, succinct, comprehensive and entertaining, this is an important book, an indispensable work of reference. It draws on the literature of many languages and quotes aptly and freshly from our own' – *The Times Educational Supplement*

The Penguin Spelling Dictionary

What are the plurals of *octopus* and *rhinoceros*? What is the difference between *stationery* and *stationary*? And how about *annex* and *annexe*, *agape* and *Agape*? This comprehensive new book, the fullest spelling dictionary now available, provides the answers.

The Roget's Thesaurus of English Words and Phrases
Betty Kirkpatrick (ed.)

This new edition of Roget's classic work, now brought up to date for the nineties, will increase anyone's command of the English language. Fully cross-referenced, it includes synonyms of every kind (formal or colloquial, idiomatic and figurative) for almost 900 headings. It is a must for writers and utterly fascinating for any English speaker.

The Penguin Dictionary of English Idioms
Daphne M. Gulland and David G. Hinds-Howell

The English language is full of pitfalls for the foreign student – but the most common problem lies in understanding and using the vast array of idioms. *The Penguin Dictionary of English Idioms* is uniquely designed to stimulate understanding and familiarity by explaining the meanings and origins of idioms and giving examples of typical usage.

The Penguin Wordmaster Dictionary
Martin H. Manser and Nigel D. Turton

This dictionary puts the pleasure back into word-seeking. Every time you look at a page you get a bonus – a panel telling you everything about a particular word or expression. It is, therefore, a dictionary to be read as well as used for its concise and up-to-date definitions.

READ MORE IN PENGUIN

REFERENCE

Medicines: A Guide for Everybody Peter Parish

Now in its seventh edition and completely revised and updated, this bestselling guide is written in ordinary language for the ordinary reader yet will prove indispensable to anyone involved in health care – nurses, pharmacists, opticians, social workers and doctors.

Media Law Geoffrey Robertson, QC, and Andrew Nichol

Crisp and authoritative surveys explain the up-to-date position on defamation, obscenity, official secrecy, copyright and confidentiality, contempt of court, the protection of privacy and much more.

The Slang Thesaurus

Do you make the public bar sound like a gentleman's club? The miraculous *Slang Thesaurus* will liven up your language in no time. You won't Adam and Eve it! A mine of funny, witty, acid and vulgar synonyms for the words you use every day.

The Penguin Dictionary of Troublesome Words Bill Bryson

Why should you avoid discussing the *weather conditions*? Can a married woman be celibate? Why is it eccentric to talk about the aroma of a cowshed? A straightforward guide to the pitfalls and hotly disputed issues in standard written English.

The Penguin Dictionary of Musical Performers Arthur Jacobs

In this invaluable companion volume to *The Penguin Dictionary of Music* Arthur Jacobs has brought together the names of over 2,500 performers. Music is written by composers, yet it is the interpreters who bring it to life; in this comprehensive book they are at last given their due.

The Penguin Dictionary of Physical Geography John Whittow

'Dr Whittow and Penguin Reference Books have put serious students of the subject in their debt, by combining the terminology of the traditional geomorphology with that of the quantitative revolution and defining both in one large and comprehensive dictionary of physical geography … clear and succinct' – *The Times Educational Supplement*

READ MORE IN PENGUIN

DICTIONARIES

Abbreviations
Archaeology
Architecture
Art and Artists
Biology
Botany
Building
Business
Chemistry
Civil Engineering
Computers
Curious and Interesting Numbers
Curious and Interesting Words
Design and Designers
Economics
Electronics
English and European History
English Idioms
French
Geography
Historical Slang
Human Geography
Information Technology
Literary Terms and Literary Theory
Mathematics
Modern History 1789–1945
Modern Quotations
Music
Musical Performers
Physical Geography
Physics
Politics
Proverbs
Psychology
Quotations
Religions
Rhyming Dictionary
Saints
Science
Sociology
Spanish
Surnames
Telecommunications
Troublesome Words
Twentieth-Century History

BY THE SAME AUTHOR

The Penguin Dictionary of Troublesome Words

Why should you avoid discussing the *weather conditions*? Can a married woman be *celibate*? Why is it eccentric to talk about the *aroma* of a cowshed? *The Penguin Dictionary of Troublesome Words* is a straightforward guide to the pitfalls and hotly disputed issues in standard written English.

Mother Tongue – The English Language

More than 300 million people in the world speak English and the rest, it sometimes seems, try to . . .

In this hymn to the mother tongue Bill Bryson examines how a language 'treated for centuries as the inadequate and second-rate tongue of peasants' has now become the undisputed global language (more people learn English in China than live in the USA). He explores the countless varieties of English – from American to Australian, from Creole to Cockney rhyming slang – and the perils of marketing brands with names like Pschitt and Super Piss. With entertaining sections of the oddities of swearing or spelling, spoonerisms and Scrabble, and a consideration of what we mean by 'good English', *Mother Tongue* is one of the most stimulating books yet written on this endlessly fascinating subject.